SOCIAL MEDIA
IN THE PUBLIC SECTOR

The Instructor's Guide for *Social Media in the Public Sector* includes a sample syllabus and PowerPoint slides. The Instructor's Guide is available for free online. If you would like to download and print out a copy of the Guide, please visit: www.wiley.com/college/mergel

Essential Texts for Nonprofit and Public Leadership and Management

SOCIAL MEDIA IN THE PUBLIC SECTOR

A Guide to Participation, Collaboration, and Transparency in the Networked World

Ines Mergel

Maxwell School of Citizenship and Public Affairs

 JOSSEY-BASS
A Wiley Imprint
www.josseybass.com

Published by Jossey-Bass
A Wiley Imprint
One Montgomery Street, Suite 1200, San Francisco, CA 94104-4594—www.josseybass.com

Cover art by Marc A. Smith, Social Media Research Foundation, http://smrfoundation.org

Jossey-Bass books and products are available through most bookstores. To contact Jossey-Bass directly call our Customer Care Department within the U.S. at 800-956-7739, outside the U.S. at 317-572-3986, or fax 317-572-4002.

Wiley publishes in a variety of print and electronic formats and by print-on-demand. Some material included with standard print versions of this book may not be included in e-books or in print-on-demand. If this book refers to media such as a CD or DVD that is not included in the version you purchased, you may download this material at http://booksupport.wiley.com. For more information about Wiley products, visit www.wiley.com.

Library of Congress Cataloging-in-Publication Data
Library of Congress Cataloging-in-Publication Data has been applied for and is on file with the Library of Congress.
ISBN 978-1-118-10994-6 (cloth); ISBN 978-1-118-22424-3 (ebk.); ISBN 978-1-118-23737-3 (ebk.); ISBN 978-1-118-26238-2 (ebk.)

Printed in the United States of America

FIRST EDITION
HB Printing   10 9 8 7 6 5 4 3 2 1

CONTENTS

PART TWO: SOCIAL MEDIA PRACTICES: PARTICIPATION, COLLABORATION, AND TRANSPARENCY   **145**

FIGURES AND TABLES

Figures

Tables

ACKNOWLEDGMENTS

This book would not have been possible for me to write without the generous support of many amazing government IT professionals who were willing to be interview partners in a longitudinal research project on the adoption and diffusion of social media applications in the agencies and departments of the U.S. federal government. They provided insights into their decisions surrounding the adoption and use of social media in their agencies. I would like especially to thank Jeffrey Levy (Environmental Protection Agency); Noel Dickover (Department of State); Tiffany Smith (Department of State); Brandon Friedman (Department of Veterans Affairs); Amanda Eamich (Department of Agriculture); Scott McIllnay (U.S. Navy); Read Holman (Department of Health and Human Services); Haley van Dÿck (formerly at the Federal Communications Commission, now at the White House); Chris Rasmussen, Don Burke, and Sean P. Dennehy (of the U.S. Intelligence Community); Neil Sroka (Department of Commerce); John Schueler (Department of Energy); Price Floyd (formerly at the Department of Defense); Scott Horvath (U.S. Geological Survey); Jeanne Holm (National Aeronautics and Space Administration); Dan Luxenberg (Food and Drug Administration); Mary Davie (General Services Administration); Katie Jacobs Stanton (formerly at the Department of State, now at Twitter); Thom Kearny and Nick Charney (of the Government of Canada); John Kamensky, Gadi Ben-Yehuda, and Mark Abrahamson (at IBM's Center for The Business of Government); and also Ben Berkowitz, Bonner Gaylord, Dustin Haisler, Steve Lunceford, John Moore, Alex Howard, Justin Herrman, Kristi Fifelsky, Jed Sundwall, Mark Headd, Pam Broviak, and Michelle Gardner.

I am especially grateful for the tireless support I received from the amazing women behind the General Services Administration's Center for New Media and Citizen Engagement, DigitalGov University, and HowTo.gov team: Lisa Nelson, Tammi Marcoullier, and Rachel Flagg, and also for the efforts of Steve Ressler at GovLoop.com, who generously introduced me over and over again to his direct contacts in government.

Many of the concepts in this book were tested and discussed with the participants in the executive education programs and students in the master of public administration program at the Maxwell School of Citizenship and Public Affairs at Syracuse University. I am very grateful for the ongoing support of my mentors Jane Fountain and David Lazer, who encouraged me along the way—even at times when social media in government was considered a fleeting fad.

I was also able to vet and try out many of my ideas with my coauthor for this book's accompanying *Social Media in the Public Sector Field Guide*, Bill Greeves, chief information officer, Wake County, North Carolina. Bill is a true government innovator and a great sparring partner in this endeavor.

At the Maxwell School of Citizenship and Public Affairs, the Dean's Office, the Center for Technology and Information Policy (CTIP), the Program for the Advancement of Research on Conflict and Collaboration (PARCC), and the Campbell Public Affairs Institute provided initial funding to cover the interview costs for my ongoing research project.

ABOUT THE AUTHOR

Ines Mergel is assistant professor of public administration at the Maxwell School of Citizenship and Public Affairs and the School of Information Studies (iSchool) at Syracuse University. She was previously a postdoctoral research Fellow at Harvard's Kennedy School of Government, Program of Networked Governance, and the National Center for Digital Government. Mergel teaches in the master of public administration program at Maxwell, where her courses address Government 2.0, new media management in the public sector, networked governance, and public organizations and management. Her research interests focus on informal networks among public managers and managers' adoption and use of social media technologies in the public sector. In particular she studies how public managers search for, share, and reuse knowledge they need to fulfill the mission of their agencies.

A native of Germany, Mergel received BA and MBA degree equivalents in business economics from the University of Kassel, Germany. She received a doctor of business administration (DBA) degree in information management from the University of St. Gallen in Switzerland and spent six years as a pre- and postdoctoral Fellow at Harvard's Kennedy School of Government.

Mergel's work has been published in a number of journals, including the *Journal of Public Administration Research and Theory*, *American Review of Public Administration*, *Journal of Public Affairs Education*, and *International Public Management Review*. Her ongoing thoughts on the use of social media applications in the public sector can be read on her blog at inesmergel.wordpress .com and on Twitter @inesmergel.

PART ONE

UNDERSTANDING SOCIAL MEDIA USE IN THE PUBLIC SECTOR

CHAPTER ONE

INTRODUCTION

Government organizations are starting to use social technologies, such as social media, social computing, and collaboration platforms, to support their mission. Social technologies have not been as widely adopted as other forms of public information and communication technologies; however, early experimentation can be observed at all levels of government as agencies make the effort to reach out to government's diverse audiences. Typically, these innovative technologies are adopted and used for three functions or purposes: (1) to increase transparency, (2) to support inter- and intraorganizational collaboration, and (3) to enable innovative forms of public participation and engagement.

Government agencies and departments are using external social networking services, where the platform is provided by a third party and data are hosted on a third-party server or in the cloud. They are also using their own websites, which allows more control over technological features and easier data archiving and access. Both models pose challenges and in many cases adoption barriers for those agencies that might potentially be willing to follow early innovators.

The use of social media applications is being driven mainly by innovative citizen use, and government organizations are slowly adopting the tools for connecting to their audiences where those audiences prefer to receive information and news on social networking sites (Schweik, Mergel, Sanford, & Zhao, 2011).

Purpose of This Book

This book is based on exploratory interviews I conducted between 2009 and 2011 with social media directors in the agencies and departments of the executive branch of the federal government and with government IT professionals working on local and state levels, as well as with social media start-up entrepreneurs who are developing applications for use in government. The initial inquiry into the ways that new technologies are diffusing through the public sector was driven by work I conducted on the web practices of federal agencies and members of Congress during my time as a doctoral and postdoctoral Fellow at the Kennedy School of Government, Harvard University, and as a member of the National Center for Digital Government and the Program on Networked Governance (Lazer, Mergel, Ziniel, Esterling, & Neblo, 2011). These projects have led to further inquiries into the informal use of new technologies among government employees to fulfill the mission of their agencies (Bretschneider & Mergel, 2010; Mergel, 2005, 2010; Mergel, Lazer, & Binz-Scharf, 2008). Many entrepreneurial government employees are driven by a passion to increase the effectiveness and efficiency of their own operations and are reaching out across organizational boundaries to learn from their peers in other agencies. They are helping each other out by sharing their local experiences with their global network and hoping to reduce redundancies (Lazer & Mergel, 2011).

Social media applications are designed with the purpose in mind to connect offline contacts online on social networking sites. My observation early in 2008 and 2009 was that many government agencies started to experiment with social media applications outside their formal IT standards and even outside their safe and sanctioned environments—with the purpose of increasing the experience of citizens involved with them and providing a new form of customer service to these audiences. Much of the innovation was sparked as a result of the successful Internet strategies during the 2008 presidential campaign, and some of the early enthusiasm was then transferred into initial experimentations by social media directors, public affairs officials, and other IT professionals. Nevertheless, the early experimentation of first movers and intrapreneurs has shown that government regulations and existing policies hindered the fast and wider spread of social media adoption. The interviews I conducted, together with my interactions online with social media professionals on Twitter using the hashtag #gov20 and the conversations I was involved in on the social networking platform Govloop.com, have resulted in several case studies. I analyzed the rich interview data with qualitative data analysis methods and social network analysis techniques. The analysis provided in-depth insights that I was able to test in order to deepen my understanding of how and why government IT professionals are adopting social media applications.

Although many of the best practices examples presented in this book come from federal agencies, the lessons learned are also applicable by local and state governments and international governments where IT professionals are starting to implement social media.

This book serves as a handbook for the use of social media in the public sector in a way that is grounded deeply in research, combining the existing practices in social media use in government with existing theories of public administration, networked governance, and information management. The intended audience includes both academics and practitioners who seek to gain a deeper understanding of the processes, intentions, managerial challenges, and actual applications of social media in government.

This book can also be used as a primer in public affairs programs, business schools, or information studies schools. The order of the chapters reflects a course I have designed, taught, and refined since 2008 at the Maxwell School of Citizenship and Public Affairs at Syracuse University. The pedagogical and theoretical approach, including in-class exercises, assignments, and a reading list for a fifteen-week course are outlined in an article published in the *Journal of Public Affairs Education* (Mergel, 2012). The syllabus is featured on education.data.gov and a frequently updated version with traditional and contemporary readings is available on my faculty page: faculty.maxwell.syr.edu/iamergel/government2-0.htm.

For practitioners this book provides a deep dive into best practices and procedural aspects of the use of social media, but it also aims to explain the underlying theoretical dimensions of the ways in which social behavior affects adoption of social media technologies. I provide ongoing updates on new cases, emerging technology innovations, and presentation slides on my blog, *Social Media in the Public Sector* (inesmergel.wordpress.com).

How This Book Is Organized

Following this introduction, this book moves in Chapter Two to an overview of social media technologies in the public sector, providing definitions and explanations of the different technologies. The unique features of major, currently adopted social media services, such as Facebook, Twitter, blogs, YouTube, and Flickr, are discussed and contrasted with traditional e-government applications.

Chapter Three then takes an in-depth look at what drives the current surge and adoption speed of social media applications in government, and Chapter Four details what are currently seen as major hurdles to the use of social media. Some of the challenges involve uncertainty regarding the applicability of existing rules and regulations. Most directives and policies cover the use of agencies' websites, but do not extend to the use of third-party portals. Chapter Five outlines the evolution of norms and necessary regulations for the safe and responsible use of new media applications in government. Norms were institutionalized with a significant time lag in relation to emergent social media behavior, and government officials set structures in place as a reactive result of continuous social media use.

The following chapters examine the organizational factors that support the implementation of social media practices in government. Findings from the adoption process of federal government agencies provide insights into how governments institutionalize the use of social media by moving from the use of early—and informal—experimentation to solid business cases in order to gain top management buy-in and then go beyond that to an institutionalized social media policy providing the context for all social computing activities. Chapter Six discusses the design of existing formal social media policies in government. A survey of publicly available documents and their year-by-year adjustments and extensions over time provide insights into the main content areas covered in policy documents. Topics include organizational roles and capacities, privacy regulations, information-vetting processes, account management, and day-to-day practices.

None of the social media activities will survive in government if they are not directly connected to an agency's mission and overall organizational goals. In order to be allocated organizational resources, such as personnel to administer social media accounts and to create content, social media activities need to be efficient and effective. Chapter Seven discusses existing impact evaluation and social media measurement techniques that are based on the current state of the art. In addition, this chapter suggests how the existing metrics can be extended with qualitative insights to increase the effectiveness of social computing activities.

Part Two of this book then showcases the three purposes for which social media applications are used in the public sector: transparency, collaboration, and participation. Each purpose is discussed in light of the existing research in public administration and the ways in which the innovative use of social media can facilitate the applications and goals of government. The current Open Government Initiative of President Obama highlights all three functions as priority goals for all ongoing, open government activities:

1. *Participation 2.0.* Public participation and, in parallel, citizen trust and satisfaction in government have dropped to historical lows (Pew Research Center for the People & the Press, 2010). At the same time, existing engagement mechanisms attract Internet *trolls*, and not the average citizen, creating what I call the *town hall divide*. The social media applications discussed in Chapter Eight provide alternative public engagement mechanisms that help support the open government mandate for innovative forms of participation and public input solicitation (Mergel, 2011).

2. *Collaboration 2.0.* Cooperation and coordination within and across government agencies is highly difficult with the current bureaucratic set of organizational norms and, at times, competing missions. Government agencies have few incentives, and they may lack the technological means to share information effectively across organizational boundaries. Chapter Nine therefore looks at collaboration platforms that enable government to increase collaboration across agencies and with diverse audiences and constituencies.

3. *Transparency 2.0.* Previous Open Government Initiatives have all attempted to increase the transparency of government records. The current use of open data and social media applications is also intended to increase the transparency of government decision- and policymaking processes. The cases provided in Chapter Ten show the first experiments in the smart reuse of public information and government datasets, without expensive Freedom of Information Act (FOIA) requests.

The goal of Part Two is to provide insights into what can be called true *lighthouse* projects—outstanding and relatively uncommon initiatives that challenge the existing understanding of transparency, collaboration, and participation for government agencies. These projects serve as illustrations and starting points for future inquiry by researchers and practitioners.

The adoption of social media applications in the public sector is still in its infancy. Even though the executive departments of the federal government were tasked in 2009 to find ways to "harness new technologies" (Obama, 2009), agencies are mostly still experimenting with the use of new technologies and are reluctant to jump on the bandwagon.

The outlook for the future of social media practices in government concludes this book, in Chapter Eleven. Additional resources, including web links, web logs, and freely accessible reports sorted according to main content areas are available in the Appendix.

Companion Learning Resource

This book has a companion field guide, *Social Media in the Public Sector Field Guide: Designing and Implementing Strategies and Policies*, coauthored with Ines Mergel by Bill Greeves, chief information officer for Wake County, North Carolina. Hands-on and practical, the *Field Guide* will help readers put into practice the concepts featured in this book.

CHAPTER TWO

SOCIAL MEDIA TECHNOLOGIES IN THE PUBLIC SECTOR

This chapter defines the terms used to describe social media use in government and provides an overview of the current applications. First, the central features and tool-specific characteristics of the main social media tools are discussed, as well as the adoption decisions for each of the tools. The chapter then compares large-scale e-government applications and their characteristics to social media applications.

Defining the Terms *Social Media, Social Software, Web 2.0*

Social technologies have made their way into the public sector: During the 2004 presidential campaign, Democratic candidate Howard Dean's presidential campaign team successfully used MeetUp, a social networking platform, to help local volunteers organize meetings of campaign helpers without having prior face-to-face interactions (Wolf, 2009). What the MeetUp experiment showed in 2004 was the successful use of online social networking services to bring people together off-line.

During the 2008 presidential campaign of then Senator Barack Obama, social media sites and content (such as YouTube videos, Facebook Fan Pages, Twitter accounts, and the like) were used to reach constituents and potential voters with an unprecedented success rate (Carpenter, 2009).

Voters who were unreachable in previous elections were reached through their social graph—the connections they built on social networking services. This development informed Transparency and Open Government, a memorandum published a day after the president's inauguration on January 21, 2009, in which President Obama instructed federal executive departments and agencies to "harness new technologies" to increase their participation, transparency, and intergovernmental collaboration activities (Obama, 2009). This mandate has started a new wave of use of social technologies on the federal government level, use that has been informed by existing local and state government initiatives that were subsequently adopted by federal departments and agencies.

Originally designed for personal networking, *social networking applications* are also open to corporate or government use and are oftentimes used as a branding mechanism. For example, the White House has, in 2011, started to collaborate with Facebook, Twitter, LinkedIn, and YouTube to host online town hall meetings. Many authors have also drawn connections between the effectiveness of the recent political uprisings in the Middle East—now known as the Arab Spring—and the use of social media applications. In countries such as Egypt and Tunisia, citizens used social media applications to organize themselves, spread messages, and discuss issues, whereas governments in these countries were not part of these conversations and were surprised by the scale of the uprisings. Similarly, the London riots during the fall of 2011 led government officials to consider shutting down and blocking Twitter access (DeRosa, 2011; Halliday, 2011).

The popularity of social networking services in Western nations has significantly contributed to a change in the business models of the music and newspaper industries and also to a significant decline in the use of traditional mail services, such as the U.S. Postal Service (USPS). With the rise of the sharing of news on the microblogging service Twitter and in Facebook's newsfeed, the numbers of subscribers to paper newspapers have dropped significantly. Although the newspaper industry recognized the trend belatedly, it has now shifted its focus to digital subscriptions (Sulzberger, 2011). The push of Apple's iTunes into digital, downloadable music has greatly changed the extent to which compact discs (CDs) are used. Government agencies are now finding they are in no way immune to these massive changes in the way that information is shared and consumed. As mentioned, the USPS is a case in point. With the increased use of electronic mail, text messaging on cell phones, and also direct messaging between users of social networking services, the number of messages on paper sent by traditional mail has declined drastically, leaving the USPS on the verge

FIGURE 2.1. INTRODUCTORY PARAGRAPH OF THE GAO
REPORT ON THE U.S. POSTAL SERVICE

October 2011

U.S. POSTAL SERVICE

Mail Trends Highlight Need to Fundamentally Change Business Model

Highlights of GAO-12-159SP, a report to the Committee on Homeland Security and Governmental Affairs, U.S. Senate

Why GAO Did This Study

By the end of fiscal year 2011, with a projected net loss of about $10 billion, the U.S. Postal Service (USPS) was expected to become insolvent. To mitigate this, Congress temporarily deferred USPS's required $5.5 billion retiree health benefit payment. Over the previous 4 years, USPS experienced a cumulative net loss of just over $20 billion. USPS expects its

What GAO Found

Long-term trends—highlighted in the data below—strongly suggest that the use of mail will continue to diminish as online communication and e-commerce expand. By 2020, USPS projects mail volume will decline to levels not seen since the 1980s: Total mail volume is projected to decrease by 25 percent, First-Class Mail is expected to decrease by 50 percent, and Standard Mail volume is projected to remain flat. While dire, USPS's projections could prove optimistic if communication continues to move to digital technologies as quickly as in the recent past. For the first time, in 2010, fewer than 50 percent of all bills were paid by mail. These trends underscore the need for USPS's business model to undergo fundamental changes to reduce personnel and network-related costs.

Source: U.S. Government Accountability Office, *U.S. Postal Service: Mail Trends Highlight Need to Fundamentally Change Business Model* (GAO-12-159SP), 2011, http://www.gao.gov/new.items/d12159SP.pdf.

of bankruptcy, according to a recent report from the U.S. Government Accountability Office (2011) (Figure 2.1).

Web 2.0 has grown to be hyped in debates about innovation in governance. As in other areas of computer technology, the designation "2.0" indicates that a new generation has been developed, in this case a new generation of Internet network. Tim O'Reilly, widely credited with launching the term *Web 2.0*, defines it this way: "The network as platform, spanning all connected devices; Web 2.0 applications are those that make the most of the intrinsic advantages of that platform: delivering software as a continually updated service that gets better the more people use it, consuming and remixing data from multiple sources, including individual users, while providing their own data and services in a form that allows remixing by others, creating network effects through an 'architecture of participation,' and going beyond the page metaphor of Web 1.0 to deliver rich user experiences" (O'Reilly, 2005).

Whereas the original purpose of social media tools was mainly for entertainment and activities oriented toward youths, such as MySpace's music and fan base, these tools and their innovative use have evolved into influential systems that mainly aim to replicate off-line connections in an online world. For government agencies these tools have added to the existing tool kit of the previous generation of unidirectional technologies, where citizens were mainly forced to play the role of passive receivers of information—assuming that they were able to recover the information they were looking for on government sites at all. However, today's social media tools empower citizens as content co-creators and as senders, not only receivers, of information who have direct interaction with government.

Moreover, as I will show in many different examples throughout the next chapters, social media applications have the potential to bridge what is often labeled the *town hall divide*: average citizens with obligations for child care or other activities who would be unlikely to come to a town hall meeting at 5:00 PM are instead now able to watch a YouTube video of the meeting, chime in through a Facebook page or tweet their opinions, and increase their participation and engagement.

Features of Social Technologies

Social technologies can be distinguished from other forms of information and communication technologies by their unique technological features that support social interactions in real time. The terms *social technologies*, *social media*, and *social networking* are oftentimes used interchangeably to describe web services that allow users to create an online profile and that also enable user-generated content, crowdsourcing, and online collaboration (Boyd & Ellison, 2007). Some social networking services are walled gardens, bounded systems that restrict access to content and contacts to subscribers only. Recent developments have shown that these boundaries have become *semipermeable*, allowing a degree of publicness that users can define for themselves. An example is the *Washington Post*'s social sharing service that automatically posts articles read by a subscriber to his or her Facebook profile, communicating that person's activities and interests directly to his or her whole network.

Recent research has shown that users do not use social networking sites to meet strangers (Boyd & Ellison, 2007). This activity is reserved for such niche sites as dating services. Instead, social media users are solidifying existing off-line relationships and are reconnecting with current and past face-to-face friends online. However, users do have overlapping friendship ties, and by articulating their social connections publicly, they may (re)discover individuals they won't necessarily meet or reconnect with in their off-line lives (Haythornthwaite, 2001). These *weak ties* may become resources for new information about jobs or other valuable information that an individual's set of local, off-line contacts might not have available (Granovetter, 1983; Granovetter & Soong, 1983).

Social technologies allow users to communicate across platforms with each other. Facebook—currently the most popular social networking platform—allows users to share details about their location, share the types and content of news they have consumed, and share information with and build on trusted recommendations from other users. Facebook status updates can be automatically reposted to other sites, such as Twitter or LinkedIn, or to applications, such as widgets.

Users on all social networking services have to create a publicly shared profile that is usually searchable through such search engines as Google or Bing. The profile page offers customizable fields, so that users can personalize their online presence to a certain degree. The only identification features are personal e-mail addresses, which are used to verify that the account belongs to a real person. Beyond that, users can choose a nickname in place of their real name to protect themselves and preserve some anonymity online. Especially during the early days of Google's social networking service, Google+, there was a fair amount of discussion about the usefulness of an enforced "real name policy" for social networking profiles (Horowitz, 2011).

Social networking services allow users to (semi-) publicly articulate their social network—sometimes referred to as their *social graph* (Narayanan & Shmatikov, 2010). For example, the per-default publicly available friends' list of a Facebook user provides insights into the number and names of network nodes that user maintains, but other users can also derive the status of their friendship, the history (through joint membership in university networks), or the types of links maintained.

The social graph—the aggregated network contacts—provides a new *social awareness stream*: users constantly update their status and share content such as newspaper articles and links to websites they pay attention to. All users who are direct contacts or who subscribe to the contents automatically receive these updates in their individual newsfeeds—alerting them to the content their contacts are paying attention to. This creates a constant influx of information and directs users to potentially valuable information that they should also pay attention to. This has two impacts: first, users tend to pay attention to information that flows through their trusted relationships; information is then snowballing through the network, becoming *viral*. Second, users move their search behavior to their social networks, their trusted relationships, instead of leaving their search results up to automated mechanisms of established search engines (Watts, Dodds, & Newman, 2008).

This form of *social search* also has consequences for government: a recent study has shown that citizens turn to their trusted contacts on social networking sites for fact-checking purposes, before they react to news or official warnings. Especially in emergency situations, this lag in reaction time and in, for example, seeking shelter during a hurricane or earthquake could have fatal consequences. As a result, government agencies need to find ways to target social hubs in networks that are able and willing to vet information through their trusted friendship ties in real time. Users can subscribe to each other's content feeds using RSS readers and thus can receive information without directly being connected to each other.

Social networking services in their basic form allow for fast, *bidirectional* exchanges, oftentimes labeled *real-time* exchanges. Most platforms provide various forms of messaging: public status updates, direct messages between a limited number of users, or private chats. Users can reply and comment on updates and share information on other users' walls, or they can use their direct contacts' user names, so that updates are also posted to their contacts feed—a feature that provides visibility and helps to build a user's reputation.

Besides messaging and self-publishing, many of the social networking services allow for the *co-creation of content* that can be shared with the whole network. This feature is inherently collaborative and participatory and can help build online communities of interest around specific issues. Examples include *wiki*s and other forms of collaboration platforms that can, for example, be used for national dialogues. For government the opportunity to tap into the collective wisdom of citizens and their user-generated innovative content is a huge latent resource that collaboration and open innovation platforms such as Challenge.gov are using (Lakhani & Wolf, 2005; von Hippel, 2005a, 2005b). Other platforms that inspire user-generated content are GovLoop and PatientsLikeMe.

In addition to the technological features, cultural norms, ethics, and processes emerge around each social networking site and vary across sites.

Major Social Networking Services Used in the Public Sector

For a long time it was not clear why government agencies felt the need to participate in information sharing outside their protected and highly regulated communication systems. When I interviewed social media directors at these agencies and asked why they made the decision to use social media applications to reach their diverse audiences, the majority replied with a very similar slogan: "We have to be where the people are if we want to reach them" (Mergel, 2010), and one of them stated: "And these tools offer some new, well, . . . to this point not quite as new, but some different ways of reaching people and engaging in those conversations."

Operating outside their protected public relations and public affairs context gives social media directors in the public sector more freedom to choose the platforms where they see most of their audience members congregate and discuss issues that might potentially intersect with the work of government agencies and departments. Moreover, especially during the initial experimentation phase in 2010, no top-down decisions were guiding the initial decisions. Early adoption decisions about social media platforms were made without a mandate, the involvement of a traditional decision hierarchy, or elaborate and sophisticated requirements negotiated with vendors.

Currently there are several hundred social media tools freely available, and the question is, How do social media directors make the decision to choose a specific tool? The majority of selection decisions happen based on quantitative measures. The more popular a tool is, the more likely it is that government social media professionals are considering its use for their mission support.

More sophisticated decision making takes the mission of the organization into account. Social media directors over time realized that some of their initial experimentation did not support the organizational goals and switched course to other more appropriate tools: one of these directors said, "Now each tool of course has specific advantages, and we try to match the specific needs or the specific goal to the particular project, to the right tool."

The U.S. General Services Administration (GSA) followed up in 2010 by negotiating terms of service agreements with social networking sites, making it safer for agencies to choose tools for their purposes (Aitoro, 2009; U.S. General Services Administration, 2010). (For a detailed discussion of regulations and directives for the use of social media in the public sector see Chapters Five and Six.)

Networking via Facebook

Facebook is currently the most popular social networking site in the world. According to Facebook's statistics page, in 2011 the site had over 800 million users (Facebook, 2011a). Facebook itself does not make any statements about the varying degrees of activity of its users, but we may assume that there are several thousand unused accounts, one-time users, or even accounts canceled because their creators are deceased (Facebook, 2011a). However, more than 50 percent of the active users log on to Facebook in any given day. The average Facebook user has 130 friends.

Facebook was founded in 2004 as an on-campus initiative to create an online address book of Harvard graduates and help them connect across dorms on campus. Initially, the site was only accessible with an @harvard .edu e-mail address, but it was then opened further—first to other dot-edu addresses and then to alumni and later on worldwide. Facebook allows a user to create a personal contact page, connect to other users through a reciprocated confirmation process, and to share content with those other users who are subscribed to the user's newsfeed.

The site has evolved during the last two years and now allows organizations to set up pages for their professional broadcasting and networking needs. Organizations' pages are set up somewhat differently from personal account pages: users can subscribe to or *like* pages, but through this action they are not opening their personal updates to a government agency. In return users can endorse updates through the like function and can leave comments on updates posted by an organization, and thereby can directly interact in near real time with government officials and other users interested in the same issue. Another difference from personal account pages is that organizational pages allow the use of specific analytics that give an agency an overview of the number of views its page has received and the demographics of its subscribers.

Facebook has quickly become the most popular social networking site used by government agencies, allowing them to get in direct contact with those parts of their potential audience that do not directly visit agencies' official government websites. Asked why government agencies prefer Facebook and how it fits into their overall communication goals, one social media director provides the following analogy:

> The mission—[we have] similar reasons to why we're in Facebook or Twitter—is again *to be where the people are.* So 400 million users now on Facebook for example [in 2010]. So you want to be there. So if people are searching for [the agency's core task] stuff on Facebook, they find us. And we're regularly posting links and stuff back to our own website, so it's a way of leading . . . it's really like being out at the mall handing out fliers saying, "Hey, come visit us." But we're at the mall, you know, we're where the people are randomly wandering by; we're not just sitting back in our office going, "Hey, come visit us; here we are." . . . [We're where everyone] can hear us.

FIGURE 2.2. THE FBI'S *NEWS BLOG*

Source: Federal Bureau of Investigation, FBI Releases Images in David Parker Ray Case [Web log post], n.d., http://www.fbi.gov/news/news_blog/fbi-releases-images-in-david-parker-ray-case.

Recently the Federal Bureau of Investigation (FBI) has joined Facebook and is using the social networking site to harness the resharing functionalities of the site. Updates are posted to the FBI's news section on its website (FBI.gov), called the *News Blog* (Figure 2.2).

The agency then reposts the same content to its official Facebook page, allowing its over 150,000 followers to reshare the post through their own networks (Figure 2.3). The reshared message then shows up in the sharers' Facebook newsfeeds and is read by all those users connected to the original person who has shared the post from Facebook's page. The message can snowball through each user's network and has a potentially unlimited reach—supporting the crowdsourcing goal of the FBI.

Asking the public to help identify the property recovered at a crime scene has led to comments from Facebook users such as the following: "Most of the jewelry that I have viewed so far on the Albuquerque page seems to be run-of-the-mill flea market and souvenir shop items. However, the necklace on the second page seems to be quite dramatic. I'm no expert

FIGURE 2.3. THE FBI'S FACEBOOK PAGE

Source: Federal Bureau of Investigation, FBI—Federal Bureau of Investigation [FBI's Facebook page], n.d., https://www.facebook.com/FBI.

on jewelry, but it looks like it may be from Nepal. I would think that a family member might remember if a missing loved one wore such an item." This comment highlights the potential insights government agencies can gain from using a crowdsourcing approach on their Facebook pages.

Microblogging via Twitter

Microblogging is a form of blogging that allows users to write brief text updates (usually 140 characters). The most popular of these services today is Twitter. The brevity of microblogs creates distinct opportunities and drawbacks different from those of a full blog. For government, Twitter messages might consist simply of references to online resources focused on an organization's news, events, or other public information—pulling audiences back to an agency's website (Mergel 2012).

In the past three years Twitter has grown significantly, to over twenty-five million unique visitors in the United States. Currently, Twitter reports 140 million active user accounts in the United States, although many accounts are not following other accounts, about 25 percent of accounts have only one follower, and according to Katie Jacobs Stanton, vice president of market development at Twitter, about 40 percent of the users are never tweeting and only listening to online conversations (Stanton 2012; Twitter, 2012). News organizations, corporations, and recently also government agencies picked up the Twitter trend. Many government agencies maintain at least one Twitter account—some even manage multiple accounts, based on their operational needs and their diverse audiences. Agencies oftentimes use their Twitter newsfeed as a *parallel publishing stream*—repurposing existing formal announcements, such as press releases, to push them out through an additional channel.

Similar to blogs, microblogging services can be used to *distribute mission-relevant information*. Beyond the distribution of information previously posted on blogs or on an agency's website, microblogs have the additional advantage of reaching followers directly to create snowball effects, so that government agencies can reach potentially unlimited numbers of people.

Twitter messages, called *tweets*, can be described as public conversations and not only are improving transparency and accountability but also, when used appropriately, are leading to increased inclusion of public opinions into policy formulation through information aggregation processes. Twitter can be used effectively to engage large numbers of citizens and create public conversations with an engaged, networked public. The outcomes of these conversations can be new insights and even innovations in the public sector, suggestions on how to make government more effective, or simply repostings of vital emergency information in areas that are beyond the direct reach of government.

> The common reputation of Twitter is that it's frivolous, which isn't the case. If it's set up right, it's a rich environment of lots of learning and sharing of important material. It's not just "what I had for breakfast."
>
> —Lee Rainie, director of the Internet & American Life Project of the Pew Research Center. (Used with permission.)

Early on, Twitter made the impression that it lacked an imposed structure. According to its founder, that was part of a strategy to allow users to
use the platform for their own purposes. Over time, Twitter has picked up
some of the social structures and routines that its users have adopted—
such as the hashtag symbol (#) and the abbreviation *RT* for a retweet—and
made them part of the platform's functionality.

Asked why their agencies have started to use Twitter—a fairly new
service whose benefit for agencies is not as intuitively obvious as that of
the social networking platform Facebook, social media directors provided
answers along the same lines: "Twitter, again [that is, like Facebook], was
a leader in its field."

Initially some agency subunits set up their own Twitter accounts and
experimented with them. As one social media director described this process: "Twitter became a tool that I became aware of, and so we started play-
ing around with it, and as we played around with it, other people across
the agency noticed and said, well, can we try this out? And we said sure,
subject to some thinking and some discussion, sure, go ahead." Across government, Twitter is used for many different purposes. Some agencies see
it as an additional promotional and broadcasting channel and are using it
mainly to recycle content that they have also posted to their website:

> One of the things that I'd been trying to push for the last, well, . . . I
> guess it's over a year now, was developing a Facebook page and a Twitter
> page, especially Twitter, just to try to notify people of major events or
> major policy kind of statements or major press statements that we're
> throwing out there. Back in . . . November, I revisited this with the senior
> executives here, and found that one of our sister organizations, the
> Office of Controller of the Currency, had been repurposing their press
> information on both Twitter and YouTube using Twitter feed, which
> just automatically sets everything; it automatically creates a Twitter and
> Facebook entry, based on an RSS feed. We coordinated our RSS feeds,
> about last . . . September . . . and after we did that, it kind of opened this
> up for us. We took a look at Twitter feed, approved [it], and I personally
> set up the Twitter and Facebook accounts, and had all that set up, and
> after I established that look, all we have to do is just really *repurpose infor-*
> *mation* that we had out there. . . . I think my senior execs were extremely
> concerned with anybody just going out there and putting anything.
> So we established strict controls over who has access to the page, how
> we're going to update the page, you know, the Twitter account and the
> Facebook page, and what we're going to use it for, for now.

Other government agencies are taking a more relaxed position on how their subunits set up Twitter accounts and reach their own audiences by providing location-specific updates, as is the case at the Veterans Administration. Brandon Friedman, the VA's director of online communications, notes:

> Another thing we're doing with those platforms is that we're rolling Facebook and Twitter out to all the VA medical centers. We've got over 150 VA medical centers, and we're getting them all to use Facebook and Twitter to communicate with their core constituencies. Because what we found when we looked at our website traffic is that half of our traffic is actually going to the VA medical centers. So when people are looking for information on VA, they typically go to their VA medical center website. So we want those hospitals to be able to communicate with their patients using social media. [Used with permission.]

Content Sharing on Blogs

Web logs, or *blogs*, are similar to microblogging services in that they provide a mostly text-based, content-sharing service for government agencies that need to update their audiences relatively infrequently, perhaps once or twice a week (Wyld, 2007). Most of the existing free blogging services, such as Blogger, Movable Type, or WordPress, allow users to easily create web content by typing into preexisting forms, hyperlinking their texts to other websites, and embedding other externally created content, such as videos or pictures.

Blogs can be integrated into an agency's website—either as a subpage of the official site or by automatically pulling updates from external blogging tools into a dedicated news section on the agency's website. Blogs allow users to subscribe to the infrequent update through an RSS feed. RSS stands for Real Simple Syndication and describes a process through which users are alerted to an update made to a web log. Users can then access the RSS feed, either through a dedicated RSS aggregator, such as Google Reader, or by receiving alerts by e-mail.

Government agencies and politicians have employed blogs as a way to offer updates and information sharing that are more informal in tone than official press releases, with their rather bureaucratic and restricted language. Blogs provide an opportunity for supplying personal accounts, sharing background stories, and using a combination of text and other visual elements to update the public. Consider for example the update

FIGURE 2.4. *ICOMMANDANT: WEB JOURNAL OF ADMIRAL THAD ALLEN*

Source: U.S. Coast Guard, *iCommandant: Web Journal of Admiral Thad Allen*, 2010, http://blog
.uscg.dhs.gov.

posted by the now retired commander of the U.S. Coast Guard, Admiral
Thad Allen, on his *iCommandant* blog, displayed in Figure 2.4.

    Although most agencies and departments are using web logs mostly to
repost content such as press releases from their websites, others are also
experimenting with blog entries that contain opinion pieces from a department's director or administrators, updates on appearances, or other types
of infrequent updates. Public users can then leave comments and discuss
the content.

Video Sharing via YouTube

YouTube is a video-sharing platform that was acquired by Google. It allows
its users to upload videos for free. Each video is assigned a unique URL
that can be shared with friends; embedded on websites, blogs, or Facebook;
or tweeted out via Twitter. Other users can rate uploaded videos, leave
comments, and discuss the content of a video. Depending on the upload
tool used, users can upload videos up to 2 GBs in size. Many videos go
viral—meaning that at times millions of users are sharing a specific video

through their social networks and accumulating millions more viewers. Currently three billion YouTube videos are watched per day, and according to YouTube's blog, forty-eight hours of video are uploaded every minute (YouTube, 2011). YouTube reports 142 million unique visitors per day, making the platform one of the most popular content-sharing social networking platforms (YouTube, 2011).

Government officials are using video sharing for multiple purposes. Some are posting videos as background information about issues, others are asking TV stations to release and post reporters' interviews with agency directors, and some are reposting third-party content on their own YouTube channels. Some politicians are posting behind-the-scenes footage, shot not with professional video production equipment but with Flip Video cameras in their offices.

Asked why government agencies are willing to post their videos on YouTube—thus storing them on Google's server, in the *cloud*, rather than keeping them at hand locally—many social media directors report similar patterns of decision making:

> It wasn't a single decision. You're now looking back through layers of time that make it look like, OK, this is the way. We started talking about YouTube three years ago, because we have quite a video library, and we wanted to find a way to socialize and make it more easy for people to find, make it more easy for people . . . to share. YouTube was one of our first targeted sites we wanted to use. We pretty quickly realized that Flickr was basically the same thing for photos, so we added that into the mix, and then we looked at social networking.

This highlights that decisions about social media adoption are not necessarily made with a broad stroke. Agencies don't necessarily populate all the most popular channels at once, but start experimenting with platforms that fit their immediate needs—in this case a platform to socialize around specific video content led an agency to also explore other social media applications; it did not begin using all of them at once.

The White House was one of the first government agencies to use its YouTube channel (Figure 2.5) to live stream a virtual town hall meeting, in 2009 (The White House, 2009).

Many members of Congress now maintain their own YouTube channels—comparable to TV channels—where they frequently provide video updates (Figure 2.6). YouTube offers a true alternative to traditional TV and press coverage. On their YouTube channels, politicians and

FIGURE 2.5. THE WHITE HOUSE YOUTUBE CHANNEL

Source: The White House, *West Wing Week: 10/28/11 or "We Can't Wait"* [Video], 2011, http://www.youtube.com/whitehouse.

FIGURE 2.6. THE YOUTUBE CHANNEL OF CONGRESSMAN MIKE HONDA, 15TH CONGRESSIONAL DISTRICT, CALIFORNIA

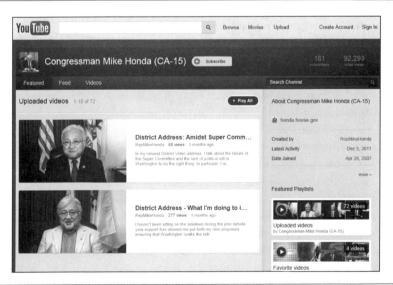

Source: M. Honda, *District Address: We Must Change Policy in Pakistan Through RSPN* [Video], October 11, 2011, http://www.youtube.com/RepMikeHonda.

government officials can keep content authority over statements they have made publicly and that might be quoted only in part or out of context elsewhere. They post their own statements or responses directly to YouTube, reshare the material on their own website and Facebook pages, and also tweet it out to their followers, including members of the press.

Some agencies allow each of their subunits to create their own YouTube accounts or channels so they can more easily reach their specific audiences and knowledge experts. This results in a wide variety of accounts. Other agencies have made a conscious decision to concentrate all their YouTube content on one channel, either because they wish to combine their various audiences or because they simply do not have enough video content to share. One social media director said that knowing how to do video, as well as Facebook and Twitter, was "inherently [a] very different skill set from being able to know how to make announcements well. And so we want to keep that kind of more under control . . . both to concentrate the community, and to make sure that we had some quality control. That's why we're only doing one account for YouTube and Flickr. But people do know how to talk to their own publics pretty well actually around the agency, and so that's why we like them to have their own Twitter and Facebook accounts."

Table A.4, in the Appendix, provides an overview of YouTube use and number of subscribers for the federal executive departments and independent agencies.

Photo Sharing via Flickr

The most prominent photo-sharing service used by government agencies is Flickr, a company acquired by Yahoo. Flickr allows its users to create profile pages, upload their own pictures, and share these pictures out to other social networking sites, such as Facebook or Twitter; it also enables users to embed Flickr pictures into blog posts, along with appropriate attribution of the source.

Flickr was heavily used during President Obama's presidential campaign, and the campaign shared behind-the-scenes pictures never seen before from a campaign trail or future president (see, for example, Figure 2.7). After the election, the White House started to use its dedicated Flickr account (www.flickr.com/photos/whitehouse), abandoning the campaign account in order to abide with the existing rules and regulations.

Flickr has quickly become the platform of choice for photo sharing for many politicians and government agencies. Asked why their agencies chose

FIGURE 2.7. ELECTION NIGHT: A CANDIDATE BEHIND THE SCENES

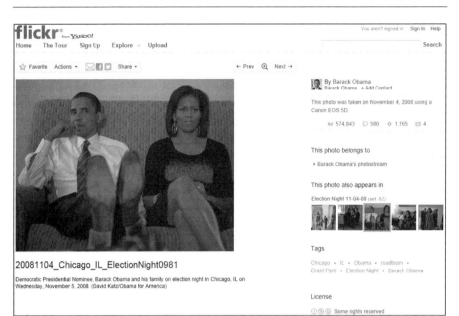

Source: Flickr, [Election night photograph], *Barack Obama's photostream*, November 4, 2008, http://www.flickr.com/photos/barackobamadotcom/3009095726.

Flickr, across the board social media directors provided compelling anecdotes, such as this:

> Flickr and video providing the rich content that shows in a vibrant way
> what it is we do . . . [and providing it] worldwide, is a great resource.
> We have a fantastic production studio here and photography support.
> We encourage students or researchers or just general interest folks to
> use whatever we have there. So it's really providing a way of digital story-
> telling . . . what a press release cannot accomplish. Much of our social
> media and new media strategy is to put a face on what has often been a
> faceless or kind of anonymous or overbearing . . . bureaucracy. We found
> that putting a voice and allowing individuals to show their personality or
> compassion through posts, photos of going out, you know, into Africa
> and various agricultural development, what we're doing in Afghanistan,
> really reaches people on a more personal level . . . you know, nobody
> sticks with a press release for more than two or three paragraphs at most.
> So [we're] trying to be more effective that way.

Differences Between E-Government Applications and Social Media

The current public administration literature mainly focuses on large-scale, government-initiated e-government projects, such as one-stop shopping portals or transaction-oriented websites (for an overview see Shea & Garson, 2010). The recent uses of social technologies were initiated mostly outside the traditional e-government realm, and government IT professionals as well as public administration scholars are still trying to understand the evolution and potential impact of this free exchange and coproduction of content. The initial use of social technologies has been a story of trial and error that has led many government agencies to stay hesitant instead of jumping on the bandwagon.

Bretschneider and Mergel (2010) defined the new wave of social technologies as the fifth wave of adoption of new technologies in government (also see Mergel, 2010, 2011). In comparison to the previous wave of e-government applications, social technologies have one main differentiating feature: they allow government to interact with its diverse audiences in a bidirectional manner. Initially, e-government applications were mostly designed to educate and inform the public. Websites were designed as portals that followed an agency's logic and mainly displayed information. In most cases government websites include a contact form through which a citizen can e-mail an agency, but that citizen rarely receives an immediate acknowledgment, and response times are relatively long. See, for example, Figure 2.8, a screenshot from USA.gov, a portal that features web links to other sites, sorted into various categories, but leaves little room for direct interactions.

The government agency information distributed by means of a portal function or any other plain website format is therefore relatively static. The content is created by content specialists, such as the staff of a public affairs office, with the help of legal counsel, in a rigorous, information-vetting procedure. The original draft of a government memo or press release goes through several iterations before the final document is ready for release to the public.

The final version of the text is then provided to a webmaster, who usually serves as the single point of access to an agency's website. The webmaster uploads the text to the site and takes it down or changes it when requested to do so by the original content specialists. Changes occur with a time lag because they follow a vetting process similar to that for the original document.

FIGURE 2.8. A TYPICAL E-GOVERNMENT WEBSITE

Source: USA.gov, U.S. Government Information, by Topic, 2011, http://www.usa.gov.

Moreover, traffic to an agency's website is usually undirected—for many content providers in the agency, it is unclear who is finding the information they have made available on the web. In rare cases agencies have the ability and the right tools to make an assessment about their audiences' behavior. Generally, agencies receive information only about click histories (that is, the number of clicks made on a specific page); rarely do they have access to the keyword searches that have led audience members to the agencies' web content, or any other in-depth statistics about the type of users interested in that content. They also do not receive any information about how their audience is reusing the content (that is, reposting it to an online community, downloading it and distributing it through other electronic means, and so forth).

More advanced forms of e-government pages include transactional functionalities, such as online payments for parking tickets, renewal of licenses, or submission of tax returns. The use of these online transactions depends heavily on citizens' perceptions of the site's ease of use.

FIGURE 2.9. PROVIDING STATIC CONTENT ON A GOVERNMENT WEBSITE

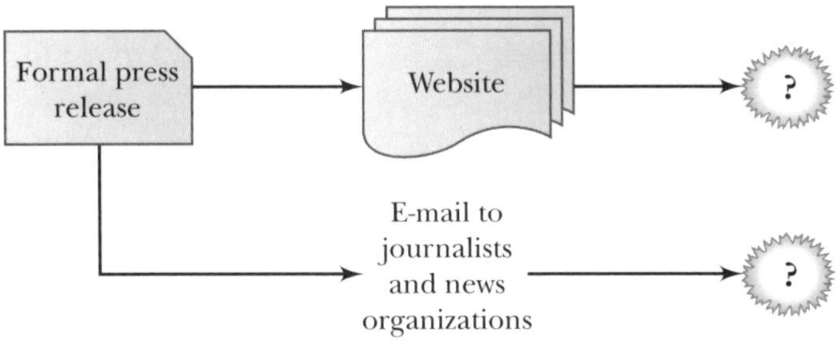

When a site does not appear easy to use, citizens will not follow through on their intentions to submit their tax returns online, participate in national dialogues, or submit their votes, and usage of these functions decreases significantly (Horowitz, 2011; Narayanan & Shmatikov, 2010; Tolbert & Mossberger, 2006).

Rarely do e-government portals and websites provide opportunities for real-time information exchanges, and information is usually pushed out, instead of interactively shared and co-created with citizens (Figure 2.9).

In contrast to e-government websites, social technologies allow for close to real-time feedback cycles. For example, subscribers receive updates posted to the social networking site Facebook in real time in their personal newsfeed. They see immediate reactions from other subscribers and can leave their own feedback for the page owner to respond to. As soon as users subscribe to a specific news source, they also receive immediate updates about who else has left comments and they can rate each other's comments. For government agencies these reflexive feedback mechanisms increase interactions with citizens and allow the agencies to engage in new forms of information sharing.

Social technologies create the potential for innovative interactions with an agency's audience. An example of this is that agencies can ask direct questions about an issue on Twitter or Facebook and invite the public to discuss the issue. Moreover, government content specialists can respond to citizens' questions immediately—the response then pops up in a citizen's newsfeed, where he or she also receives updates from social contacts, newspapers, brands, favorite TV shows, and so forth.

The main distinction between relatively static e-government sites and highly interactive and self-updating government social media accounts is the directionality of information sharing. In the case of e-government sites, the agency is the sole provider of authorized information, pushing it out through the website, with no direct interaction with the information consumer. In the case of social media technologies, government is still the provider of authorized and vetted information, but in addition citizens are able to reuse, reshare, and discuss the content provided by the agency. Government is the main actor in the information process but allows citizens to interact with the content—potentially creating additional value as they discuss issues and provide innovative insights for government. Consider for example the screenshot of the social media hub of the Department of Defense in Figure 2.10. Price Floyd, former special advisor for international

FIGURE 2.10. SOCIAL MEDIA HUB OF THE DEPARTMENT OF DEFENSE

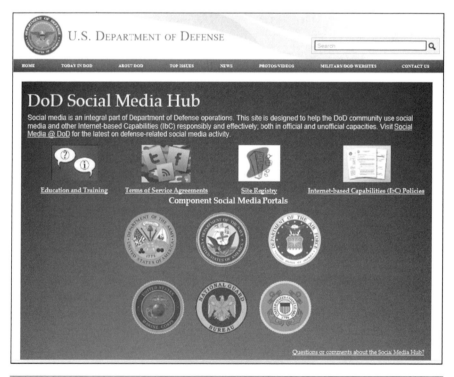

Source: U.S. Department of Defense, Social Media@DoD, January 20, 2010, http://www .defense.gov/socialmedia.

communication at the U.S. Department of Defense, points out that social technologies not only permit government to push out information into the ether but also allow government to listen to ongoing conversations, respond when necessary to provide correct information in case rumors are spreading, and generally feel the temperature surrounding the issues discussed (Watts et al., 2008).

Overall the initial content creation process of formal government information stays the same. What the additional social media channels provide are innovative conduits through which information (often the same information that is available on a website) is provided on third-party platforms. Interaction with that content is bidirectional (Figure 2.11). In addition to carrying out the educational and informative purpose of supplying information, social media applications allow discussions about that information. Moreover, agencies can proactively start dialogues, allowing informal exchanges very close to the formal processes and outcomes of the formal work government agencies conduct. Innovative insights and also results from general polls can help to create actual value for government; ideas about cost cutting or suggestions for process change can inform future government decision making.

FIGURE 2.11. PROVIDING FOR SOCIAL TECHNOLOGY INTERACTIONS ON A GOVERNMENT WEBSITE

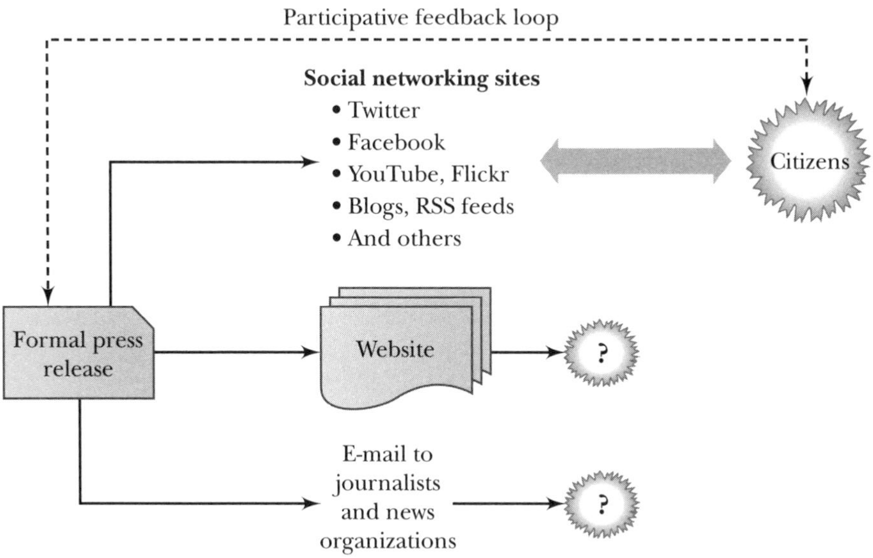

Consider for example the following incident. Travelers discussed varying treatment they received from security personnel at airports on the Transportation Security Administration's blog (at blog.tsa.gov) and highlighted procedural differences in their comments. TSA responded with the blog post shown in Figure 2.12, showing that the agency listened to citizens and used the concerns raised by bloggers as an indicator for necessary change in its internal procedures.

FIGURE 2.12. "HOORAY BLOGGERS!": A TSA BLOG POST

Source: Transportation Security Administration, Hooray Bloggers! [Web log post], February 6, 2008, http://blog.tsa.gov/2008/02/hooray-bloggers.html.

Unstructured and emergent social media content is oftentimes disconnected and disintegrated from the formal work government agencies are
conducting on a daily basis. The TSA showed that its use of social media is no
longer disconnected from its formal, structured, and predefined processes;
instead, this usage has delivered business value and changed formal procedures. Publicly announcing the impact citizens' contributions to an agency
blog had on that agency's standard operating procedures might in turn lead
to increased transparency and accountability—and might also increase the
willingness among citizens to engage with government in the future. Trust in
government operations may increase as a result.

Government 2.0 Ecosystem

Agency use of social technologies did not emerge in isolation from other
developments. Instead, following their first experiments with social media,
government IT professionals labeled their movement *Government 2.0*—
reflecting Web 2.0 applications and indicating that they are (oftentimes
outside the formal government context) experimenting with the use of
social media. The term *Government 2.0* was coined by William Eggers in
the pre-Web 2.0 era (Eggers, 2005; Eggers & Dovely, 2008). In his use
of this term, Eggers focused generally on the use of technology to increase
transparency and participation in government but did not mention social
media. Tim O'Reilly then picked up the term and extended its original
definition, promoting the view that government serves as a platform: agencies provide the data and the public is free to reuse it, design web and
mobile phone applications around innovative use of public data, and provide the applications for free to the public and to government (O'Reilly,
2005, 2010).

I define *Government 2.0* as the use of social technologies to increase participation, transparency, and interagency collaboration in the public sector.
Prominent tools are, among others, social networking platforms, content
creation and sharing tools, web logs, and microblogging tools that allow
for a *bidirectional information exchange* within government organizations
and in government interactions with citizens. The main differences from
previous e-government web applications are a higher degree of interactivity and of content production by both government and citizens (Cormode
& Krishnamurthy, 2008). These new technologies are being used both
internally and to target Internet-savvy citizens and can reach users who are
not using the traditional ways of interacting with government. The U.S.

General Services Administration has negotiated and signed agreements with social media providers so that agencies can use these services for free to reach out to citizens (Aitoro, 2009).

DEFINITION OF GOVERNMENT 2.0

The use of social technologies to increase participation, transparency, and interagency collaboration in the public sector. Prominent tools are, among others, social networking platforms, content creation and sharing tools, web logs, and microblogging tools that allow for a *bidirectional information exchange* within government organizations and in their interactions with citizens.

The first two years of this Government 2.0 movement have shown that the use of social media applications challenges the existing standard operating procedures: A new information-sharing paradigm has evolved, moving from a need-to-know to a need-to-share basis (Dawes, Cresswell, & Pardo, 2009). The existing bureaucratic, linear, and relatively restricted information-sharing procedures are disrupted by information created outside the defined organizational reporting structure: Citizens and other stakeholder groups are coproducing innovative knowledge by leaving comments on blogs, tweeting government information, informing each other using Facebook pages and groups, posting YouTube videos, or reaching out to government organizations through citizen-initiated applications such as SeeClickFix. These rather disruptive activities occur in innovative environments, such as the university-public partnerships at Manor Labs, Texas, or are incentivized by government awards and contests, such as Apps for Democracy or Apps for America. Moreover, the "rock stars" of this new use of social networking are those who spend their free time developing and coproducing applications and websites to reuse government-produced data (such as MyTweet311, GovLoop, or MuniGov2.0); these apps and websites serve as incubators for innovation in government (Kamentz, 2010).

One of these influential developments is the Open311 movement—a collaborative effort to create open standards for 311 services (see www .open311.com). Open311 services connect 311 data collected by governments with location-based data to create more effective public services. For example, CrimeReports.com works with data police departments collect and displays it on maps of neighborhoods (Figure 2.13).

FIGURE 2.13. A CRIMEREPORTS.COM MAP

Source: CrimeReports, New York City, 2010, http://www.crimereports.com.

The Government 2.0 movement therefore does not include only government innovations but also innovations that are crowdsourced among citizens or civic hackers. Government 2.0 Barcamps, or *unconferences*, helped to organize the movement and resulted in initiatives, such as CrisisCommons, and also start-up opportunities, such as SeeClickFix, to engage citizens in community issues. These examples show that Government 2.0 has developed itself from a "Wild West" in the use of open data and social media applications to an organized movement and has even produced a convergence and consolidation with tangible outcomes, such as public services, with value for all citizens.

Summary: Social Technologies in the Public Sector

Table 2.1 summarizes the differences between e-government approaches to technology and the use of social technologies by government agencies (that is, Government 2.0).

TABLE 2.1. OVERVIEW OF DIFFERENCES BETWEEN E-GOVERNMENT AND GOVERNMENT 2.0

	E-Government	Government 2.0
Main goal	• Delivery of government services online (transactional).	• Creation of emergent, bottom-up initiatives: Citizen-driven. Employee-centric.
Status	• Content consists of final, tested, and vetted versions. • Most of the time, requires large financial investments and is long-term.	• Approach is *perpetual beta*, subject to changes by third-party website providers. • Is typically low-cost and short-term.
Feedback mechanisms	• Surveys of focus groups done infrequently and with limited customers.	• Continuous detailed feedback received from online publics.
Authority over knowledge and information	• Authority held by knowledge experts. • Higher levels of control over content; developer-centric.	• Both government experts and members of the public hold authority: co-creation is desirable; control is held by both government and public participants; final decision to use knowledge is limited to government. • Lower levels of control and managerial coordination.
Interaction	• Push. • One-way communication. • Low interactivity.	• Pull. • Listen; engage; allow comments, polls, and voting. • Possibility of bidirectional interactions.
Targeting of audiences	• Aimed at broad masses: "the public."	• Personalized. • Channel approach. • Clear understanding.
Measurement	• Purely quantitative, with limited access to detailed user behaviors and identities.	• Real-time data, "temperature," reach, numbers, qualitative data about opinions, attitudes. • Analysis of audience and demographic data possible.
Tactics	• Informational and educational. • Reactions based on e-mail responses, press coverage, and anecdotes.	• Strategic campaigns. • Evaluation conducted on a continuous basis, with direct intervention possibilities. • Reflexive feedback mechanism exists: offering immediate impact and real-time information.

CHAPTER THREE

DRIVERS FOR THE USE OF SOCIAL MEDIA IN THE PUBLIC SECTOR

What is driving adoption of social media among public sector agencies? Use of social media is slowly growing and evolving in government, but too often social media are still considered merely a fad. When adoption does occur, the drivers include the ease of social media use, existing adoption decisions made at the individual level (by citizens and many government employees), and emergent social behavior that is resulting in new social structures related to the use of innovative technologies. This chapter takes a closer look at the behavioral, technological, and economic drivers that influence the adoption of social media in the public sector. It includes some of the perceptions of current social media directors in federal agencies, highlighting their reasons for adopting new technologies to support their agencies' missions.

The current use of social media applications in the public sector suggests two distinct trends. Some government organizations are extremely hesitant to jump on the bandwagon and provide only a single online access point—a web contact form—for the public. Other agencies are diving headfirst into the use of social media channels and are distributing their web presences across multiple accounts on social networking sites, extending their reach and digital visibility across the web. The following observation from a federal social media director highlights how some agencies worked through their initial hesitance: "Initially some thought it was just a fad and would detract from the press mission. But I was able to argue for social media as a supplement—to supplement our communication as an 'and also' approach as opposed to an 'and/or' approach."

What the apparent popularity of social media tools in the public agencies where they are being used indicates is that government has an increasing need to create, distribute, and collect information outside the traditional communication mission.

Government agencies know the importance of informing or educating the public about an agency's mission. The communication strategy that relies on press releases is heavily hierarchical and its information-vetting processes are outlined clearly, leaving little room for informal exchanges with either public affairs personnel or knowledge experts located deep in an agency's hierarchy. Clearly the most recent Internet technologies are creating dramatic changes in the way people communicate and collaborate at a peer-to-peer level (Benkler, 2006). Moreover, these changes have potentially transformative implications for the way public sector organizations fulfill their missions and communicate with each other and with citizens (U.S. Government Accountability Office, 2011). But they also create potential difficulties and challenges that have their roots in the institutional context within which these technologies are or will be deployed. (Read more about these hurdles and challenges in Chapter Four.) In other words, it is not the technology that might keep public sector organizations from transforming and innovating—it is the organizational and institutional hurdles that need to be overcome (Fountain, 2001; Tolbert, Mossberger, & McNeal, 2008).

In many ways, social media use in the public sector can be seen as a wicked problem (Rittel & Webber, 1973); having little or no initial formal guidance, government IT professionals have had to experiment with the application of social media. This has exposed them to a very high degree of uncertainty and risk taking. At first, norms and regulations covered only online practices on official and institutionalized government websites or e-mail traffic. But after several years, regulations and policies for the use of third-party sites followed. Once government organizations start to use social media sites, they find themselves in a continually reactive mode as information and feedback from the public arrive. Moreover, platform providers are changing their services and privacy settings, so that new government policies and standard operating procedures have to follow as soon as the provider-based changes are discovered. Innovative behavior and social structures are user driven. Overall, the responsible and effective use of social media applications represents a complex problem that necessitates high degrees of experimentation. As a result, government is only slowly adopting social media use into its standard operating procedures. As one government IT professional responsible for social media use says: "For me, social media is about one one-hundredth of my time. I just do it on the side."

Even though social media comes with a lot of challenges and risks, government agencies have started to dive into online social networking. Three categories of drivers foster the adoption of social media applications in the public sector: behavioral, economic, and technological. Each of these sets of drivers is discussed in the following sections.

Behavioral Drivers

Behavioral, or social, drivers are indirectly reflected in the desire of the generation of so-called digital natives to create their own content and share it with their friends and online contacts—oftentimes with few hesitations about how their public selves will be displayed (Gasser & Palfrey, 2008). Citizens have been setting up online presences, often on multiple social networking sites, such as MySpace, Friendster, or Facebook, or on microblogs and blogs, such as Twitter, Blogger, WordPress, or others. These sites allow every citizen, with or without programming skills, to set up a public representation and stay connected to friends.

A case in point is the use and sharing of digital video or pictures. Previously, the creation and dissemination of this kind of online content was primarily reserved for highly skilled and tech-savvy early adopters. User-generated videos are still being produced by a relatively small number of people, but through low-tech distribution and access procedures (such as YouTube), these videos are being viewed by a very large number of people. Increasingly, this development is also spreading across age groups and is no longer unique to the MySpace generation. Especially during the 2004 and 2008 presidential campaigns, more and more citizens were becoming involved in political engagement such as political opinion building through social networking sites and blogs and the integration of online and off-line contacts (consider, for example, Moveon.org, Barack Obama's and John McCain's Facebook groups and profiles, and causes applications). This movement in electoral politics convinced public sector organizations to consider the use of YouTube, Facebook, and Twitter as well (Jordan, 2009).

Strength of Weak Ties Supporting Social Media

A recent research study published by the Pew Internet & American Life Project shows that Americans have various motivations for using social networking sites. Most of them are creating an online profile to stay in touch with existing friends (67 percent) or family members (64 percent) or to reconnect with friends they have lost touch with (50 percent) (Fretwell, 2010). Social networking sites are therefore being used to replicate some of the off-line interactions with friends with whom users are maintaining strong ties.

Social networking sites are used to reinforce already existing (off-line) relationships. In addition the study shows that half of the users included in the study also use social networking services to reactivate ties that have become weak over time. These are ties that bind people based on a common attribute that allows them to connect to each other frequently or feel a strong connection to each other. Based on this sense of likeness, people then tend to communicate more often—or because they have a strong sense of belonging they can provide emotional support for each other even though they do not have the opportunity to meet in person (Granovetter, 1973, 1983). For example, Facebook is often used to reconnect with college friends who have moved to other parts of the country or to stay in touch with friends in one's former hometown. These weak ties can be reactivated with the help of Facebook or even Twitter. Even though the frequency of interaction might not change because of mere online contact, the potential resources that might exist in a weak tie—such as social or professional support—can be helpful for future interactions. Figure 3.1 illustrates how strong and weak ties combine in the social networks of most individuals.

Social networking sites are less frequently used to meet strangers. As a graphic from the Pew research report mentioned earlier shows (Figure 3.2), people have various motivations for using these sites, and online dating or connecting to new online contacts who were not previously off-line contacts plays only a minor role for users as a motivation to create an account on a social networking site (affecting only 3 percent of users).

Increased Social Awareness Among Government Officials

Following this apparent trend among citizens and private users, many public sector organizations have started to build a virtual representation of their organization on social networking services. They use the technologies that their constituents already use, rather than making their constituents

FIGURE 3.1. STRONG AND WEAK TIES IN A SOCIAL NETWORK

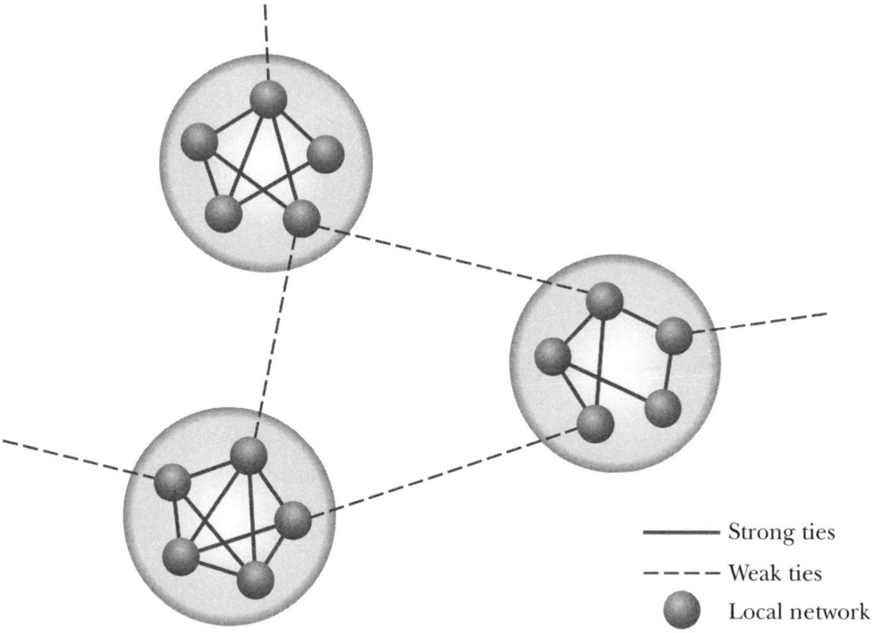

——— Strong ties
----- Weak ties
● Local network

come to them (for example, through an e-government website), and thus they allow people to communicate with them by using Facebook or Twitter or other social networking sites. As one social media director in the federal government explained in 2010: "Why we are on Facebook or Twitter: to be where the people are. So [there are] 400 million users now on Facebook for example, so you want to be there. When people search for . . . stuff on Facebook, they find us."

Nevertheless, as I have discussed, adoption of social media applications by U.S. government agencies is happening only after a significant time lag, and it is triggered by events, rather than by a conscious, top-down decision by top management. For example, the so-called social media revolutions during the Arab Spring in 2011 have increased awareness among government officials that social media applications can be used successfully to coordinate and manage citizens and represent their needs with one voice (Lazer, Mergel, Ziniel, Esterling, & Neblo, 2011; Mergel, 2012).

FIGURE 3.2. MOTIVATIONS FOR USING SOCIAL NETWORKING SITES

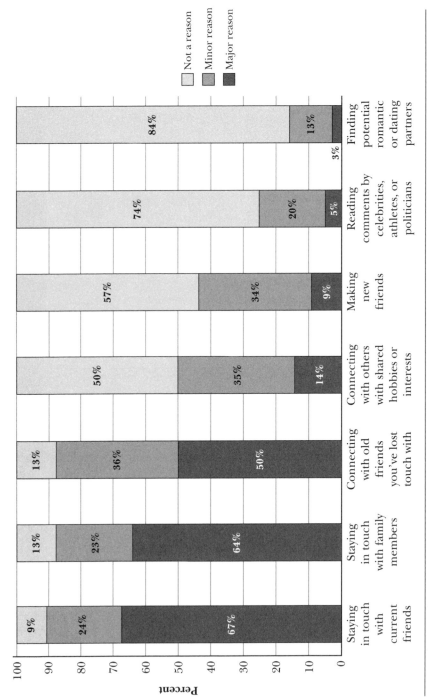

Note: Findings are from the Pew Research Center's Internet & American Life Project, April 26 to May 22, 2011, Spring Tracking Survey; *n* = 2,277 adults ages eighteen and older, including 755 cell phone interviews. Interviews were conducted in English and Spanish. Margin of error is +/–3 percentage points for social networking site users (*n* = 1,015)—adults who use sites such as Facebook, MySpace, LinkedIn, and Twitter.

Source: A. Smith, *Why Americans Use Social Media* (Pew Research Center, 2011), http://www.pewinternet.org/Reports/2011/Why-Americans-Use-Social-Media.aspx. All PEW graphics are used with permission.

The trends in motivations and generally in the use of social networking sites are also evident in the change in Internet use during the last ten years. Although the use among teens has increased slowly (from 75 percent to now 93 percent), the major increase has happened in the older age groups, who represent the majority of voters and taxpayers, as shown in Figure 3.3.

These trends have led to increased acceptance of social media tools in government. Many public officials understand that their diverse audiences are no longer looking at government as the only authority to provide valuable information but are turning to their peers and vetting official information through their social networks. As one social media director in the U.S. federal government states: "Get the message out to the audiences that might not normally hear it and [that] have a lower engagement with government."

Recent polls have shown that the use of social media by government agencies has increased each year since the 2008 elections. As an example, in 2010 only 14 percent of government workers were willing to use social

FIGURE 3.3. CHANGE IN INTERNET USE BY AGE, 2000–2010

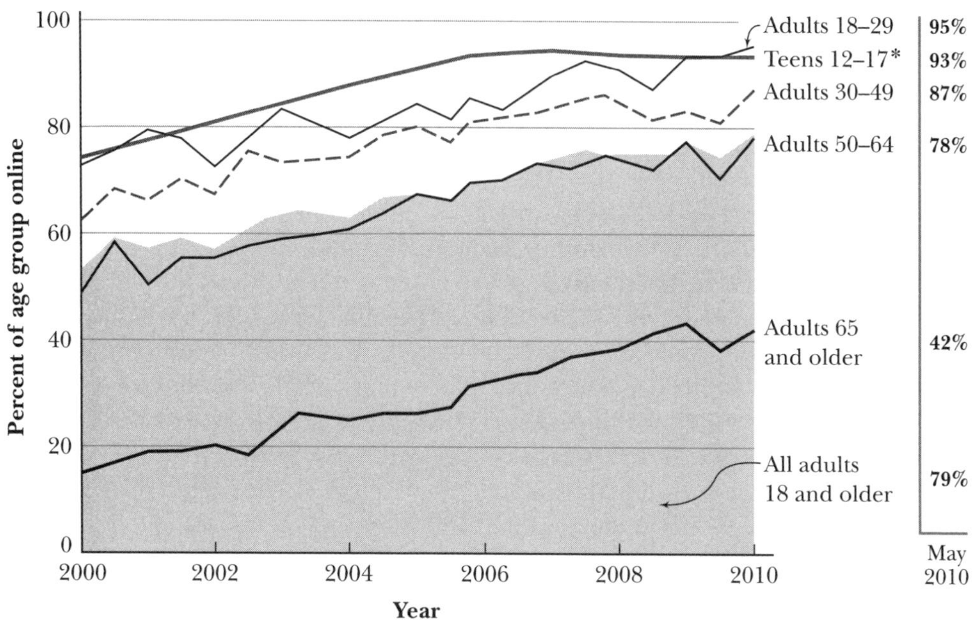
Percent of age group online
100
80
60
40
20
0
2000
2002
2004
2006
2008
2010
Year
Adults 18–29
95%
Teens 12–17*
93%
Adults 30–49
87%
Adults 50–64
78%
Adults 65 and older
42%
All adults 18 and older
79%
May 2010

Note: Teens' data are from September 2009.

Source: Pew Internet & American Life Project, *Updated: Change in Internet Access by Age Group, 2000–2010*, 2010, http://pewinternet.org/Infographics/2010/Internet-acess-by-age-group-over-time-Update.aspx. Used with permission.

media. By 2011 this number had increased, and now 79 percent of government workers are willing to use social media to support the mission of their agency (Lipowicz, 2011). This is a trend that can also be seen among members of Congress (Lazer & Mergel, 2011). As Marks reported in October 2011 on Nextgov, more than 80 percent of congressional websites now link to external social media sites. By comparison, in 2009 only 20 percent of members of Congress had linked their websites to a personal Twitter or Facebook account. In addition, 50 percent of all congressional committees link to a committee Twitter account, up by 30 percent since 2009, and 40 percent of the committees also provide a link to a committee Facebook page. Although most of the activities on these accounts are focused on traditional broadcasting and sharing of information, a small percentage of members and committees allow interaction and engagement to a certain degree and have opened their Facebook pages for comments from the public.

Changes in News and Information Consumption Behavior

The increased acceptance of Internet use and greater access to social networking sites have also changed the way that users search and access information online. Government officials recognize that parts of their audiences are no longer accessing official government information through federal websites. Instead, users want to receive valuable information either through a friendship network or delivered directly into their Facebook newsfeed. Says one social media director, "There is part of our stakeholder group out there that uses Twitter exclusively or Facebook as their main website to get information, to disburse information, to communicate with people. . . . It's easier for people to get notified of things if they're using Facebook. If they're logged in all the time, or have Twitter open all the time, it's easier to tell them about that. I mean people are using that almost as much they're using e-mail now."

Other media consumption patterns support the move to social media as a major source of information. The mere popularity of Facebook's newsfeed has reduced direct website hits and subscriptions to paper versions of newspapers. As a matter of fact, the rise of social media has resulted in major income loss in the news industry. Many people have stopped subscribing to newspapers. Indeed, 41 percent of respondents to a Pew Research Center survey said they received their news on the web (Pew Research Center's Project for Excellence in Journalism, 2011), a shift that has had major impacts on the news industry (including radio and television news sources as well as newspapers). As a result the *New York Times* has instituted a paid digital subscription model, the first national newspaper to do so.

Both Twitter and Facebook newsfeeds are catering to all information needs of their users: social news from friends, civic and government news, and also professional and instrumental news in the form of work-related updates.

Moreover, user communities on social networking sites are posting updates faster than single news reporters are able to write up their stories or prepare TV-ready versions of their reports. For example, in crisis situations, such as earthquakes or dorm shootings, news travels faster and is vetted faster by thousands of participants in the Internet community than it can be by a breaking news reporter, who must file the updates for traditional delivery mechanisms (Johnson, 2011). Figure 3.4 shows the trends in where citizens go to access news.

FIGURE 3.4. TRENDS IN INDIVIDUALS' SOURCES OF NEWS (BY PERCENTAGE OF RESPONDENTS)

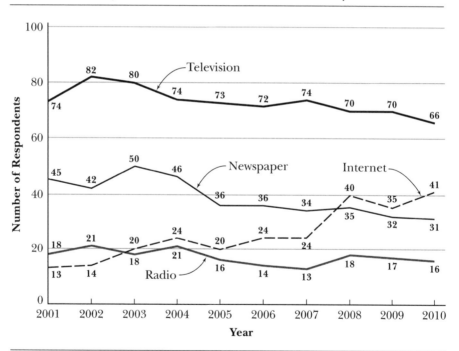

Note: Findings from the Pew Research Center, December 1–5, 2010. The question asked was, "Where do you get most of your news about national and international issues?" Figures for each year add to more than 100 percent because respondents could volunteer up to two main sources.

Source: Pew Research Center for the People & the Press, *Internet Gains on Television as Public's Main News Source*, 2011, http://www.people-press.org/2011/01/04/internet-gains-on-television-as-publics-main-news-source. Used with permission.

Federal government departments recognize that their traditional websites are not the places where citizens search for information: "We hold no illusion that the U.S. government site is going to be the first place that any American citizen will go to get their information," says one social media director. And another points out:

> I think it is a fundamental shift: instead of asking people to come to government, it is government going to the people. So people are, for a lack of a better term, hanging out on Facebook, people are hanging out on Twitter. And so we want to be sure that our messages can get to people where they want it, when they want it, and in the form that they want it. I think it is both a fundamental shift in our approach to that, and also a reaction to just the nature of the technology changing the way people get information.

The recognition that government is not the only authority for information is also reflected in a changing public sector information paradigm: the traditional need-to-know information paradigm is now reserved for national security or intelligence topics, and a new paradigm of need-to-share is opening government up and allowing public officials to proactively disclose and share information with the public (Dawes, Cresswell, & Pardo, 2009).

Technological Drivers

Even though the underlying technology itself is not new, the recent increase in social media applications can be attributed to their ability to support people's social networking needs: people have the need not only to share success stories but also to report negative events in order to receive emotional support. The direct and quick feedback cycles on social networking sites create a form of social justification that exists in the off-line world typically through face-to-face interactions (Boyd & Ellison, 2007; Joinson, 2008). Part of the current success of tools such as Twitter and Facebook can be attributed not only to the psychological traits that support the use of social media applications but also to a relatively high degree of technological literacy—that is, *slack capacity* within society for using social media applications for private purposes (for example, by sharing pictures or videos or by writing web logs). A social media director in the U.S. federal government highlights how social media help outreach: "Our social media strategy is to put a face on what has often been a faceless, kind of anonymous or overbearing bureaucracy. Nobody sticks with a press release for more than two to three paragraphs [at] the most."

Not only are citizens outside government looking to share their stories on social networking sites, but also younger government employees are increasing the pressure on government to implement social media applications, in the same way previous generations pushed for e-mail or web access. Demographic shifts will change the makeup of the government workforce as baby boomers retire and are replaced by a younger generation (the digital natives mentioned earlier) with a high level of familiarity with these new technologies plus a lower threshold for exposing themselves on the Internet (Gasser & Palfrey, 2008; Liikanen, Stoneman, & Toivanen, 2004).

Today, in addition to a growing comfort level among formal agencies, a parallel movement is observable on the citizen side. So-called civic hackers, citizen journalists, or citizen scientists, or what some might call *alpha geeks* with a vested interest in government, are using social media tools with ease and are creating mashups using free and open source tools (such as wikis to co-create content).

The main technological drivers for the adoption of new technologies include the rapid diffusion of broadband to households, which enables an increasing number of citizens to create their own content, post it (for example, on video- or photo-sharing websites), and in return to download larger content, such as media files. Prior limitations of dial-up connections did not allow these developments. According to a relatively recent Pew study, this trend will become even more widespread when newer generations of high-speed wireless broadband become more widely available (Pew Internet & American Life Project, 2007). Moreover, higher processing speeds and greater memory capacities, as well as access to higher-quality production equipment, such as digital cameras, video recorders, and mobile phones, allow almost synchronous production and distribution on the go. A past hindrance has been turned into a facilitator of the interactive web tool generation. Also applications are more accessible and have a low learning curve, and enable users to create and share their content without any professional technological background. These technological drivers have the advantage that they allow a broader audience to create, share, and access online.

Peer Production

Search engines such as Google, the web-based encyclopedia Wikipedia, the video-sharing site YouTube.com, and the online store Amazon.com are well-known examples of platforms that support content that is produced using peer production methods. Each time we are searching for keywords or book titles with a search engine and are making an active choice by selecting one of the results, the search mechanism remembers the choice for the next search. Thus every user is contributing his or her knowledge to improve the search experience for future users. Similarly, users of social networking websites such as MySpace.com or Facebook.com, news-sharing sites such as Digg.com and Slashdot.com, or social bookmarking sites such as del.icio.us are using individual choices to improve their content.

On all these high-profile, interactive websites, users connect to some degree with the content of the site, rather than just reading static text, and are using their choices to aggregate an attention network of topics, contacts, and information. What these sites have in common is that they harness the productive power of their users. Yochai Benkler (2006) refers to this as "commons-based peer production." To Benkler, *peer production* describes a special kind of production system where individuals act in response to their own needs and interests and in a decentralized manner. In the case of Google, users are actively searching for things they want to find for whatever work they are doing. But behind the scenes, Google's PageRank algorithm uses the hyperlinks created by individual web authors as a "vote" for the importance of such pages (Page, Brin, Motwani, & Winograd, 1999). I will return to this in the discussion later on task granularity.

A similar situation exists with Amazon.com. Users, following their own self-interests, actively search for, review, and purchase products: for example, books. As this is done, Amazon's technology keeps a database of the kinds of books that each person bought and provides recommendations of other books he or she might like based on the purchase history of others who have bought the same or similar books. The review function through which every user can add feedback and book reviews to any page creates a public value for the overall community. The PageRank technology in Google and the book recommendation system in Amazon are examples of efforts to employ the work of end users who are carrying out tasks motivated by their own interests to create systems of accreditation and relevance (Benkler, 2006).

The other important attribute of commons-based peer production, besides the fact that it relies on information collected through the activity of users who are motivated by their own information collection activities, is that it thrives in crowd-like situations, where a huge number of potential users exist (Surowiecki, 2005). Most, if not all, of the high-profile websites mentioned earlier have users providing content from across the globe. This leads us to the next foundational topic: open source.

Open Source and Open Content

Open source describes a phenomenon that began in the mid-1980s in computer programming software. To summarize, open *source* software differs from traditional proprietary software in that the computer source code—the internal logic of the program—is made available for anyone to access and read. The innovation made in the early days of open source software (then called *free* or *libre* software) involved its use of copyright law and a concept sometimes referred to as *copyleft* (Deek & McHugh, 2008). A copyleft license provides the user with the right to copy, modify, and redistribute new derivatives of open source software, but mandates that the derivative be licensed under the same copyright as its "parent" software. This, in and of itself, was a great innovation, and has inspired others to develop similar licenses for digital products other than software. The most famous of these are the Creative Commons licenses developed by intellectual property scholar Lawrence Lessig and others associated with the organization of the same name (Creative Commons, 2008). Creative Commons licenses are now ubiquitous on the net, attached to products such as papers, images, music, and photographs.

Benkler (2006, p. 63) refers to open source software collaboration as the "quintessential instance of commons-based peer production." As he puts it, open source "depends on many individuals contributing to a common project, with a variety of motivations, and sharing their respective contributions without a single person or entity asserting rights to exclude either from the contributed components or from the resulting whole." However, several recent studies, beginning with Krishnamurthy (2002) and Schweik and English (2007), show that many open source projects are the work of not large teams but rather small teams of developers. Yet in some instances these projects do deploy their user base to help with some of their activities, such as testing or the production of documentation.

User-Centered Innovation

In addition to the copyleft licensing of innovation, there are two other surprising points to make related to the open source phenomenon. First, at least until about five years ago, the majority of software developed (which was a sizable amount) was written by volunteer developers. These were people with technical skills who wrote software in their free time, and who may or may not have been gainfully employed as well. They were providing a public good labeled by Stebbins (2001) as "serious leisure." Now, however, more developers are paid, as businesses, governments, and nonprofit organizations have entered the open source space, leading to a significant change in the composition of the open source participant ecosystem.

The second important point is that historically, the majority of the software produced has been developed by programmers who are also *users* of the software (von Hippel & von Krogh, 2003). The idea of users as innovators adds significantly to the incentives driving people to contribute, as well as to the quality of their contribution (von Hippel, 2005a). The existence of open source collaborations that are "user-centered innovation networks" (von Hippel, 2005b) is somewhat of a surprise to many in that these innovators freely reveal their innovations. But the open source community demonstrates that this does indeed happen and in a significant way (Schweik & English, 2007).

Research over the last five years has helped to explain the incentives that drive volunteer contributors to behave this way (Ghosh, 2005; Lakhani & Wolf, 2005). Solving a specific need (the user-centric component) is one common motivation. Others are the enjoyment of a challenging problem (serious leisure), learning and skill building through collaboration with others, and signaling skills to others for ego gratification or possible future job opportunities. In addition, studies by Krishamurthy (2002), Riehle (2007), and Deek and McHugh (2008) show how firms are making a profit using a business model built around or upon open source products. For example, there are businesses that (1) build complete systems to solve a client need (system integrators); (2) provide technical support services; (3) distribute open source products; (4) create new software products built with open source components; and (5) dual license their software (one open source and one proprietary). For our purposes a detailed understanding of these business models is not important. What is important is that these businesses also have their own user-centric needs and as a result are increasingly committing their own resources (such as employees or monetary donations) to open source projects.

Crowdsourcing

The idea of business needs leads us to another relevant concept touched on earlier—*crowdsourcing*. Howe (2008) defines it this way: "Crowdsourcing is the act of taking a job traditionally performed by a designated agent (usually an employee) and outsourcing it to an undefined, generally large group of people in the form of an open call." In other words, a company posts a problem it is facing on the Internet, individuals submit solutions, winning ideas are rewarded, and the company mass produces the innovation for profit (Brabham, 2008a). Crowdsourcing is an idea that tries to capture the value of mining ideas from large groups of people, as highlighted by James Surowiecki in his 2004 book *The Wisdom of Crowds.* The idea in its current form embraces the peer production and user-centric innovation concepts but differs from open source in that the request for help comes from a firm and the innovation becomes its product, compared to open source where the product remains in the public domain (Brabham, 2008a). In a more recent study of participants in iStockphoto .com (described later), Brabham (2008b) finds that, like open source participants, they are motivated by enjoyment and fun but also, naturally, by the prospect of making money. However, unlike what is thought to be true in open source, they do not appear to participate for peer recognition or to build a network of collaborators. So there appear to be motivational differences, at least for some, between crowdsourcing and open source. Crowdsourcing also differs from peer production efforts such as those that support Wikipedia and the other website examples given earlier, in that in the former an organization is creating a kind of contest for help, whereas in the latter, the actions are driven solely by the users' own interests, needs, and motivations.

But not only the corporate sector can use crowdsourcing as a way to innovate. Recently, Lukensmeyer and Torres (2008) proposed to apply the idea of crowdsourcing to government citizen engagement efforts. They acknowledge that there are several reasons to be cautious or skeptical. First, citizens are more sensitive when it comes to privacy when dealing with their government. Second, government problems are often more challenging compared to problems found in the private sector. Third, getting acceptance of these kinds of innovative practices is harder in government agencies than in the private sector. Fourth, the present *policy framework* for citizen engagement makes it hard to implement such a radical idea, and potential policy reform is moving at a glacial pace. But Lukensmeyer and Torres also note one reason to forge ahead: the gap between how citizens and industry use the Internet and government will continue to widen, leaving a disenchanted citizenry. These authors emphasize this point with the example of a very useful peer production–like application used in the wake of Hurricane Katrina. Called PeopleFinder, it is a relatively simple Google Maps mashup application to help people locate family and friends. PeopleFinder was implemented by a company rather than a government agency. The recent Open Government Initiative of the Obama administration appears to take this kind of example into account and is mandating that government agencies include citizens in their processes in an effort to make processes more transparent but also in an effort to tap the wisdom of the crowds to become more innovative (The White House, 2009).

In short, these fundamental concepts—peer production, open source and open content, user-generated innovation, and crowdsourcing— provide many of the drivers for the use of social media applications in the public sector.

Economic Drivers

The economic drivers accounting for the rise of social media technologies in the public sector include investments in advertising and investments in the future value of popular social networks, such as Facebook or MySpace, by corporations such as Microsoft (McCarthy, 2007). Moreover, media companies are actively producing added value to free online services and are therefore catering to customers in the so-called long tail, (see Figure 3.5), where companies distribute small quantities of many products cheaply (applications on Facebook or the iPhone, for example) rather than putting large investments into expensive software versions and upgrades (Anderson, 2008).

FIGURE 3.5. THE LONG TAIL OF SOCIAL MEDIA TOOLS

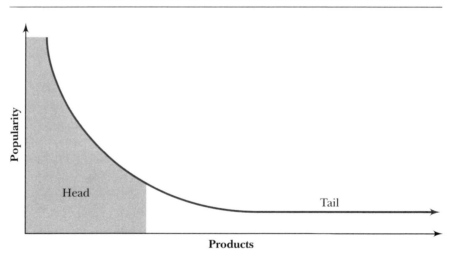

Source: C. Anderson, *The Long Tail: Why the Future of Business Is Selling Less of More* (Rev. and updated ed.) (New York: Hyperion, 2008).

The economic advantage of using social media in comparison to traditional e-services in the public sector is that most of the social media services are free of charge and are usually provided by external private sector organizations—mainly because they are labeled as lifelong beta versions (O'Reilly, 2005). Only a few "gated" services charge a monthly fee for premium services. Users and their online behaviors—instead of expensive development and marketing teams—contribute to technology innovations. Users' acceptance of "perpetual" beta versions is extremely high. Even when Facebook announced major privacy setting changes that were highly criticized, the general opinion was that users should not complain about a free service that tries to make a profit through its users' willingness to produce and share content.

The long-tail model in media has also motivated similar business models in other areas of e-government. For example, the interest in cloud computing, or shared service centers, evolved as a consequence. Services that are already hosted on third-party websites and servers have become a more acceptable form of e-government and are now openly discussed as a means of reducing the amounts of resources and investments necessary in government.

With most households operating one or more personal computers and the wide-scale use of mobile phones with direct access to the Internet, I expect a future where most individuals have immediate access to some computing capacity. Trends in software also make it possible for even relatively low-skilled individuals to create their own software applications and to make use of applications newly developed by others as they become available (consider, for example, BlackBerry or iPhone applications for constant connectivity). In a world where each individual has computing capacity, has access to software applications, and is networked, mobile phones and the Internet allow individuals immediate communication with all other individuals and organizations. Similarly, this type of decentralized computing, access to software, and networked communication allow organizations to have immediate access to all relevant individuals and information sources. Finally, all of these trends are leading to major changes in both data capturing and data retrieval. Each individual may now act as an input source of data about himself or herself, other individuals, and his or her and others' environments. These developments underpin the increasing ability of citizens to report events as they happen, including but not limited to fires, crimes, and traffic accidents (Gillmore, 2006).

CHAPTER FOUR

BARRIERS TO THE USE OF SOCIAL MEDIA IN THE PUBLIC SECTOR

The growth in public sector social media use comes at a time when government online practices generally are under heavy criticism. Two recent initiatives of the Obama administration in particular have shown that government agencies are wasting money on some aspects of their online presences. For example, the IT Dashboard that tracks government spending on IT projects is revealing that costs have been exploding over time (U.S. Government Accountability Office, 2011). Initially, projected expenses skyrocketed due to a lack of expert knowledge during the proposal phase as well as too little guidance and the addition of new requirements during the project implementation phase. The second source of excessive costs is the exploding number of government websites. In a recent blog post titled "TooManyWebsites.gov," the White House social media director pointed out that U.S. federal government departments and agencies altogether have established over 2,000 top domain websites; the smaller subsites and microsites associated with these main websites total up to 24,000 sites (The White House, 2011). Both these sources of high costs highlight the decentralization of web authority in the federal government. Each agency, subunit, or even team or informal group can set up a web presence with little or no formal top-down guidance or oversight of even its large IT projects.

At the same time, polls find that citizens deeply distrust their government, and this lack of confidence in government operations has led to movements such as Occupy Wall Street, voicing grievances about government failures to confront bank practices, the volume of foreclosures from defaulting mortgages, income inequality, and the worldwide financial crisis. A recent Pew Research Center study finds that 89 percent of U.S. citizens distrust the government's ability to do the right thing (Zeleny & Thee-Brenan, 2011). The existing government communication and information systems have not proven their expected value (Moon, 2002). The use of government communication sites shows that trust in government can only be increased when citizens have the impression that their government is sharing information well. Otherwise trust in government will decrease even further than the levels shown in Figure 4.1 (Rainie, Purcell, Siesfeld, & Patel, 2011).

FIGURE 4.1. TRUST IN GOVERNMENT AND VIEWS ON NATIONAL CONDITIONS

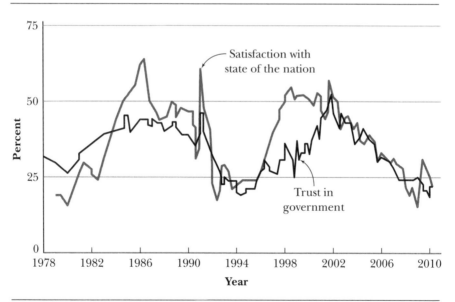

Source: Pew Research Center for the People & the Press, *Distrust, Discontent, Anger and Partisan Rancor: The People and Their Government,* 2010, http://www.people-press.org/2010/04/18/distrust-discontent-anger-and-partisan-rancor.

In this climate of distrust in government, the factors of exploding costs for IT projects, a movement toward reducing the number of online accounts and digital government presences, a desire to centralize IT spending and coordinate IT practices, and the burgeoning use of social technologies are combining to produce a new wave of digital government (Bretschneider & Mergel, 2010).

Yet numerous challenges can hinder the adoption of social technologies; this chapter focuses on four central categories of these challenges: (1) systemic challenges, including the fact that power is highly distributed in the U.S. government system; (2) organizational and cultural challenges arising from bureaucracy and existing standard operating procedures; (3) informational challenges owing to information-vetting and justification processes; and (4) legal challenges arising from the use of innovative (and relatively untested) technologies in the public sector.

Systemic Challenges

This first challenge is inherent to the American political system. Government operations are highly distributed as a result of the federal system. The decentralization of U.S. government operations—and the consequent decentralization of e-service provisions and interactions—is anchored in the U.S. Constitution, particularly in the concept of the separation of powers. Government tasks are separated into the legislative, executive, and judicial branches. The functions of these branches are distinct and the sources and spheres of power and authority in each branch are specifically defined. The "checks and balances" in this design are meant to prevent the concentration of power in a single branch of government.

Federalism also implies the separation of power between national, state, and local governments. It is designed to prevent the centralization of government by curtailing the power of the federal government in order to uphold the rights of the individual states, through a system where rights and responsibilities are divided among the federal government, the fifty state governments, and approximately 90,000 local governments (Kettl, 2006; Kettl & Fesler, 2009). This system results in overlapping and intersecting lines of responsibility, authority, and participation but also a large degree of autonomy for government units, with a considerable amount of freedom to decide their extent of transparency, information sharing, collaboration, and participation in the forms of engagement activities.

In terms of technology adoption, each individual agency has maximum freedom to adopt its own software practices. Often, IT functions are decentralized, and intersect little with communication or public relations authority within an individual agency. The result can be "wild" experimentation with social technologies outside the given organizational context or in the cloud. This distribution of functions in the overall system combined with the autonomy of each department, subunit, and agency has implications for where the responsibility for social media use should be located in an organization and where formal guidance should be coming from. For example, should responsibilities for technology and for content be located in the IT department, in the public affairs office, or with individual knowledge experts much deeper in an organization? A problem also occurs when top-down decisions are directed at one branch but ultimately affect all levels of government. For example, the adoption and acceptance of the transparency and open government memorandum is only recognized in those units to which the memo is directed: the departments of the executive branch.

Another challenge is that the emergent application and popularity of social technologies and the increasing use of social technologies by individuals is creating dramatic changes in the way people communicate and collaborate at a peer-to-peer production level over the Internet, and this in turn is driving a need within government units to create, distribute, and collect information by means outside the traditional hierarchical information structure if these units wish to communicate with citizens (Benkler, 2006). For example, citizens are expecting instant feedback when they are willing to interact with government on social media sites. However, government's standard operating procedures are not designed to provide instant—and oftentimes informal—feedback. The expected reciprocation creates a reflexive feedback cycle that cannot be met with the current standard operating procedures and formal communication structures.

The evolving social technologies coupled with the changing behavior of citizens and government employees form a reality that is completely mismatched with government's required yearly print schedules of formal reports. Organizational processes need to follow new forms of interactions and task fulfillment in a networked government. Removing the constraints of existing technology and introducing new technological means are requiring government to think about new rules, acceptable use standards, organizational institutions, resource allocation, and adjustments of existing resources to the new requirements.

Organizational and Cultural Challenges

The traditional *press mission* of government organizations focuses on press conferences; press releases; interviews; speech writing; the provision of printed information in the form of government reports, brochures, and flyers; official websites; podcasts; and also of course public service announcements and public hearings (Nabatchi & Reeher, 2012; Veteritti, 2008). These traditional forms of informing the public about government operations and decision-making processes oftentimes lead to high degrees of guardedness in public employees' communications. The learned, on-the-record, scripted communication style favored by government officials is a barrier to their use of informal conversational technologies. *Confidentiality agreements* and sworn secrecy statements prevent open exchanges on third-party platforms. The principles of using *discretion* about what a public sector employee does on the job and maintaining confidentiality about private data concerning citizens as agency clients protect public sector employees and citizens alike. For example, police officers are not allowed to talk about the details of last night's arrests, social workers are not allowed to reveal specifics about their cases, and service members are expected to keep classified information from being leaked to the public on the Internet.

As part of the mandate set by the transparency and open government memo, President Obama asked agencies to use new technologies in the hope of promoting efficiency and effectiveness in government. In order to accomplish this goal, agencies are opening their organization's communication channels not just to the public but also across organizational boundaries—inviting other government organizations and also corporate and nonprofit sector organizations to collaborate in innovative ways. Although this phenomenon can be seen from an audience perspective, it much more highlights how government transforms to a networked organism (Figure 4.2). Interagency collaboration has been in the center of attention for scholars such as Fountain (2001, 2007) who argue that agencies, with their mandated interactions, have overlapping interests and need the technological infrastructure to effectively collaborate across organizational boundaries. At the current state of enacting the Open Government Initiative, however, most collaboration still happens informally, and interagency exchanges still need to be formalized. Social media platforms can serve as effective mechanisms to facilitate these exchanges and improve bureaucratic governance structures in the public sector.

As social media are adopted, the boundaries between government agencies as the sole authorities for information and other organizations

FIGURE 4.2. NETWORKED GOVERNMENT

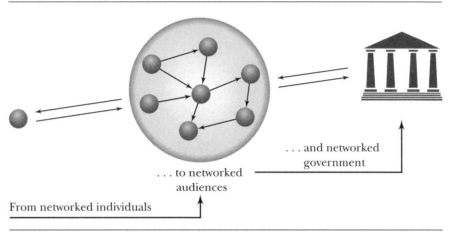

... and networked
government

... to networked
audiences

From networked individuals

and individuals start to blur. These blurring boundaries are increasing organizational complexity (Bughin, Byers, & Chui, 2011). At the same time, an agency's audience members are becoming more clearly identifiable, down to the individual citizen, rather than being an undefined, broad group of potential listeners or stakeholders. Although there is a huge potential for an influx of innovative knowledge as a result of blurring and thus extending the boundaries of agencies, the informal nature of online conversations does not match the highly formal nature of government records and processes.

One social media director summarizes the organizational and cultural barriers to the adoption of social media as follows:

> I would say that the biggest hurdle is probably a culture issue. There are some government agencies that are extremely liberal with their use of social media. They allow people to participate constantly, doesn't matter who they are. I guess from my perspective that is a wonderful thing. However, they are a very, very small minority. The majority of government agencies are extremely conservative, and very centralized or controlling. And it goes for [my agency] too, I'll be perfectly honest. Every one of the staff, the employees, or the contractors has access to the Internet through the network. They do not have access to Facebook. . . . They have access to Twitter but they can't tweet. I think that once this becomes really part of the mainstream, and people get more and more

used to it, and there becomes a real business reason to have access to it, I think that executives all over the federal government will loosen up. I'm not just talking about [my agency] here. So I think that once that loosens up . . . there will be more of a culture of trust about the software itself.

Social technologies can have disruptive effects on the existing organizational norms and procedural elements of government organizations. Examples of these kinds of effects can be found in the publishing industry: the so-called blogosphere has created an immense threat to the existing business model of news creation and distribution in the corporate sector. Information sharing about news and events is no longer reserved for the traditional news channels of television, radio, and print media. On the contrary the publishing industry, in particular, has suffered an immense drop in subscriptions and sales (Carr, 2008; Pew Research Center's Project for Excellence in Journalism, 2008; Thottam, 1999). There is a tendency for people to think that news is more reliable when it is replicated and verified through citations and linkages on blogs or Twitter or shared through trusted friendship ties—so-called social news sources—by means of social networking sites (Goode, 2009).

In a fully networked government, social technologies can be used to scan the environment and match issues that citizens are discussing online and off-line with agency priorities. A networked agency then has to try to match the use of social technologies to its mission and to actually accomplish the tasks.

Identity of Government Audiences

The mission statements of agencies are usually relatively broad and include audience definitions such as "all Americans" or "the public." Understanding the diverse group of stakeholders a government department has to cater to is especially challenging in an environment in which measuring online activities and tracking user behavior of citizens is highly restricted.

Within that diverse group may be not only citizens, government clients, customers, communities, interest groups, and elected and other officials at all levels of government but also vendors, service providers and contractors, foreign governments, other government organizations, nonprofit organizations, and corporate sector organizations. Traditionally, all these groups were defined broadly and identifiable only as large stakeholder groups with whom government communication was only indirectly possible. Social technologies—with the ability to create a personalized profile of each user—now provide the challenging opportunity for government officials to humanize and individualize their direct exchanges, literally down to the individual level. Now the possibility of direct communication as part of both traditional service and e-service delivery has the potential to create an overwhelming amount of information access and influx and a situation in which government officials might not have the capacity to extract or customize their exchanges.

Only recently the federal policy that agencies were not to use *persistent cookies*, which would allow them to track individuals' use of an agency site, was slightly lifted, and agencies are now allowed to track mission-critical use of government websites to a certain extent. The actual practices have not yet caught up with the regulations, and agencies still tend to measure only global trends, instead of individual citizen behavior (see Chapter Six for detailed measurement techniques).

Disincentives

An important characteristic of social technologies is the emerging collaborative and integrative voluntary element. For example, Intellipedia, a recent wiki application for the Intelligence Community, has grown faster than Wikipedia during the same time period due to the contributions of a set of highly motivated and engaged employees (Gross, 2006). One of the challenges for an agency that has decided to integrate a wiki, for example, into its daily routine of knowledge creation and knowledge dissemination is how to motivate employees to voluntarily share their knowledge with everyone in the organization. Interactive web technologies such as Intellipedia challenge the organization as a whole: standard operating procedures might have to be reengineered or well-established routines completely scrutinized. It is difficult, however, to engage a critical mass of employees to contribute to an additional organizational system (Mergel, Lazer, & Binz-Scharf, 2008). As Behn (1995) puts it, it is difficult to motivate public sector employees to go the extra mile beyond the established job descriptions and immutable payment structure (also see Kirlin, 1996).

In order to increase the motivation to participate in or to start to use social technologies in government, it is necessary to go beyond traditional incentive systems. User-centered innovation is a potentially important tool. For example, when social technologies are developed and put in place by employees who are trying to solve work challenges or improve the functioning, collaboration, or interaction of employees and other stakeholders, those employees have a desired outcome as a major incentive. Incentivizing also needs to focus on the baby boomers and digital immigrants who have little or no experience with social technologies. The Intellipedia experience showed that SWAG ("stuff we all get," such as coffee mugs, lanyards, or shovels) works as an initial incentive to activate and reward the first generation of users. However, SWAG cannot incentivize resistant government employees whose work environment and workplace culture incentivize them to conduct their tasks within learned routines. In all forms of organization, but especially in government, there is a culture of maintaining the status quo, and employees might take a defensive stance against innovation. For this reason, additional needs-based incentives might have to be considered, such as professional development rewards and mechanisms to encourage sharing and collaboration through employee performance reviews (see for example Schweik, Stepanov, & Grove, 2005), to satisfy the need for self-esteem and self-actualization or to recognize contributors as experts based on, for example, the number of articles added to a wiki.

In addition an official measurement of efficient knowledge sharing via social technologies can be integrated into annual performance reviews and evaluation systems. This might help to enhance the status of technology adoption and show that top management is buying into new routines. The biggest challenge is therefore to understand what motivates individual employees to contribute to innovation, and then adapt the existing human resource policies and systems accordingly. (See Chapter Six for an in-depth view of metrics and measurement for social technology activities.)

Foci of Decision Making and Entrepreneurship

In the previous four waves of IT adoption in government, including the most recent wave of Internet services (e-government), organizational decision making was directed from the top down (Figure 4.3). Top-management decision making led to allocation of necessary resources, acquisition of skills through vendors, and investment decisions. Implementation and use were then accepted and applied broadly.

As this book has argued, social technologies have the advantage of being widely distributed and accepted among citizens and among public servants as citizens. Tools such as YouTube, Wikipedia, Flickr, and Facebook have lowered the learning curve for content production and sharing online. The resulting ease of use stimulates self-regulation and self-organization. The interactive web can be used as an additional set of tools and channels for citizen participation and interaction with elected officials. However, this has potentially disruptive effects on power balances in the sense that it

FIGURE 4.3. DECISION MAKING AND IMPLEMENTATION IN E-GOVERNMENT PROJECTS

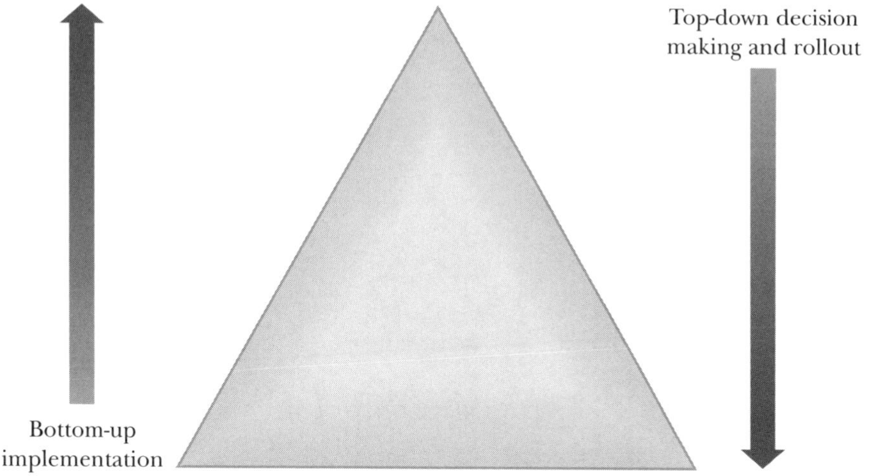
Top-down decision making and rollout
Bottom-up implementation

Source: Copyright © 2012 by Ines Mergel. All rights reserved.

might undermine government's mandate and sovereignty. The result of many undirected interactions then leads to the emergence of new structures and use patterns that consolidate over time and become the new status quo in the interaction between public sector organizations and their stakeholders, which O'Reilly calls the "architecture of participation" (2004).

Figure 4.4 illustrates how lighthouse projects appear as informal experimentation—oftentimes driven by demands from outside the organizational boundaries. In this phase, top management reacts to successful business cases with more hesitation and far fewer resources than it did in the previous transaction- and service-oriented e-government phase.

Informational Challenges

Another set of challenges in using social technologies in the public sector involves defining the relevance of content and information-vetting processes. Public administration researchers are propagating a new information paradigm as a result of the Open Government Initiative (Dawes, Cresswell, & Pardo, 2009). In the public sector the advent of the faster and

FIGURE 4.4. BOTTOM-UP EXPERIMENTATION WITH THE USE OF SOCIAL MEDIA APPLICATIONS

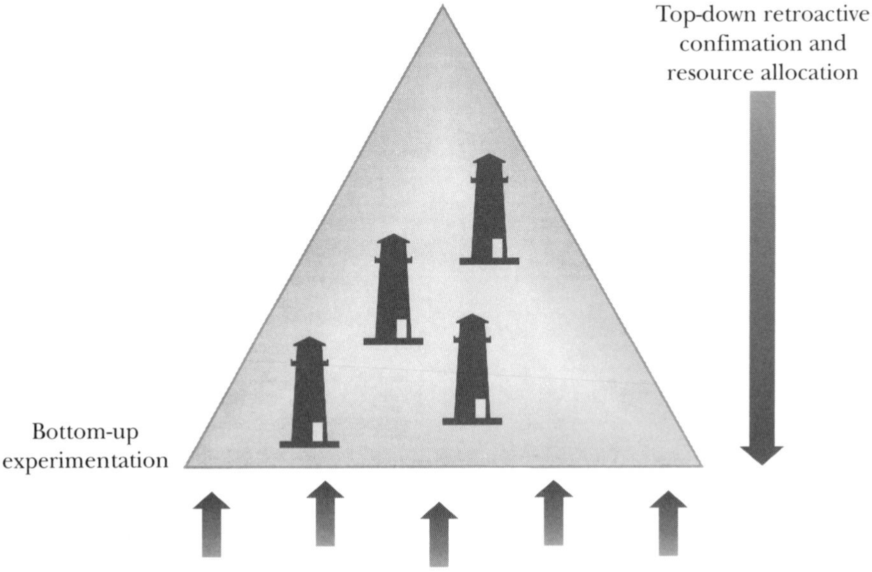

Top-down retroactive confimation and resource allocation

Bottom-up experimentation

more interactive publishing mechanisms of social technologies is helping government to move from a *need-to-know* to a *need-to-share* information paradigm. The unprecedented openness and fast back and forth conversations envisioned in the open government paradigm are designed to lead to new forms of inclusion, co-creation of content, bidirectional information flows, and close to real-time feedback cycles. The traditional information-vetting procedures can therefore be used only for initial versions of press releases and similar announcements. Responses to blogs or Facebook comments or retweets and replies on Twitter challenge any orchestrated information-vetting procedure.

This informational challenge can be extended to third parties, including contractors, outside government. The potential of interactive web tools to support ease of collaboration and informal horizontal and vertical information sharing among all collaborators also creates an obligation to coordinate, manage, and control information dissemination. A specific issue here is that government actors might feel the threat of losing control over the information creation and dissemination process.

As one of the social media directors I interviewed says, controlling the message has become a challenging task:

> I mean, you've got to walk a fine line. I mean, people have to understand that the age of being able to control how you are seen and viewed and talked about is gone. People are going to talk about us, and they are going to talk about us publicly whatever we do. So, what I try to do is guide the conversation. We allow people to comment on our stuff, whether it is positive or negative, and when we get negative stuff, I do a couple things. If they are wrong and the criticism is incorrect, then I will say, you are [incorrect], here is why. If the criticism is valid, we address it and say it is something we are working on. But I think we are beyond the point of trying to just avoid the fact that there is bad news out there and people are going to say bad stuff about us.

Other, perhaps related, recent developments at the federal government level, such as enhancements to the Freedom of Information Act (U.S. Department of State, 2007), revised information-sharing strategies in the Intelligence Community (Office of the Director of National Intelligence, 2008), and the U.S. Army's new knowledge management principles (U.S. Army, 2008) are softening the traditional need-to-know culture and replacing it with a need-to-share attitude, and are doing so in some rather surprising parts of the government (Dawes et al., 2009). Organizations such as the Army are struggling with the official use of social technologies. On the one hand, sites such as Facebook have proven to be important sources of emotional support and connection for deployed soldiers with their families and friends (Wells, Sorenson, Justice, Castilo, & Lin, 2009). On the other hand, misdirected use of these applications has led the U.S. Marine Corps to ban access to social networking services on their network (Beizer, 2009a, 2009b).

The new realities challenge the standard operating procedures of traditional information creation and access for the public. Previously information was kept in specific information channels, such as e-mail folders and shared hard drives, condensed into reports and memos, and stored in isolated databases that have tended to lock information within agency silos (Wylie, 2007). These traditional practices are now being challenged. They could be enhancing or disrupting information flows in three areas: (1) individuals' ability to exercise access rights to existing information, (2) individuals' ability to participate in the creation of information and knowledge, and (3) individuals' needs for archiving and searching.

Social technologies are also changing the way information is publicly created and who creates information. For example, applications such as wikis and blogs are providing opportunities for external participants to easily create comments or submit opinions and questions. So far, there is little regulation available that states how this information has to be archived or made publicly available upon request, or even how it constitutes government information in the first place. This creates a challenge for public records management but might also hinder public sector organizations from starting to use more interactive ways of integrating comments and feedback from the public in the first place.

Moreover, although comments on blogs and entries on wikis could create public value through the "wisdom of crowds" phenomenon (Surowiecki, 2004), they could also lead to the creation of new forms of information silos, with information stuck in specific channels. The back end of government might not be designed in a way that allows it to efficiently integrate the incoming information in an effective knowledge management system. A meaningful extraction of the created knowledge and its integration into the existing knowledge base is necessary to turn created knowledge into actionable knowledge. So far there exist only limited possibilities for automatically extracting and combining created knowledge (Mergel, 2011; Schweik, Mergel, Sanford, & Zhao, 2011). Government still needs to find ways to automatically extract sentiments or innovative knowledge from the massive amounts of information that citizens are willing to leave in comments or retweets on platforms such as Facebook or Twitter. Government in turn has the opportunity to show how citizens' input has affected innovations in government and thus new policies or decisions that affect citizens directly.

Moreover, several questions arise as more knowledge is created publicly and through the citizens' peer production processes: Who owns the content created by citizens? Is the privacy of those who contribute protected? Who determines how the content or data are used? The current information proprietary rights do not provide sufficient answers to these questions and are challenging existing assumptions about transparency approaches in government.

The declining trust in government affects more than the way that citizens wish to interact with government. The already mentioned Pew Research Center study shows that citizens also do not trust their elected officials or media organizations to provide trustworthy information. Instead, citizens tend to vet the information they receive with a diversity of other resources, including their trusted friendship networks, before they act on it. Individuals are using social technologies to collect, vet, and discuss news and information, instead of turning to formally scripted content provided by government. Although this might seem like a challenge solely for government, it also highlights major opportunities for the responsible use of social media to increase citizen satisfaction (ForeSee, 2011). Social technologies can potentially fill the trust gap and help in the triangle between government, mass media, and citizens to fulfill a critical civic function and increase trust in elected government officials. The interactive nature of social media applications allows immediate reaction to citizen inquiries— be it as a fact-checking mechanism or as a true customer service function. Citizens will know immediately what happened to their concerns and how the information was processed, and they might perceive that their comments and complaints are taken seriously by government officials.

Technological Challenges

Government is facing technological challenges on several levels. On the one hand agencies with significant information infrastructure that are using pre-web technologies have the challenge that their existing IT systems are not integrated and that knowledge cannot be accessed and shared in an efficient way (Brewin, 2008). For example, a recent report from the U.S. Government Accountability Office (2009) found this situation at the U.S. Food and Drug Administration. As a result the agency was unable to fulfill its mandate to access and integrate existing (legacy) databases and to inform the public about potential threats.

Adding social technologies has also led to security concerns, as one social media director reports: "I think the other hurdle is IT security. We have a group here that is dedicated to providing IT security—firewall, virus prevention, everything is their responsibility. I think that until some of the social media sites really stress prevention, and take care of their own problems as far as creating havens for viruses or any other problems like that, I think that once that happens, then the IT security people will say that it's OK to do some [social technology] stuff." And another social media director adds: "The only issue we have had at all is security. We were afraid at the very beginning that if we opened up the whole department to Facebook and Twitter that we . . . [might] crash the system. We were worried about the whole . . . security issue. But we worked through all that within a few months last year."

In the fast-developing landscape of social media providers, it is not clear which applications might survive and still be available six months from now. The current example of the URL shortener that was taken off the market (Nambu's tr.im) is a case in point. In response the U.S. federal government created its own URL shortener (a beta version is at go.usa.gov). Nevertheless, the fast pace and arguably uncontrollable evolution of third-party tools might discourage public sector organizations from jumping on the bandwagon and adopting new services if they have to fear that their mission-specific content might disappear together with the technology.

Agencies' internal vetting processes, security checks, and IT support are slow and hinder successful and rapid adoption of new technologies:

> Currently the biggest roadblocks that we face are really more from a resource and from an internal perspective. So, for example, if I want to set up a blog externally on an externally hosted site, that's easier than getting, for example, WordPress installed here at the [agency] so that we have an ability to host blogs as needed and evaluate plug-ins and add new features. One of the things I would like to see more here is to have more internal capability for things. But roadblock-wise, that's probably the biggest challenge here. I think other than that, using Facebook, Twitter, there haven't been any major hurdles, because we have been fortunate that [the department] is leading the way. We have been able to work with them, take their guides, best practices, adapt it to our work. We have very supportive folks down at [the department] who want to see this happen and move forward, so that environment is really great for us.

Finally, social technology adoption faces challenges beyond those in the back office or on the infrastructure side. One of these is *digital illiteracy*. As large parts of the population become more and more familiar with social media tools, a huge gap is growing between adopters and nonadopters. In fact, some of the reluctance to adopt social media applications in the public has come from incidences of ineffective or irresponsible use of social networking services by public officials themselves (Associated Press, 2011; Morozov, 2009; Sutter, 2009; Wildstrom, 2009). The low degree of digital literacy in relation to social media can be explained by the newness of these media. As Figure 4.5 illustrates, social technologies provide an informal interaction that comes very close to the richness of face-to-face interactions. However, users might be unaware of how they are connected through their social media networks and how others can reuse their posted content in a way that can snowball through the system.

FIGURE 4.5. RICHNESS OF INTERACTION FOR DIFFERENT COMMUNICATION MEDIA

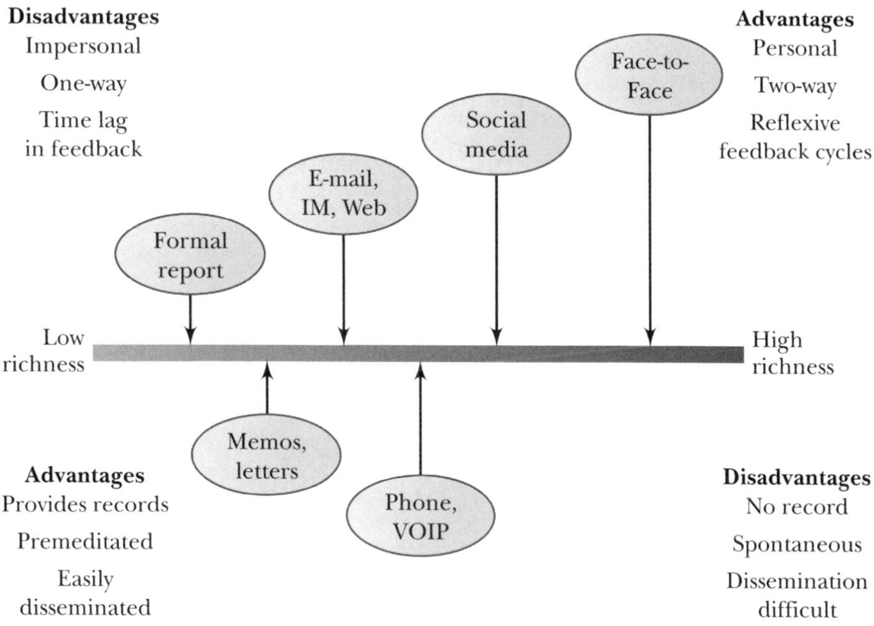

Disadvantages
Impersonal
One-way
Time lag
in feedback

Advantages
Personal
Two-way
Reflexive
feedback cycles

Face-to-Face

Social media

E-mail, IM, Web

Formal report

Low richness

High richness

Memos, letters

Phone, VOIP

Advantages
Provides records
Premeditated
Easily
disseminated

Disadvantages
No record
Spontaneous
Dissemination
difficult

Legal Challenges

An ambiguous legal environment has hindered many government organizations from adopting social media applications. Starting out, agencies had little formal guidance, top-management engagement, or even regulations or acceptable use policies. Instead, existing regulations covered only e-mail use and Internet presences and did not address social media applications on third-party websites. The following statement of a social media director in the federal government suggests the contradictions found in existing laws and regulations, which do not meet the needs of the new technological and behavioral realities:

We want to encourage participation and collaboration, and social media tools are great tools to encourage participation and collaboration. And hopefully all the regulations and laws will catch up with where we are headed. So to the extent that we can, we want to be able to, for example, leverage the power of the crowds to come up with some ideas for how we are doing some things at the [agency]. And so we'd like to see an ideation tool, where folks can put their ideas out. There are contests to help spur innovation. So, we are trying to follow the presidential direction, and I think our senior leadership here supports that. The roadblocks that we find internally are that there are just other rules in place, and there are requirements that we have to meet, and sometimes these are at odds. But we always try to make sure to look at the bigger picture, and try to move all the tools forward.

This apparent gap between evolving practices and nonexistent or outdated rules and regulations has hindered or prevented many agencies from starting to use social technologies. Slowly, guidelines are catching up with the apparent need for regulation.

CHAPTER FIVE

REGULATIONS AND DIRECTIVES FOR THE USE OF SOCIAL MEDIA IN THE PUBLIC SECTOR

The use of social media applications by government agencies is connected with many uncertainties. Third parties create and maintain social networking services outside of government. Increasingly, the data and records that government employees create on behalf of their agencies and departments are not stored on a local government server but in the cloud. Although a great deal of early experimentation occurred and several lighthouse projects emerged when government started to use social media, most agencies remain hesitant to experiment outside existing rules and regulations. This hesitation has led to a series of new rules and regulations and updated standards and directives to bring policy into alignment with the use of social media. Most regulations are, however, upgrades or adaptations of existing rules for government websites.

Interactive web technologies and accompanying behavioral changes among users also have legal drivers: emerging distribution platforms allow easy, relatively low-tech creation and sharing of work. The collaborative culture of open source software development, driven by an innovation in the use of copyright so that licenses may mandate a sharing culture rather than proprietary protection, has led to joint product creation in which thousands of programmers voluntarily produce a product for free (Lerner & Tirole, 2005). Traditionally, software was produced with substantial investments in staff and organizational overhead by existing media companies. Each new version opened a new revenue stream for the creators. By contrast, Creative Commons licenses—inspired by the example of open source software production—now allow for flexible licensing and copyright schemes that encourage open access, sharing, and the prospect of creating new derivative works in digital format, rather than treating content as closed and proprietary (Creative Commons, 2008). This trend is in line with the information policy innovation taking place currently in the Obama administration (The White House, 2009).

The combination of agency use of existing communication media tools with changing user behavior on the citizen side has enabled a productive and technologically empowered public sector community with potentially disruptive effects on existing government communication models. This is connected with high expectations among the public concerning access, information distribution, and freedom of interaction. As both citizens and government employees are becoming more tech savvy and are informally learning from each other, innovations are emerging that are solely user driven and that increase the level of demand for interactivity with government agencies and public sector units. Government regulations had to be developed to respond to these changes and make it safe for departments and agencies to use social media tools. The rest of this chapter presents a close look at the evolving body of regulations that exists today, established in reaction to innovative social networking services and their increased used by government.

The Evolution in Directives and Rules

The direction in which the use of social media services in the U.S. government has been evolving stems in part from rule changes made for political and regulatory reasons and from new policies about *acceptable use*. However, it is also being driven by an increased level of maturity in social media tools. To highlight just the most prominent tools: LinkedIn, Friendster, and MySpace were launched in 2003, followed by Facebook in 2004, YouTube in 2005, and Twitter in 2006. We can add to this development the emergence of a whole conglomerate of other Web 2.0 tools, such as wikis, blogs, and virtual worlds.

The platforms that are now collectively called social media have roots that stretch back almost ten years. Many local and state government information technology (IT) professionals tried early on to find ways to integrate social media into their existing communication, collaboration, and community approaches. For example, in 2007, the then chief technology officer (CTO) of Washington, DC, Vivek Kundra, used a wiki to present requests for proposals in the acquisition process. In 2008, as part of the Government 2.0 ecosystem, over 800 local government IT professionals found a way to share lessons learned and best practices by participating in a virtual group called MuniGov2.0. At about the same time, GovLoop—the "Facebook for government"—was created; it now has over 50,000 government professionals sharing information about Government 2.0–related topics.

E-Government Act of 2002

The E-Government Act of 2002, which deals with the "federal management and promotion of electronic government services," helped to pave the way for the responsible use of web services by government. In this Act, federal agencies and departments were instructed on the organization, accessibility, usability, and preservation of government information on the Internet. An interagency committee was put in place to share best practices across organizational boundaries and to create recommendations for the adoption of standards for electronic government information, interoperability, and electronic records management.

Policies for Federal Agency Public Websites (2004)

The demands articulated in the E-Government Act of 2002 resulted in "Recommended Policies and Guidelines for Federal Public Websites," published in a final report of the Interagency Committee on Government Information and submitted to the Office of Management and Budget (OMB) in June 2004. The recommendations of the committee were then distilled into an OMB memorandum, Policies for Federal Agency Public Websites, directing executive departments and agencies to apply these new policies (Office of Management and Budget, 2004). The memorandum outlined the importance of efficient, effective, and appropriately consistent use of federal agency public websites to promote a citizen-centered government in compliance with federal information resource management law and policy.

Specifically, the memo highlights that public websites are considered information resources and information dissemination products and have to be managed as part of an agency's information resource management program. The memo specifies the following policies in detail:

- Establish and maintain information dissemination product inventories, priorities, and schedules.
- Ensure information quality.

- Establish and enforce agency-wide linking policies.
- Communicate with the public and with state and local governments.
- Search public websites.
- Use approved domains.
- Implement security controls.
- Protect privacy.
- Maintain accessibility.
- Manage records.

Third-party websites, including social networking services such as Facebook or MySpace, are not mentioned in this Act in the policies established for public records management, privacy protection, or linking of materials.

Open Government (2009 to Present)

It was not until 2009 that President Obama—encouraged by his successful Internet campaign strategy that included the use of social networking services—started to talk about the use of social networking services in government (Carpenter, 2009).

Transparency and Open Government Initiative (2009)

In 2009, agencies and departments in the executive branch of the U.S. federal government started to use social media applications such as Facebook pages, Twitter updates, YouTube videos, blogs, and RSS feeds. This development was triggered by President Obama's memorandum titled Transparency and Open Government, published one day after his inauguration on January 21, 2009 (Obama, 2009b). In this memo President Obama highlights three distinct areas of open government that he directs executive departments and agencies to increase: participation, collaboration, and transparency.

The administration made these three areas its priority to increase openness in government. Although the tools to accomplish these goals are not specified, the memo does state the need for information disclosure in an easy and accessible manner, increased speed of disclosure, additional opportunities for citizen input, and the use of innovative tools, methods, and systems for intergovernmental collaboration. President Obama has emphasized the use of innovative tools in many subsequent speeches (Obama, 2009a).

The memo provides a mandate for the executive departments and agencies in the federal government. At the same time, a movement that is self-inspired, driven by the need for more transparency and community building at the local and state government levels, can also be observed.

Although every administration in the past forty years has developed a variation of open government, the Obama administration has redefined information as a public asset that needs to be shared with citizens. The transparency and open government memo specifically urges executive departments and agencies to "harness new technologies to put information about their operations and decisions online and readily available to the public" (Obama, 2009b). What becomes clear in this memo is that the current administration does not see government as the sole provider of relevant and actionable information—on the contrary, all constituencies are regarded as important contributors in helping to create, share, and disseminate information.

The Open Government Directive

Government 2.0 has quickly become a synonym for the use of the second generation of Internet technologies in government: highly interactive social networking services that allow real-time information sharing, crowdsourcing, and bidirectional communication between citizens and government (Bretschneider & Mergel, 2010). In the first year of the Government 2.0 movement most federal government agencies were hesitant to dive into social media. On the federal level the transparency and open government memo was quickly followed by a series of regulations and policy documents to provide necessary detailed guidance to agencies. In December 2009, the OMB followed up with the Open Government Directive, which ordered executive departments and agencies to take specific actions to implement the principles of transparency, participation, and collaboration along the lines of the following activities (Office of Management and Budget, 2009; also see The White House, 2009):

- Publish government information online.
- Improve the quality of government information.
- Create and implement the culture of open government.
- Create an enabling policy framework for open government.
- Create an open government plan, including a flagship initiative.

In April 2010, each federal executive department and agency published its open government plan. The administration's chief technology officer and chief information officer were charged with evaluating the results of these plans on an *open government dashboard*—publicly highlighting the performance of each agency (Figure 5.1).

Terms of Service Agreements with Social Networking Services

The Obama administration found that more regulations and conditions were necessary to foster the adoption of new technologies. A pivotal precondition for federal agencies to start using social media tools was negotiating *terms of service* (ToS) agreements with new media providers, a task undertaken by the General Services Administration (GSA), Office of Citizen Services (U.S. General Services Administration, 2010). The ToS arranged by the GSA resolves any legal concerns that agencies discovered in the standard terms and conditions in relation to liability limits, endorsements, the Freedom of Information Act, and governing law. The GSA provides the model agreements that can be adapted by all other government agencies to negotiate their own terms of service agreements with new media providers.

Similarly, state government authorities have participated in successful negotiations with service providers in order to modify social media service terms. For example, in 2011 the National Association of State Chief Information Officers (NASCIO) negotiated model agreements with Facebook for state government use (Bertot, Jaeger, & Hansen, 2011; Price, 2010). These negotiations have made social media ToS requirements more appropriate to the needs of local and state governments.

The Presidential Records Act and Social Media Information

The hesitation of agencies to adopt social media applications also was fueled by uncertainty about records management for social media content created by government units on third-party websites.

The White House made a first push toward discussing social media content records by viewing them in light of the Presidential Records Act of 1978 (Phillips, 2009). Written more than three decades ago, the Act does not address social media, e-mail, or web content. In his communications with the executives of the National Archives and Records Administration (NARA), the director of new media for the White House, Macon Phillips, verified that postings to online social networking profiles or postings of videos or photos

FIGURE 5.1. DASHBOARD EVALUATING PERFORMANCE ON THE OPEN GOVERNMENT DIRECTIVE

Key:
- Meets Expectations
- Progress Toward Expectations
- Fails to Meet Expectations

					Open Gov't Plan					
Agency	High-Value Data	Data Integrity	Open Webpage	Public Consultation	Overall Plan	Formulating the Plan	Transparency	Participation	Collaboration	Flagship Initiative
Agency for International Development	Progress	Progress	Progress	Progress	Meets	Meets	Meets	Progress	Progress	Progress
Department of Agriculture	Progress	Progress	Progress	Progress	Meets	Progress	Meets	Progress	Meets	Meets
Department of Energy	Progress	Progress	Progress	Progress	Progress	Progress	Progress	Progress	Progress	Progress
Department of Education	Progress	Progress	Progress	Progress	Progress	Progress	Progress	Progress	Progress	Progress
Department of Commerce	Progress	Progress	Progress	Progress	Meets	Progress	Meets	Progress	Meets	Meets
Department of Defense	Progress	Progress	Progress	Progress	Progress	Progress	Progress	Progress	Progress	Progress
Department of Health and Human Services	Progress	Progress	Progress	Progress	Progress	Progress	Progress	Progress	Progress	Progress
Department of Homeland Security	Progress	Progress	Progress	Progress	Progress	Progress	Progress	Progress	Progress	Progress
Department of Housing and Urban Development	Progress	Progress	Progress	Progress	Progress	Progress	Progress	Progress	Progress	Progress
Department of the Interior	Progress	Progress	Progress	Progress	Progress	Progress	Progress	Progress	Progress	Progress
Department of Justice	Progress	Progress	Progress	Progress	Progress	Progress	Progress	Progress	Progress	Progress
Department of Labor	Progress	Progress	Progress	Progress	Meets	Progress	Meets	Progress	Meets	Meets
Department of State	Progress	Progress	Progress	Progress	Meets	Meets	Meets	Progress	Meets	Meets
Department of Transportation	Progress	Progress	Progress	Progress	Progress	Progress	Progress	Progress	Progress	Progress
Department of the Treasury	Progress	Progress	Progress	Progress	Progress	Progress	Progress	Progress	Progress	Progress
Department of Veterans Affairs	Progress	Progress	Progress	Progress	Meets	Progress	Meets	Progress	Meets	Meets
Environmental Protection Agency	Progress	Progress	Progress	Progress	Progress	Progress	Progress	Progress	Progress	Progress
General Services Administration	Progress	Progress	Progress	Progress	Progress	Progress	Progress	Progress	Progress	Progress
National Aeronautics and Space Administration	Progress	Progress	Progress	Progress	Progress	Progress	Progress	Progress	Progress	Progress
National Science Foundation	Progress	Progress	Progress	Progress	Meets	Meets	Meets	Meets	Meets	Progress
Nuclear Regulatory Commission	Progress	Progress	Progress	Progress	Progress	Progress	Progress	Progress	Progress	Progress
Office of Personnel Management	Meets	Progress	Progress	Progress	Progress	Progress	Progress	Progress	Progress	Progress
Small Business Administration	Progress	Progress	Progress	Progress	Meets	Progress	Meets	Progress	Progress	Progress
Social Security Administration	Progress	Progress	Progress	Progress	Progress	Progress	Progress	Progress	Progress	Progress
Council on Environmental Quality	Meets	Progress	Progress	Progress	Meets	Progress	Meets	Progress	Progress	Progress
Office of Management and Budget	Progress	Progress	Progress	Progress	Meets	Progress	Meets	Progress	Meets	Progress
Office of National Drug Control Policy	Progress	Progress	Progress	Progress	Meets	Progress	Meets	Progress	Progress	Meets
Office of Science and Technology Policy	Progress	Progress	Progress	Progress	Progress	Progress	Progress	Progress	Progress	Progress
Office of the United States Trade Representative	Progress	Progress	Progress	Progress	Progress	Progress	Progress	Progress	Progress	Progress

Source: The White House, Open Government Initiative: Around the Government, n.d., retrieved from http://www.whitehouse.gov/open/around.

FIGURE 5.2. TWITTER PROFILE FOR MACON PHILLIPS, WHITE HOUSE DIRECTOR OF NEW MEDIA

Macon Phillips (EOP) ✓

@macon44

An official WH twitter account. Comments & messages received through official WH pages are subject to the PRA and may be archived. Learn more wh.gov/privacy

Washington, DC · http://www.WhiteHouse.gov

Source: M. Phillips, [Twitter profile], n.d., http://twitter.com/#!/macon44.

on White House social media sites are considered presidential records and must be preserved. In a blog post (Phillips, 2009) the White House stated that its automatic archival procedure does not include the tracing and tracking of individual activities of citizens; instead only voluntarily provided content has to be archived, according to the Presidential Records Act .

As a result, many White House (WH) social media sites and profiles include a statement alerting users that the content is subject to the Presidential Records Act. For example, Phillips's Twitter profile (Figure 5.2) includes this statement: "An official WH twitter account. Comments & messages received through official WH pages are subject to the PRA and may be archived."

On April 14, 2010, the Library of Congress announced that it had acquired the entire Twitter archive (Figure 5.3)—a step forward in reducing some of the hesitation social media directors, especially in federal departments, were facing. Up to that point it had been unclear how to retain Twitter messages—or any messages created on social networking services—for public record-keeping purposes. The Library of Congress's collaboration with the microblogging site Twitter now creates a lifetime archive of all Twitter messages ever sent, although that does not relieve government agencies of the mandate to archive their own records. It does, however, help Twitter users to access all their data, given that Twitter displays only the previous two weeks' worth of messages on its website.

Information Collection Under the Paperwork Reduction Act (2010)

Following up on President Obama's 2009 transparency and open government memo, the Office of Information and Regulatory Affairs at the

FIGURE 5.3. LIBRARY OF CONGRESS ANNOUNCEMENT ABOUT TWITTER ARCHIVE

Source: Library of Congress, [Tweet about acquisition of Twitter archive], April 14, 2010, http://twitter.com/#!/librarycongress/status/12169442690.

OMB published an executive directive that offered additional guidance to agencies to specify the transparency and openness requirements for record keeping (Office of Management and Budget, 2010b). This directive reiterates the original purpose of the Paperwork Reduction Act (PRA) to "improve the quality and use of Federal information to strengthen decisionmaking, accountability and openness in government and society." Under the Open Government Initiative and in accordance with the PRA, information collected from the public includes "any statement or estimate of fact or opinion regardless of form or format, whether in numerical, graphical, or narrative form, and whether oral or maintained on paper, electronic or other media" (U.S. Government Accountability Office, 2010).

Even though the directive does not explicitly list the information solicitation and sharing that occur when government agencies interact with the public on social media sites, it can be interpreted as applying to the use of social media applications as well. Government records include information collected "regardless of the form or format" according to the PRA. Generally, record keeping therefore includes pictures, videos, and any type of opinion statements posted to or solicited from government agencies on social networking sites—under specific provisions.

The Office of Management and Budget (2010b) reduces the burden on agencies to collect and archive public information to incidences where ten or more persons submitted their opinions or facts solicited from an agency or department over a period of twelve months.

Social Media, Web-Based Interactive Technologies, and the Paperwork Reduction Act (2010)

Paralleling the updated interpretations of the Paperwork Reduction Act, the Office of Management and Budget (2010c) also published a memorandum: Social Media, Web-Based Interactive Technologies and the Paperwork Reduction Act. This memo responds to the Open Government Directive's demand to "review existing OMB policies, such as Paperwork Reduction Act guidance and privacy guidance, to identify impediments to open government and to the use of new technologies and, where necessary, issue clarifying guidance and/or propose revisions to such policies, to promote greater openness in government."

The memo highlights that the Paperwork Reduction Act does not apply to many of federal agencies' uses of social media and web-based interactive technologies. Every time an agency sponsors public information collection, the following three types of information solicitation do not have to be archived:

- *General solicitations.* 5 C.F.R. 1320.3(h)(4) excludes "facts or opinions submitted in response to general solicitations of comments from the public, published in the Federal Register or other publications, regardless of the form or format thereof, provided that no person is required to supply specific information pertaining to the commenter, other than that necessary for self-identification, as a condition of the agency's full consideration of the comment."
- *Public meetings.* 5 C.F.R. 1320.3(h)(8) excludes certain "facts or opinions obtained or solicited at or in connection with public hearings or meetings."
- *Like items.* 5 C.F.R. 1320.3(h)(10) reserves general authority to OMB to identify other "like items" that are not "information."

In the same vein, e-mail addresses used by the public to subscribe to updates from government agencies and departments are not subject to the PRA, but any additional information that agencies require for the subscriptions, such as race, gender, citizenship status, or employment, is covered under the PRA.

Guidance for Online Use of Web Measurement and Customization Technologies (2010)

In 2010, the OMB published Guidance for Online Use of Web Measurement and Customization Technologies, a memo to help agencies in their engagement efforts with the public (Office of Management and Budget, 2010a). The guidance memo outlines the usefulness and benefits of "web measurement and customization technologies to allow users to customize their settings, avoid filling out duplicative information, and navigate websites more quickly and in a way that serves their interests and needs." Benefits occur for both citizens and agencies: agencies can easily trace and track the kinds of information provided on their websites that are useful for the public and can change agency information provision according to the collected web measurement results. The guidance document indicates how agencies can avoid invading the public's privacy while at the same time benefiting from the use of tracking mechanisms that archive and store users' online interactions on a government website.

Under this guidance, agencies are *not* allowed to use these tracking and measurement tools for the following activities:

- to track user individual-level activity on the Internet outside of the website or application from which the technology originates;
- to share the data obtained through such technologies, without the user's explicit consent, with other departments or agencies;
- to cross-reference, without the user's explicit consent, any data gathered from Web measurement and customization technologies against PII [personally identifiable information] to determine individual-level online activity;
- to collect PII without the user's explicit consent in any fashion; or
- for any like usages so designated by OMB [Office of Management and Budget, 2010a].

Moreover, whenever user data are to be saved, agencies must give clear notice and provide a personal choice to their users. Agency-side opt-out tools allow the agency to remember that a user has opted out earlier, and client-side opt-outs allow users to change their local computer setting so as to opt out of measurement and tracking mechanisms (that is, users may disable cookies in their browsers).

Accountable Government Initiative (2010)

In September 2010, President Obama updated the members of the Senior Executive Service on the Open Government Directive and renamed his Open Government Initiative the Accountable Government Initiative

(The White House, 2010). In this memorandum he specifically highlights the inefficiencies of existing technologies and processes in government: "You also are aware what happens when your best efforts are thwarted by outdated technologies and outmoded ways of doing business. You understand the consequences of accepting billions of dollars in waste as the cost of doing business and of allowing obsolete or underperforming programs to continue year after year."

The president's memorandum was coupled with an update from the OMB that pointed out two technology-related performance indicators. First, it directed agencies to push for more transparency and accountability through data-driven interactions with the public and asked agencies to provide increased access and customer service to the public through their websites. For example, the Department of Veterans Affairs (VA) Blue Button project, by letting veterans download their personal health records, serves as a model for enhanced customer service. Second, it pointed to the IT Dashboard as a means of tracking inefficient IT projects and saving costs by stopping unproductive IT projects. Figure 5.4 displays the visual clarity of this dashboard.

NARA's Social Media Record-Keeping Guidelines (2010)

The initial social media record-keeping discussions and early experimentation at the White House were followed by the National Archives and Records Administration's social media record-keeping guidelines published in October 2010 (U.S. National Archives and Records Administration, 2010). The NARA guidelines reiterate the definition of federal records according to the Federal Records Act (44 U.S.C. §3301): "All books, papers, maps, photographs, machine readable materials, or other documentary materials, regardless of physical form or characteristics; made or received by an agency of the United States Government under Federal law or in connection with the transaction of public business, and; preserved or appropriate for preservation by that agency or its legitimate successor as evidence of the organization, functions, policies, decisions, procedures, operations, or other activities of the Government or because of the informational value of data in them."

Institutional Changes: GSA's Office of Innovative Technology

The Open Government Initiative also made a few organizational changes necessary, building capabilities to better guide the use of new technologies

FIGURE 5.4. THE IT DASHBOARD

Source: IT Dashboard, n.d., http://www.itdashboard.gov.

in light of the new directives and regulations. In testimony before the Committee on Oversight and Government Reform of the U.S. House of Representatives in July 2010, GSA's associate administrator, David L. McClure, outlined how the General Services Administration can help the federal government with implementation of new technologies for citizen inclusion and collaboration (U.S. General Services Administration, 2010). The GSA has established the Center for New Media and Citizen Engagement as the central entity to provide guidance on the use of new media. The effort culminated in HowTo.gov, a new website that provides agencies with step-by-step guides on how to present web content, a list of selected and vetted tools to use for different types of initiatives, software downloads, and instructions on how to customize and administer social media tools from a strategic and administrative perspective. A similarly important website for guidance, Challenge.gov, helps agencies to set up crowdsourcing and ideation applications. Other guidance comes from

PlainLanguage.gov on how to present content on different social media channels to increase inclusion and diffusion of government practices.

Knowledge is not only crowdsourced from citizens—innovative knowledge needs to make its way into government from many different constituents. An example of this is the effort of the White House's Open Government Initiative in 2011 to attract useful knowledge through a wiki, with the goal of crowdsourcing expert opinions on how to increase transparency, collaboration, and participation. (Figure 5.5 displays a page from a website intended to gather public input about this wiki.)

Adoption or diffusion of Government 2.0 practices on the state and local level can be observed only on a case-by-case basis, and these activities display a "just do it" mentality and a lot of trial and error. There is little guidance beyond that available from the federal and state levels, and local governments are under no obligation to emulate federal or state guidelines on the adoption of social media applications and oftentimes set their own standards for this process. Recently, NASCIO has published toolkits and some guidance for state-level chief information officers (Price, 2010).

Nevertheless, Government 2.0 is still in its infancy and can be observed mainly in form of highly public flagship initiatives on the federal

FIGURE 5.5. EXPERTNET: A WIKI FOR THE OPEN GOVERNMENT INITIATIVE

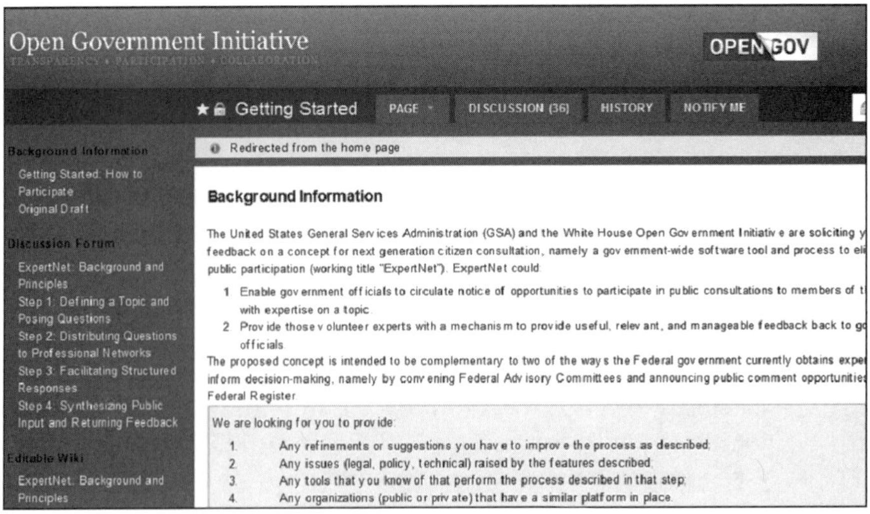

Source: ExpertNet, n.d., http://expertnet.wikispaces.com.

TABLE 5.1. OVERVIEW OF GUIDING REGULATIONS AND DIRECTIVES FOR THE USE OF SOCIAL MEDIA IN THE PUBLIC SECTOR

Title	Date Enacted	Description	Link
Paperwork Reduction Act of 1995	May 1995	Aims to minimize the burden on the public of supplying information to the government. Makes participation in government easier and more understandable. Improves the quality of government information for further accountability.	http://www.gpo.gov/fdsys/pkg/PLAW-104publ13/pdf/PLAW-104publ13.pdf
Government Paperwork Elimination Act	October 21, 1998	Addresses using alternative technology to initiate paperless interactions with the government.	http://www.gpo.gov/fdsys/pkg/PLAW-105publ277/pdf/PLAW-105publ277.pdf
E-Government Act of 2002	December 17, 2002	Aims to ensure that all agencies and branches of government enhance their use of the Internet as a resource for interacting with individuals and organizations. Creates the post of chief federal information officer, whose job is to implement the Act.	http://www.gpo.gov/fdsys/pkg/PLAW-107publ347/pdf/PLAW-107publ347.pdf
Policies for Federal Agency Public Websites (OMB memorandum)	December 17, 2004	Establishes guidelines for websites and the ways they can be used to implement the E-Government Act of 2002 in order to create a more "citizen centered" government.	http://www.whitehouse.gov/sites/default/files/omb/memoranda/fy2005/m05-04.pdf
Management of Federal Information Resources (Circular A-130 Revised; OMB memorandum)	May 2005	Defines websites as a source of information to the public. Because they contain information, that content must be maintained and recorded, like other forms of information.	www.whitehouse.gov/omb/circulars_a130_a130trans4
Transparency and Open Government (presidential memorandum)	January 21, 2009	Sets three goals: government will be transparent, participatory, and collaborative.	http://www.whitehouse.gov/the_press_office/Transparency_and_Open_Government
A Strategy for American Innovation	September 2009	Presents a plan to push open innovation of new technology to drive America's future and economy. Paves a path for future Government 2.0 initiatives, such as challenges and prizes.	http://www.whitehouse.gov/administration/eop/nec/StrategyforAmericanInnovation

(continued)

TABLE 5.1. OVERVIEW OF GUIDING REGULATIONS AND DIRECTIVES FOR THE USE OF SOCIAL MEDIA IN THE PUBLIC SECTOR (*continued*)

Title	Date Enacted	Description	Link
Open Government Directive (OMB memorandum)	December 8, 2009	Outlines specific actions federal agencies must take to fulfill the president's January 21, 2009, memo, Transparency and Open Government.	http://www.whitehouse.gov/sites/default/files/omb/assets/memoranda_2010/m10-06.pdf
Responsible and Effective Use of Internet-Based Capabilities (Department of Defense memorandum)	February 25, 2010	Establishes DOD's specific policy on new media and the Open Government Initiative.	http://www.defense.gov/NEWS/DTM%2009-026.pdf
Guidance on Use of Challenges and Prizes to Promote Open Government (OMB memorandum)	March 8, 2010	Describes the use of competitions open to the public to drive innovation. Members of the public participate in solving the problems facing the government.	http://www.whitehouse.gov/sites/default/files/omb/assets/memoranda_2010/m10-11.pdf
Terms of Service Agreements (ToS negotiated by the GSA)	Beginning in February 2009	Establish terms of service for using multiple social media web platforms, terms that do not conflict with government agencies' policies.	http://www.gsa.gov/portal/content/104320
Information Collection Under the Paperwork Reduction Act (OMB memorandum)	April 7, 2010	Explains what does and does not count as information to be collected under the Paperwork Reduction Act. This is relevant as e-government tools increase public interaction with agencies through websites and new media.	http://www.whitehouse.gov/sites/default/files/omb/assets/inforeg/PRAPrimer_04072010.pdf
Social Media, Web-Based Interactive Technologies, and the Paperwork Reduction Act (OMB memorandum)	April 7, 2010	Offers specific guidance on how new media fit in with older laws like the Paperwork Reduction Act.	http://www.whitehouse.gov/sites/default/files/omb/assets/inforeg/SocialMediaGuidance_04072010.pdf

Title	Date	Description	URL
Guidance for Online Use of Measurement and Customization Technologies (OMB memorandum)	June 25, 2010	Offers OMB guidance on appropriate government use of web technologies.	http://www.whitehouse.gov/sites/default/files/omb/assets/memoranda_2010/m10-22.pdf
Guidance for Agency Use of Third-Party Websites and Applications (OMB memorandum)	June 25, 2010	Discusses how agencies should go about using web technology hosted by a third party: for example, websites such as Facebook or Twitter or an application such as a blog.	http://www.whitehouse.gov/sites/default/files/omb/assets/memoranda_2010/m10-23.pdf
Accountable Government Initiative (OMB memorandum)	September 14, 2010	Discusses closing the IT gap and generally making government overall more efficient through the use of technology.	http://www.whitehouse.gov/sites/default/files/omb/memoranda/2010/AccountableGovernmentInitiative_09142010.pdf
Plain Writing Act of 2010	October 13, 2010	The provisions of this law apply to all government publications (including websites and information accessed through links on those websites); they must be clear and written in easy-to-understand language.	http://www.gpo.gov/fdsys/pkg/PLAW-111publ274/pdf/PLAW-111publ274.pdf
Guidance on Managing Records in Web 2.0/Social Media Platforms (NARA bulletin)	October 20, 2010	Gives advice on how agencies can comply with current mandatory record-keeping requirements while operating in a Government 2.0 and e-government world.	http://www.archives.gov/records-mgmt/bulletins/2011/2011-02.html
America COMPETES Act	January 4, 2011	This law makes it significantly easier for all federal government agencies to legally host challenges and prizes using new web platforms.	http://www.whitehouse.gov/blog/2010/12/21/congress-grants-broad-prize-authority-all-federal-agencies

government level. A recent report of the U.S. Government Accountability Office (2011) states many of the still existing challenges in federal agencies' use of Web 2.0 technologies. GAO recommendations include directions to federal agencies to set up social media policies, which will be addressed in the following chapter.

Summary Timeline

Table 5.1 reviews the major federal documents that affect government use of social media.

CHAPTER SIX

SOCIAL MEDIA POLICY CONSIDERATIONS

This chapter focuses on the organizational, managerial, and administrative dimensions that government organizations need to consider as a prerequisite to implementing social technologies. It includes topics that span the whole spectrum of early strategizing, from policy handbooks to minute-by-minute implementation tactics for social media accounts.

Formal Guidance and Institutionalization

As mentioned earlier in the book, formal guidance for the use of social technologies in government was lacking early on. Instead, regulations and executive orders emerged retroactively to apparent needs, in order to move the adoption of social technology forward. For many social media directors it was clear from the presidential mandate that they had to plunge into new terrain. As one of them states, "We had to use social media to accomplish the goals of the Open Government and Transparency initiative." What was less clear was how these tools could be used in effective and efficient ways with as little risk as possible for the organization and individual account administrators. A social media director described the process in his agency this way: "Well, we just started messing around with—well, not messing around—we just started utilizing a wiki and we may or may not go forward with using it more." This strong degree of experimentation shows how social technologies emerge as new forms of e-government. As opposed to previous forms of technology implementation in government, progress comes from trial and error, instead of formal, top-down strategic planning.

The key hurdles when adopting social media practices are the location of the social media director within the organizational hierarchy and the resources dedicated to the use of social media applications. When well resolved, these same factors become drivers of social media use. In departments in which social media are regarded as a technological problem, social media responsibility stays with the IT department. In departments where social media use is seen as part of the mission and included in strategic communication efforts, social media responsibility is located in the public affairs office and oftentimes knowledge experts in subunits are included in the social media efforts. Over time, the importance of social media efforts in early adopter agencies has resulted in business cases that helped the innovators behind these efforts to provide top management with facts and figures that justified allocation of resources, and organizational structures oriented to social media use were created as a result. Most executive departments now have an official social media, or new media, director, who actively works on the creation of such institutional norms as policies to govern the day-to-day administration of social media accounts or strategies that provide guidance on how social media can best support the mission of the organization.

As opposed to the informal guidance social media directors either search for or can access through their informal networks, there is very little formal guidance provided within each agency. Although many have been looking to the White House Office of New Media, the Federal Web Managers Council or, more recently, the Center for Excellence in Digital Government of the U.S, General Services Administration (GSA), formal guidance issued in a top-down fashion was developed and made available only after a significant lag time of over two years (from 2009 to 2011). For example, the Social Media Navigator is described by the GSA as providing government agencies and employees with information about using the many available social media tools and can be considered a formal advice mechanism. Another guideline source is HowTo.gov, set up by the GSA in 2011, which now gives federal agencies access to concrete guidelines concerning which social media tools to use for what kind of purpose. Two recent U.S. Government Accountability Office (GAO) reports (2010a, 2011) clearly state that federal executive departments and agencies still lack formal guidance for their use of social media and Web 2.0 applications.

None of the social media directors mentioned that they received formal guidance through the existing hierarchy in their agency or their top management. Instead they were waiting for regulations and guidelines to be set up, such as the terms of use agreements with social networking services that were established by the GSA in 2010. In some cases this has delayed adoption decisions. Others observed how their counterparts in the U.S. federal government approached social technology usage, observed their behavior online, and then emulated some of these practices. The network diagram in Figure 6.1 summarizes the responses of these directors when they were asked which departments they perceived as proactive and having the best social media practices in government. The departments listed on the left were not mentioned by any other department and

FIGURE 6.1. INFORMAL NETWORK OF ATTENTION AMONG SOCIAL MEDIA DIRECTORS IN THE FEDERAL GOVERNMENT

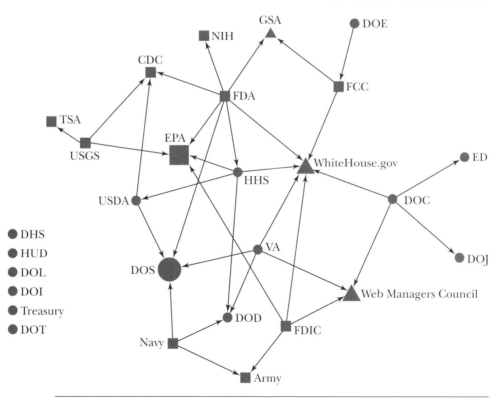

are therefore—at least for the purpose of this question—isolated from the information flow on social media.

Building Organizational Institutions

The U.S. federal government has over time taken a highly centralized approach in providing organizational resources and institutions to guide the implementation and responsible use of social media technologies. The GSA Center for Excellence in Digital Government is tasked with the responsibility to "provide government-wide support, training and solutions that help agencies deliver excellent customer service to the public via social media." The center includes many subsections that focus on a variety of content areas. For example, the Center for Citizen Engagement and New Media provides guidance on social media terms of service agreements, runs Challenge.gov (a contest platform), and supports citizen engagement activities, such as public dialogues (see the organization chart in Figure 6.2).

FIGURE 6.2. ORGANIZATION CHART FOR THE GSA'S CENTER FOR CITIZEN ENGAGEMENT AND NEW MEDIA

Federal Citizen Information Center	Center for Citizen Engagement and New Media	Center for Innovative Technologies
USA.gov	Social media ToS	Federal Cloud PMO
Federal content center	Open government	e-Gov projects
Print distribution	Public dialogues	Mobile platform
	Challenges	Data.gov
		Cloud platform

Center for Customer Service Excellence

Best practices
Education and training
(Web Manager University)

Center for Information Technology Services and Solutions

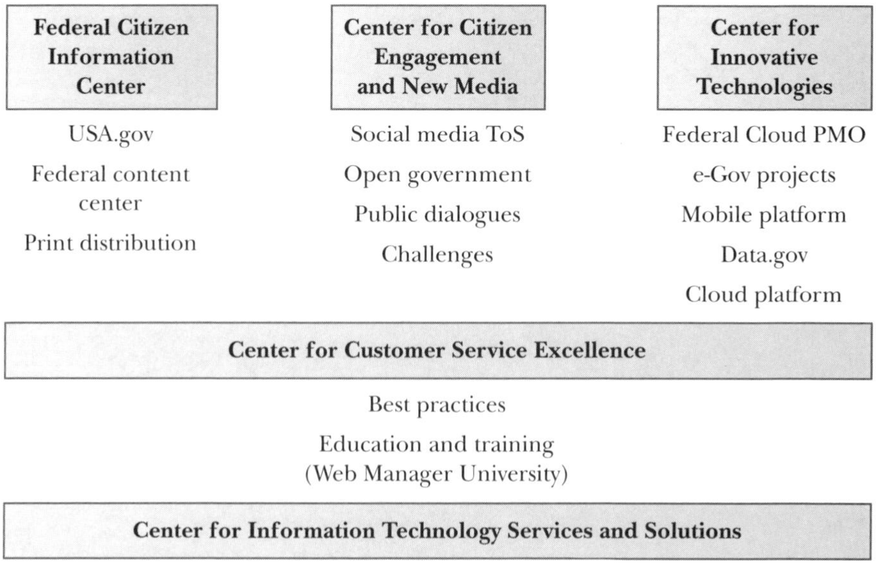

Source: Adapted from U.S. General Services Administration information, http://www.gsa.gov.

In addition, the GSA has developed a set of institutional resources that provide formal guidance for those subunits in government seeking advice or role models in the form of best practices examples. Under the umbrella HowTo.gov, GSA combines its DigitalGov University and web content guidance. DigitalGov University runs free webinars and conferences in which government employees can learn about content and implementation challenges of social technologies. The GSA's Web Content website (www.howto .gov/web-content) aggregates formal requirements, best practices, directives, and policies in one central location. Topics such as effective management and governance, web analytics, and accessibility issues, as well as usability and design topics, are covered to provide initial guidance and lower the burden and risks for beginners (Figure 6.3).

Although these resources provide guidance in one centralized place, GSA's guidance does not have regulatory or directive authority to instruct other government agencies. In many cases federal agencies are

FIGURE 6.3. THE GSA'S WEB CONTENT SITE ON HOWTO.GOV

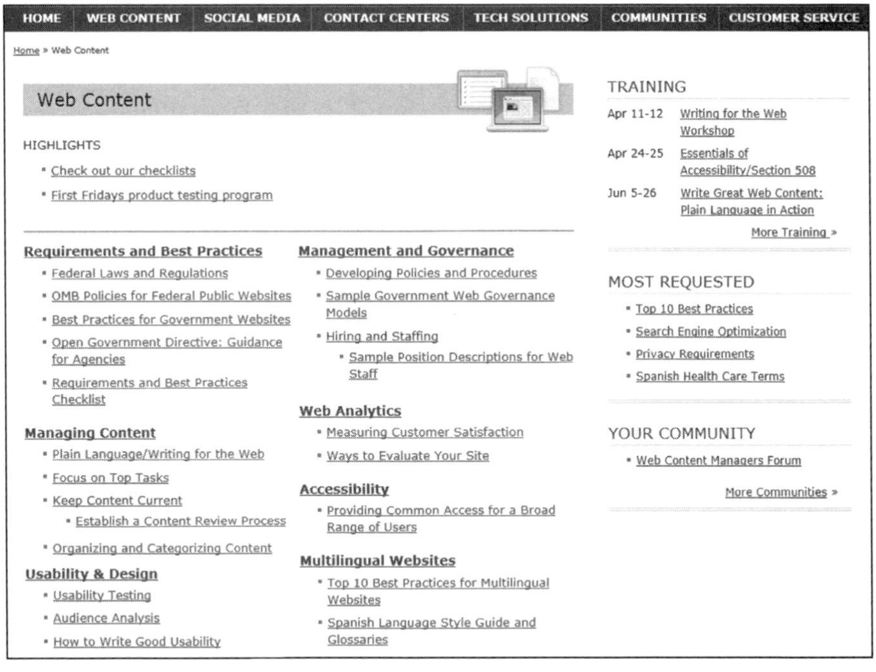

Source: U.S. General Services Administration, HowTo.gov, July 11, 2012, http://www.howto.gov.

not even aware of the resources provided by GSA and are experimenting on their own.

Organizational Responsibilities

Departments need to decide where the internal function for the responsible and effective use of social technologies should be located within the organization. On the one hand, historically all formal communication efforts are located in the public affairs department. On the other hand, the introduction and vetting of new technologies is positioned in the central IT department. Social technologies bridge the gap between these two areas of authority. Public affairs no longer presents the only interface with government's diverse audiences, and exchanges on social media can no longer follow a scripted, formal, press release approach. The technology is web based, and data and infrastructure are located in the cloud, so IT departments do not necessarily have to vet compliance with internal security mandates. As a result, organizational responsibility has evolved in different locations in departments and agencies. A majority of agencies have left the organizational responsibility with the public affairs shop; a minority have added it as a responsibility to the central IT department and appended it to web content responsibility. More advanced departments have taken a decentralized approach, assigning a task force to work on setting the context for the responsible use of social technologies, a move that allows content specialists to set up their own issue- or content-related social media accounts. Resources in the form of financial support and staff will then follow these initial decisions.

Social media responsibilities will then include the administration of a social media operations plan that lays out activities on a daily, weekly, and monthly basis and assigns responsibilities to specific individuals in the organization. It also details how to monitor responses to online activities and how to deal with comments. In addition, the management responsibilities will include implementing the social media strategy and classifying each needed activity into a category: research, design, implementation, administration, optimization, or impact measurement.

The Social Media "Ringmaster"

As organizational responsibilities evolve, staff, titles, and workgroups follow as a need develops to institutionalize the activities and assign specific authority for their management and successful administration.

The position of social media director—or what Spenner calls a social media "ringmaster"—is so far not fully defined in many government organizations or even in the corporate sector where social media were embraced much faster and earlier than in government (Spenner, 2010). Some of the activities or responsibilities will require a vision of how the organization's mission can be implemented and how social media technologies will be able to support the mission. The position will also require the ability to take a holistic view of all the different elements, seeing how they can fit together and can be integrated with existing communication, collaboration, and participation channels. This will most likely mean that the executive in the social media director job will have to be able to work collaboratively across teams, subunits, and even department boundaries in support of the organizational mission. Acquiring and then administering collaborative skills in a top-down hierarchy with predefined standard operating procedures will require talent and the willingness to rely not only on persuasion and emotional intelligence but also on an in-depth knowledge of processes, needs, and organizational routines in government organizations.

Many current social media directors were directly recruited out of the 2008 presidential campaign and were used to a fast pace from working toward a weekly election goal. They already had the social media skills required in place but needed to adjust to the standards in government, working around and with restrictive modes of operations. And they have needed to convince their counterparts to buy into the use of social technologies, which has been a slow process.

Personal Responsibilities

As social media policies and strategies evolve, many agencies have included a paragraph in their formal guidance to direct the individual use of social media applications. Personal responsibilities for the use of social technologies are twofold. One aspect focuses on the individual as a representative of the organization and the second focuses on private use of social networking services.

The first aspect involves public sector employees who are officially assigned to represent their organization on one or several social media accounts. This assignment comes with a set of responsibilities. For example, account holders have to make sure they understand the type of content that is acceptable to communicate to the public, what tone is acceptable for online exchanges, and what processes are in place in case they are unsure about the acceptable practice. The U.S. Environmental Protection

Agency's commenting policy (shown later in Figure 6.11) provides guidance for newcomers on how to evaluate these questions ad hoc.

The second aspect of personal responsibilities addresses the individual and private use of social networking services by public sector employees. A succinct example of private use regulations is the recent update of the *U.S. Navy: Social Media Handbook for Navy PAOs* (U.S. Navy, 2011). In comparison to the initial *Navy Command Social Media Handbook*, published in 2010 (U.S. Navy, 2010a), the updated version now includes guidance on how to use social media responsibly—not only at the workplace but also in the private sphere. In addition, it includes guidance for family members, to mitigate the risk of exposing confidential information when using location-based services that can potentially identify the geographical location of a vessel.

One social media director explains the reasons for supplying these types of directions as follows: "We had to take steps . . . [in the form of a] directive, which is really addressing or formalizing the policy, which should have been common sense. But it is formalizing this policy to make sure that all the employees and contractors understand how to behave, even if it's just [their] own personal account."

As shown in Figure 6.4, in its social media strategy the Department of Defense (DOD) explicitly defines personal as opposed to organizational use of social technologies by its employees. And the U.S. Navy recommends that Navy personnel use LinkedIn (as opposed to Facebook) to share and talk about their profession in a professional way (Figure 6.5).

FIGURE 6.4. THE DOD'S POLICY ON RESPONSIBLE USE OF INTERNET CAPABILITIES

5. Limited Authorized Personal Use. Paragraph 2-301 of Reference (b) permits limited personal use of Federal Government resources when authorized by the agency designee on a non-interference basis. When accessing Internet-based capabilities using Federal Government resources in an authorized personal or unofficial capacity, individuals shall employ sound operations security (OPSEC) measures in accordance with Reference (g) and shall not represent the policies or official position of the Department of Defense.

Source: U.S. Department of Defense, Responsible and Effective Use of Internet-Based Capabilities (Directive-type memorandum), 2011, http://www.dtic.mil/whs/directives/corres/pdf/DTM-09-026.pdf.

As opposed to strategies for public officials who are elected to a public office, organizational social media strategies are less focused on constant campaigning or on image and reputation building (Dutta, 2010). For further readings about the use of social media by representatives of corporations consider the example of Best Buy's CEO, Brian Dunn, and his use of Twitter to spot trends and communicate with employees and customers (Dunn, 2010) or Disney's CEO, Robert A. Iger, embracing "mommy bloggers" as a vehicle to engage with customers (Ignatius, 2011). Many high-level government officials have also started to use Twitter, using accounts in their own name in their official capacity as a director or an administrator of their agency or department. Most common, however, are agency-wide or initiative-related government Twitter accounts.

FIGURE 6.5. LINKEDIN FOR NAVY PERSONNEL

LinkedIn is not just an online resume database, it's a place where we can better tell the Navy story and increase awareness of what the Navy does

- We know that veterans have a difficult time educating the civilian world of how their job translates outside of the military
- We can help foster understanding between the civilian and military worlds by describing our own jobs and skill sets in a public forum and participating in discussions about our subject matter expertise
- You can also use LinkedIn to do research and reach-out to people you or your leadership may be meeting with to increase productivity and impact (*think: embarks, interviews, etc.*)

 SOCIAL MEDIA SNAPSHOT

Source: U.S. Navy, *LinkedIn. U.S. Navy Social Media Snapshot* [Slide show], 2011, http://www .slideshare.net/USNavySocialMedia/linkedin-for-navy-personnel.

FIGURE 6.6. INFORMATION CLEARANCE PROCESS

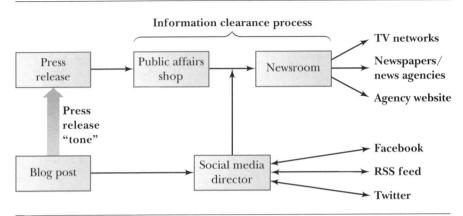

Information-Vetting Processes

The clearance process established for content on government social media sites also needs to cope with information vetting, a responsibility made especially complex by the informal nature of comments, blog posts, and Twitter updates. Figure 6.6 displays the standard steps in information clearance before an agency sends information to news organizations. First, content specialists or public affairs specialists write a press release. It is then proofread and confirmed in the public affairs department (informally known as the *public affairs shop*), then forwarded to the agency newsroom, where it is uploaded to the agency website as well as sent to television networks and news agencies. The process includes several steps and readers and provides an audit trail for future records management purposes.

In contrast, blog posts that are not written in a press release tone are vetted by the social media director. If, however, the tone is close to that of a press release, blog posts are forwarded to the public affairs specialists for verification. If the tone and content of press releases fit the requirements of a blog post, they are also published on the organization's blog and replicated on social media accounts, such as Twitter or Facebook. Although many agencies use a commonsense approach to publishing social media content (for example, following the guideline "when in doubt, leave it out"), the U.S. Navy (2010b) provides a specific content guide with detailed instructions about appropriate content for social media outlets.

Social Media Guidelines

Given the lack of formal guidance distributed directly to them, many government agencies have started to design their own rules and regulations, to mitigate risks for the organization and its individual employees. Initially, most social media policies were informal collections of commonsense pointers intended to increase awareness among those employees who had started to set up social media accounts for their teams or subunits. An important purpose of these first drafts has been to articulate a formal justification and purpose for the use of new technologies and a plan for how social media can be integrated into overarching communication priorities, as well as specific campaigns and initiatives.

As practices have evolved, common approaches to mitigating risks have arisen. A review of the existing social media guidelines used in federal agencies produced the following list of questions. It sums up the topics that all the guideline documents address in seeking to use social media successfully.

Questions to Use in Developing a Successful Social Media Strategy

- What are your overall organizational objectives and goals?
- How will mission accomplishment be measured?
- What content are you going to create or curate to gain interest?
- Where will that content come from?
- What alternatives for access to and representation of information are available?
- What schedule should you use?
- Who will be responsible for content creation?
- Who will have management oversight of the content?
- Who is going to be your target audience?
- What is acceptable online conduct, or netiquette?
- What self-identifying audience characteristics will you look for?
- What networks are these audience members on?
- For whom will you build your network?

Fitting with the Existing Organizational Mission and Norms

The guiding principle for an agency's use of social technologies can be directly derived from that agency's overall mission. For example, the

FIGURE 6.7. THE TSA'S MISSION STATEMENT

Source: Transportation Security Administration, Mission, Vision, and Core Values, n.d., http://www.tsa.gov/who_we_are/mission.shtm.

mission statement of the Transportation Security Administration (TSA) clarifies (in broad strokes) the organization's priorities (Figure 6.7). It focuses on the American public ("people") and industry ("commerce"). Every U.S. agency and department has a specific focus, thus mission statements vary widely. Some are very specific and outline in detail niche audiences—such as lawyers, farmers, educators, recipients of food stamps, and so forth—whereas others see the American public in general as their core audience. As technologies evolve and the behavior of audiences diversifies, it is increasingly necessary to align social technology use with organizational mission and strategy, instead of using a one-size-fits-all approach (Narayanan & Shmatikov, 2010).

Government agencies are setting their social media goals based on their mission statements and also their existing communication strategies (Hrdinova, Helbig, & Peters, 2010; Wilson, Guinan, Parise, & Weinberg, 2011). For example, these goals might involve informing the public in general about food safety alerts; providing legal guidance by announcing new regulations to specific communities, associations and unions, industry sectors, or professions; providing scientific data for researchers; or supplying educational support for teachers.

Defining the Audience(s)

As outlined in the previous step, the audiences of an agency are usually described in the mission statement. After generally understanding who their audiences are, using a traditional communication strategy approach, agencies can identify these audiences and their needs more precisely by asking the following questions:

1. Who are our audiences?
2. What are we going to communicate to each of our audiences? When will we communicate it? And how much will we communicate?
3. Where and how will we communicate with each of our audiences?
4. What are the preferred media of each audience?
5. Who will play what role in the team's communications with our audiences?
6. How will we react to inquiries?

The following statement from a social media director shows how his agency has approached the definition issue:

> We have a variety of target audiences at the [agency]. From a social media perspective, it depends upon what we are trying to do. So for example, one of our audiences is definitely the American public, especially when it comes to safety and crisis risk communication. We definitely want to be able to get the word out about the [specific issue]. But there is an industry audience, and I don't do a lot of work with that personally here at the [subunit], but for example our devices center has a lot of folks involved in the regulation related to specific medical devices for example, and they are communicating with that audience. And they have been using Twitter successfully to communicate with that [audience]. So we have a lot of different audiences depending on which different groups we are talking about there. But definitely the consumers, the public is a big audience. . . . But we don't want to lose sight of the other smaller audiences. When I say smaller, I mean the niche audiences that might be interested in, say, the regulatory aspects that the average public might not be interested in.

Because a government agency's audience is no longer just the general public, one-way or one-size-fits-all approaches are not sufficient for successful interaction. Instead, agencies are recognizing that different audiences have different information and interaction needs, are using different types of tools, and are paying attention to different types of content.

Selecting Tools

As mentioned in Chapter Five, the GSA worked with new media providers to develop terms of service that federal agencies can agree to (Figure 6.8). The new agreements resolve the legal concerns found in many standard terms and conditions that posed problems for federal agencies, such as liability limits, endorsements, freedom of information requirements, and governing law. The GSA has negotiated agreements with Flickr, YouTube, Vimeo, and blip.tv, and is in discussions with many other providers that offer free social media services. Federal agencies that want to use these services to meet their mission can now choose to sign these agreements. There is no necessity for each single agency to negotiate separate, no-cost agreements.

Moreover, GSA's Apps.gov platform provides step-by-step guidance for implementation of each social media tool (Figure 6.9). For example, if an agency wants to increase participation, it can choose from a list of approved tools and then be guided through the implementation process, including

FIGURE 6.8. INTRODUCTION TO THE GSA'S DISCUSSION OF ITS TERMS OF SERVICE AGREEMENTS

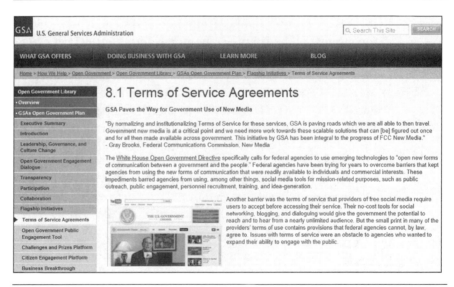

Source: U.S. General Services Administration, Terms of Service Agreements, 2011, http://www .gsa.gov/portal/content/104320.

signing the terms of service agreement, setting up an external account, and branding the account page to reflect the agency's corporate branding. The site also provides guidance and best practices examples for daily administration.

A decentralized approach toward tool selection in the U.S. federal government has resulted in some agencies moving much more quickly than others. Some agencies have an advanced and mature understanding of social technologies. Their specifications are not derived from general guidelines that were set top down. Their choices are tool agnostic. When they ask themselves what tools they should be using, they are not looking for formal guidance or where worldwide trends are going; instead they are looking specifically at the needs of their own niche audiences: "You know, we are not loyal to one platform over another," says one social media director. "We are just trying to go where [our audiences] are. If they are

FIGURE 6.9. THE GSA'S APPS.GOV

Source: U.S. General Services Administration, Apps.gov, n.d., https://www.apps.gov/cloud/main/start_page.do.

on Facebook, that is where we want to be. [If] they are on Twitter, that is where we want to be."

Implementing Daily Routines and Account Administration

One of the most critical issues when it comes to social media use in government is daily administration. Earlier in this chapter, organizational responsibilities were defined. Now it is important to understand how daily routines are implemented, so that the expectations of the public for near real-time answers and conversations are met. A challenge in government is the difference between a nine-to-five work schedule and the always-on mentality of the social media world.

Two instruments have proven successful in supporting the expectations and the reflexive feedback cycle of social technologies: a set of daily, event-driven routines and a clearly articulated commenting policy.

Daily routines beyond the scripted press release schedule can be either standard routines to broadcast news and inform the public about ongoing events or purely event driven, intended to include an audience in ongoing activities within a certain time frame. One of the social media directors I interviewed shares her daily routines to populate social media channels:

> So the [department] blog is our primary public facing blog. And this is really all about the department, and it's open to every single agency in the way we staff it. Because I don't have the staff to actually sit down and write something that might be of interest and consideration for the master's degree students. So what we do is draw upon existing resources in press shops or other constituent relations. We have the benefit at [this department] of having over 100,000 employees all over the world. Most are not in Washington, DC, they're working in states and counties. So those are the individuals who have the greatest understanding of what information is important for the stakeholders, and also having the best vocabulary to talk about it, in an accessible manner. We really open it up to anyone. And then the clearance just goes through the typical clearance process for any public statement. So typically it follows the same track as a press release, but, um, less stringent. When blogs are sent to me that read like a press release, I send it back and tell [the writer] to send it to the press shop, and they can post it on the newsroom. So it's really a mix. We have some standing features; on Tuesday we always

FIGURE 6.10. THE IMPORTANCE OF A COMMENTING POLICY

Source: J. Levy, [Tweet about writing a commenting policy], 2011, http://twitter.com/#!/levyj413/
status/126647619492655104.

have a Science Tuesday, where we talk about various research or studies posted—different things that we're doing here . . . that folks might not be aware of. And Fridays we focus on people's gardens and farmer's markets. We have a great deal of engagement there. And also it's just pop culture really. It's shifting to get people more focused on buying local and what they can do and get out in their community. But a lot of it is also timely and newsworthy, so it will often follow the pace of our newsroom or various events that the [department] secretary or other officials will be attending.

The second element in administering accounts in a safe and efficient way is establishing a *commenting policy*; the EPA's social media director, Jeff Levy, recently sent a tweet to reinforce this (Figure 6.10). A commenting policy highlights how an agency or department engages with its diverse audiences on social media channels. Some agencies have decided to disable comments—which means that the agency itself can post updates but members of the public are not allowed to respond to updates, endorse updates, or reuse, retweet, or share updates on their own networks.

Other agencies leave the commenting function open and allow the public to engage directly with status updates. In this case a guideline with clear rules for acceptable behavior is provided. Consider for example the U.S. State Department's Facebook commenting policy, which is embedded in its Facebook terms of service agreement along with information on privacy policy, security, member conduct, information quality, and so forth.

THE U.S. DEPARTMENT OF STATE FACEBOOK TERMS OF SERVICE

1. Acceptance of Terms

Welcome to the U.S. Department of State on Facebook! The U.S. Department of State provides this service to you, subject to the following Terms of Use ("TOU"), which may be updated by the U.S. Department of State from time to time without notice. You can review the current version of the TOU at any time on the U.S. Department of State Facebook page.

2. Purpose

The purpose of the U.S. Department of State on Facebook is to engage audiences on issues relevant to U.S. foreign policy.

3. Description of Service

The U.S. Department of State on Facebook operates on the Facebook platform. It provides its members with a variety of features, including but not limited to: video and photo sharing, access to a community blog, discussion forum, messaging, and notifications of developments in U.S. foreign policy. The U.S. Department of State reserves the right to alter the types of features that the U.S. Department of State on Facebook provides at any time with no notice.

4. Facebook's Privacy Policy

By using or accessing Facebook, and this site, you are accepting the practices described in the Facebook Privacy Policy. For more information on Facebook's privacy policy, go to http://www.facebook.com/terms.php#/policy.php.
The Information Facebook Collects
When you visit Facebook you provide them with two types of information: personal information you knowingly choose to disclose that is collected by Facebook and Web Site use information collected by Facebook as you interact with our Web Site.

When you register with Facebook, you provide them with certain personal information, such as your name, your email address, your telephone number, your address, your gender, schools attended and any other personal or preference information that you provide to them. The U.S. Department of State on Facebook does not store any of this personal information nor any additional member information beyond that which is already stored for your account by Facebook.

You post User Content (as defined in Facebook's Terms) on the Site at your own risk. Although Facebook allows you to set privacy options that limit access to your pages, please be aware that no security measures are perfect or impenetrable. We cannot control the actions of other Users with whom you may choose to share your pages and information. Therefore, we cannot and do not guarantee that User Content you post on the Site will not be viewed by unauthorized persons.

5. Security

Participation in the U.S. Department of State on Facebook is voluntary. You are responsible for maintaining the confidentiality of your login, and are fully responsible for all activities that occur under your login. You agree to (a) immediately notify the U.S. Department of State on Facebook community manager of any unauthorized use of your login or account or any other breach of security, and (b) ensure that you exit from your account at the end of each session. The U.S. Department of State on Facebook cannot and will not be liable for any loss or damage arising from your failure to comply with this section.

6. Member Conduct

The U.S. Department of State on Facebook is moderated. That means all comments will be reviewed before posting. In addition, the U.S. Department of State on Facebook expects that participants will treat each other, as well as U.S. Department of State employees, with respect. The U.S. Department of State on Facebook will not post comments that contain vulgar or abusive language; personal attacks of any kind; or offensive terms that target specific ethnic or racial groups. The U.S. Department of State on Facebook will not post comments that are spam, are clearly "off topic" or that promote services or products. Comments that make unsupported accusations will also be subject to review.

Any references to commercial entities, products, services, or other nongovernmental organizations or individuals that remain on the site are provided solely for the information of individuals using the U.S. Department of State on Facebook. These references are not intended to reflect the opinion of U.S. Department of State, the United States, or its officers or employees concerning the significance, priority, or importance to be given the referenced entity, product, service, or organization. Such references are not an official or personal endorsement of any product, person, or service, and may not be quoted or reproduced for the purpose of stating or implying U.S. Department of State endorsement or approval of any product, person, or service.

> Only comments that comply with the U.S. Department of State on Facebook TOU will be approved for posting.

> The use of vulgar, offensive, threatening or harassing language is prohibited.

(*continued*)

THE U.S. DEPARTMENT OF STATE FACEBOOK
TERMS OF SERVICE *(continued)*

Public comments should be limited to comments related to the posted topic. The U.S. Department of State on Facebook is not the proper place to express opinions or beliefs not directly related to that topic.

The U.S. Department of State on Facebook is not open to comments promoting or opposing any person campaigning for election to a political office or promoting or opposing any ballot proposition.

The U.S. Department of State on Facebook is not open to the promotion or advertisement of a business or commercial transaction.

Communications made through the U.S. Department of State on Facebook e-mails and messaging system will in no way constitute a legal or official notice or comment to the U.S. Department of State or any official or employee of the U.S. Department of State for any purpose.

7. Copyright Information

Links to U.S. Department of State on Facebook as well as U.S. Department of State websites and blogs are welcomed. Unless a copyright is indicated, U.S. Department of State on Facebook information is in the public domain and may be copied and distributed without permission. Citation of the U.S. State Department as source of the information is appreciated.

If a copyright is indicated on a video, photo, graphic, or other material, permission to copy these materials must be obtained from the original source.

8. Information Quality Guidelines

Every effort is made to provide accurate and complete information. However, we cannot guarantee that there will be no errors. Please read the U.S. Department of State's guidelines pursuant to the Data Quality Information Act before submitting inquiries under this Act.

If you would like verification or a hard copy of original information released on U.S. Department of State websites and blogs or if you have any questions or comments about the information presented here, please contact the public information staff in the U.S. Department of State Bureau of Public Affairs.

You acknowledge that the U.S. Department of State does not pre-screen all Content, but that the U.S. Department of State and its designees shall have the right (but not the obligation) in their sole discretion to edit, delete, refuse or move any content that is available via the site. Without limiting the foregoing, the U.S. Department of State and its designees shall have the right to remove any Content that violates the TOU or is otherwise objectionable. You agree that you must evaluate, and bear all risks associated with, the use of any Content, including any reliance on the accuracy, completeness, or usefulness of such Content.

You acknowledge and agree that the U.S. Department of State may preserve Content and may also disclose Content if required to do so by law or in the good faith belief that such preservation or disclosure is reasonably necessary to: (a) comply with legal process; (b) enforce the TOU; (c) respond to claims that any Content violates the rights of third-parties; or (d) protect the rights, property, or personal safety of the U.S. Department of State, its users and the public.

You understand that the technical processing and transmission of the site, including your Content, may involve (a) transmissions over various networks; and (b) changes to conform and adapt to technical requirements of connecting networks or devices.

You agree that if you post content that contains statements or depictions of violence against a person, group of people, or country, that the U.S. Department of State will report this incident and its content to the appropriate law enforcement agency.

9. Special Admonitions for International Use

Recognizing the global nature of the Internet, you agree to comply with all local rules regarding online conduct and acceptable Content. Specifically, you agree to comply with all applicable laws regarding the transmission of technical data exported from the United States or the country in which you reside.

10. Content Submitted or Made Available for Inclusion on the Site

The U.S. Department of State does not claim ownership of Content you submit or make available for inclusion on the site. The Department only claims ownership over self generated content created by the Department of State for inclusion on this site. It does not take responsibility for the inclusion of third party links or other third party content such as articles.

11. Indemnity

You agree to indemnify and hold the U.S. Department of State, and its affiliates, officers, agent, grantees or other partners, and employees, harmless from any claim or demand, including reasonable attorneys' fees, made by any third party due to or arising out of Content you submit, post, transmit or make available through the site, your use of the site, your connection to the site, your violation of the TOU, or your violation of any rights of another.

(continued)

THE U.S. DEPARTMENT OF STATE FACEBOOK
TERMS OF SERVICE *(continued)*

12. General Practices Regarding Use and Storage

You acknowledge that the U.S. Department of State may establish general practices and limits concerning use of the site, including without limitation the maximum number of days that message board postings or other uploaded Content will be retained by the site, and the maximum number of times (and the maximum duration for which) you may access the site in a given period of time. You agree that the U.S. Department of State has no responsibility or liability for the deletion or failure to store any messages and other communications or other Content maintained or transmitted by the site. You further acknowledge that the U.S. Department of State reserves the right to change these general practices and limits at any time, in its sole discretion.

13. Modifications to Service

The U.S. Department of State reserves the right at any time and from time to time to modify or discontinue, temporarily or permanently, the site (or any part thereof). You agree that the U.S. Department of State shall not be liable to you or to any third party for any modification, suspension or discontinuance of the site.

14. Links

The U.S. Department of State on Facebook provides external links solely for our readers' information and convenience. When readers select a link to an external website, they are leaving the U.S. Department of State on Facebook and are subject to the privacy and security policies of the owners/sponsors of the external website. The U.S. Department of State on Facebook may provide, or third parties may provide, links to other websites or resources. You acknowledge and agree that the U.S. Department of State is not responsible for the availability of such external sites or resources, and does not endorse and is not responsible or liable for any Content, advertising, products, or other materials on or available from such sites or resources. You further acknowledge and agree that the U.S. Department of State shall not be responsible or liable, directly or indirectly, for any damage or loss caused or alleged to be caused by or in connection with use of or reliance on any such Content, goods or services available on or through any such site or resource. Facebook may contain links to other websites. The U.S. Department of State is not responsible for the privacy practices of other websites. You are encouraged to be aware that when you leave our site to read the privacy statements of each and every website that collects personally identifiable information. This Privacy Policy applies solely to information collected by Facebook. U.S. Department of

State officers continually review the external links for their ongoing value to the issues and topics presented within the U.S. Department of State on Facebook. The process for adding an external link is the same as for clearing information for public dissemination, as described in the U.S. Department of State's Information Quality Guidelines:

"Clearances on information for dissemination generally are obtained from any office within the Department or any other agency within the U.S. Government that has a substantive interest in the information."

15. English Language

In order to assure that members adhere to the TOU, the language of the U.S. Department of State on Facebook site is English. Content posted in languages other than English may be subject to removal. An accurate translation into English must be provided if a member chooses to post content in other languages.

Terms of Use, Notices and Revisions

The U.S. Department of State reserves the right to change our Privacy Policy and our Terms of Use at any time. If we make changes, we will post them and inform the community of the changes. If we make significant changes to this policy, we will notify you through notice on our home page. We encourage you to refer to this policy on an ongoing basis so that you understand our current privacy policy.

Contacting the Website

If you have any questions about this privacy policy, please contact the U.S. Department of State on Facebook Community Manager.

Source: U.S. Department of State. U.S. Department of State Facebook Terms of Service, 2010, http://www.facebook.com/usdos.

The EPA prominently highlights its Facebook commenting policy on the left-hand sidebar of its Facebook page, making it always accessible to highlight its importance (Figure 6.11). The policy is strictly enforced and reminders, with links to the policy, are frequently reposted as status updates. To help employees decide when to respond to a comment left on one of the social media outlets, the EPA provides the guide shown in Figure 6.12.

FIGURE 6.11. THE EPA'S COMMENTING POLICY FOR FACEBOOK

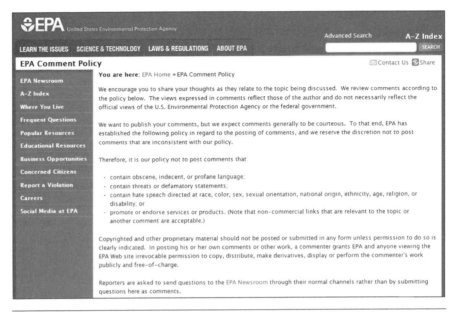

Source: U.S. Environmental Protection Agency, EPA Comment Policy, n.d., http://www.epa.gov/epahome/commentpolicy.html.

Designing Social Technology Policy and Strategy

In this chapter we have examined the different modalities that social media directors are using to access information about best practices, experiences, and guidance for their own use of social media applications. The factors that are driving the decisions to adopt innovative web practices include passive observation and comparisons of government and corporate best practices, the informal attention network among departments, and to a certain extent, formal guidance. The design process is outlined in Figure 6.13.

Social Media Tactics

In my interactions with new media directors in the federal agencies and departments, I differentiated three types of social media use to promote transparency, participation, and collaboration.

FIGURE 6.12. SHOULD I RESPOND ONLINE ON EPA'S BEHALF? AN EMPLOYEE GUIDE

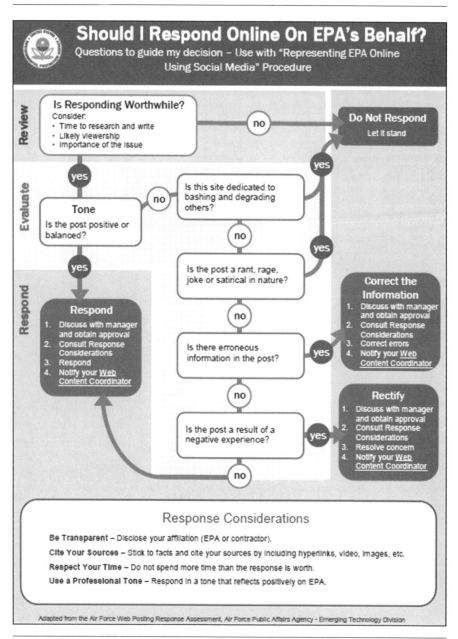

Source: U.S. Environmental Protection Agency, Should I Respond Online on EPA's Behalf? n.d., http://yosemite.epa.gov/OEI/webguide.nsf/socialmedia/representing_epa_online#flowchart.

FIGURE 6.13. DESIGNING SOCIAL TECHNOLOGY POLICY AND STRATEGY

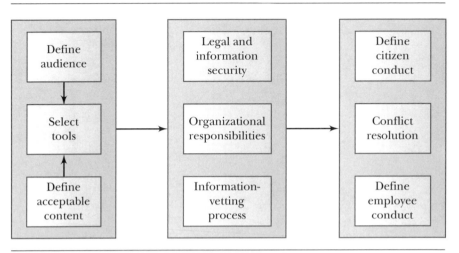

The first strategy can be called the *push* strategy: the new medium is seen as an extension of the existing (usually relatively static) Internet presence and is used as an additional communication channel "to get the message out." This results in unmoderated Twitter updates that are used mainly to publicize press releases or appearances of agency secretaries, unattended Facebook walls that are blocked for public comments, and sparsely populated YouTube channels.

The second strategy can be called the *pull* strategy: social media applications are used to bring audiences to the organization's website, where agency news is aggregated (to avoid losing control of what happens with the information). Pull strategies actively involve audiences by using some degree of interaction that results in a few comments on Facebook walls and a few retweets (reuses of messages by other Twitter users) or answers to comments on responses from Twitter followers. Examples include the Centers for Disease Control and Prevention's use of social media tools to alert and inform the public about a salmonella outbreak from contaminated peanut butter or that agency's H1N1 flu prevention campaign.

The third strategy—and at the same time the least observable—can be called a *networking* strategy. Here, the use of social media tools is highly interactive, with a lot of back and forth between the agency and its diverse constituencies. The social media directors usually have a sense of who is following the agency and whom it wants to reach. They are using Facebook, Twitter, and the like strategically, not only to control and direct messages to their audiences but also to have their ears and eyes on the channels where the actual issues are being discussed that might be of relevance to the agency's or department's mission. Social media tools are not used merely for publishing purposes and are not viewed as a time sink for the already overworked IT staff but as strategic information-sharing and knowledge creation tools involving social media champions from a variety of content areas.

One agency that stands out for its networking strategy is the GSA. Managers there used the informal social networking site GovLoop.com to create a group and discuss the department's Acquisition 2.0 strategy. The discussions among a diverse audience of government employees led to the creation of the BetterBuy Wiki project (see betterbuy.fas.gsa.gov) that is truly transforming the GSA's multibillion-dollar acquisition process. Tenders are now crowdsourced, meaning that vendors and agencies are asked to submit proposed revisions to the final tender document before it is officially released for solicitation.

Representation

The overwhelming reason to participate in social media spaces can be summarized this way: to achieve representation of the department or agency on all potential interaction channels. The success of Facebook and Twitter has convinced social media directors that they want to be where citizens are. The following statement, which I also mentioned in Chapter Three, is representative of the view of the majority of my interview partners: "Why we're on Facebook or Twitter: to be where the people are. So [there are] 400 million users now on Facebook for example, so you want to be there. When people search for . . . stuff on Facebook, they find us."

All agencies maintain several different social media accounts, including accounts on YouTube, Facebook, and Twitter, and also have blogs and RSS feeds. Many agencies are experimenting with additional—less mainstream—social networking services, such as alternative video and photo-sharing services and wikis. The reason for choosing several different channels was stated by several social media directors: "We wanted to be active in various social media spaces." Only those agencies that are targeting younger audiences or their representatives, such as teachers or professors, also maintained a MySpace account in 2010. A social media director explains his agency's tactic: "We have multiple goals. Initially, the work we have done pretty much so far was just to basically get a toe in the water and to be active in the various social media spaces. Having said that, we have to take very small measured steps."

The representation objective confirms the need for maximum inclusiveness. Government agencies want to reach audiences in those social spaces they frequent on a daily basis. Several interview partners recognized the need to reach audiences that do not routinely interact with federal agencies and are therefore excluded from decision-making and policymaking processes. They see the use of organizational channels on social media sites as a way to institutionalize interactions and bring citizens' knowledge into government.

Agencies that are following a representation tactic as their main social media strategy are described by their social media directors as "by nature very conservative organizations," and they are repurposing existing content. They are using social media channels to notify audiences about existing policy statements or major press releases but are not creating content catering specifically for these social media audiences. This again emphasizes that their only purpose is to represent the agency or department on multiple channels: "There is part of our stakeholder group out there that uses Twitter exclusively or Facebook as their main website to get information, to disburse information, to communicate with people. . . . It's easier for people to get notified of things if they're using Facebook. If they're logged in all the time, or have Twitter open all the time, it's easier to tell them about that. I mean people are using that almost as much they're using e-mail now."

The resulting social media tactic is the push strategy described earlier, where minimal additional resources are invested into tailoring the content specifically for social media channels and active bidirectional interactions (Figure 6.14). Social media directors in these types of organizations have low confidence in the usefulness of social networking applications and some of them actively shut off the commenting function for their Facebook accounts and do not track how their Twitter updates are reused or retweeted through their followers' own networks. Social media channels are used because these agencies understand expectations and online destinations where their audiences are interacting and have started to repurpose existing, press-release-style information through social media channels. This centralized approach allows for little innovative interactions or engagement. Instead it simply makes existing content more acceptable or appropriate for various audiences.

FIGURE 6.14. AN EXAMPLE OF THE PUSH STRATEGY: A WHITE HOUSE TWEET

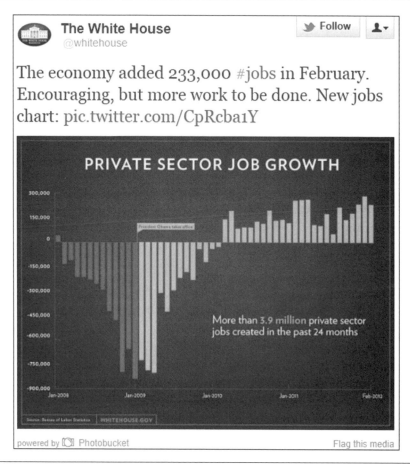

Source: The White House, [Tweet about the economy], 2012.

Engagement

The second most frequently mentioned objective in maintaining social media accounts is *engagement*. Social media tools are still new to most agencies, and therefore examples of best practices in the public sector are rare. Most social media directors perceive their actions as an experiment in an unknown problem space. They recognize that their departments' traditional websites are not the place where citizens search for information:

> I think it is a fundamental shift: instead of asking people to come to government, it's government going to the people. So people are, for a lack of a better term, hanging out on Facebook, people are hanging out on Twitter. And so we want to be sure that our messages can get to people where they want it, when they want it and in the form that they want it. I think it is both a fundamental shift in our approach to that, and also a reaction to just the nature of the technology changing the way people get information.

Departments following an engagement tactic have recognized the need of their audience to interact with government in a natural conversational style, instead of passively receiving government reports or memos: "Much of our social media . . . strategy is to put a face on what has often been a faceless or kind of anonymous or overbearing . . . bureaucracy. . . . Nobody sticks with a press release for more than two or three paragraphs at most."

Even though social media managers and policy entrepreneurs are constantly exploring best practices outside government (such as Starbucks' My Starbucks Idea or Best Buy's Twitter-based customer service, Twelpforce), there are very few role models within government for an interactive engagement approach.

Most social media directors are restrained by the institutional hurdles they need to overcome, and early experimentation has led to using social media tools in the same way that traditional, static website content is provided: "We wanted to engage," said one director. "But, when we started a year ago, a lot of things were just push. Recognizing that we should be engaging, more so to push a listen-type of strategy." Several directors report that they decided to create a business case with one specific tool first, experiment, and gain experiences and insights from that use. Only when they felt they had collected enough insights and were able to make their case did they present their findings to their top management and ask for additional support.

Recognizing the shortcomings of push strategies, some agencies have switched to an active pull strategy (Figure 6.15). As described previously in this chapter early practices indicate that content produced for the core website was duplicated and pushed through social media channels. Although these practices can still be observed, some agencies have recognized the additional value of social media services: bidirectional interaction.

FIGURE 6.15. AN EXAMPLE OF THE PULL STRATEGY: A CHALLENGE.GOV TWEET

Source: Challenge.gov, [Tweet offering a challenge], March 16, 2012, https://twitter.com/#!/ChallengeGov/status/180758778692644864.

Citizens are invited to coproduce content that is then replicated on the agencies' websites: "One side of the communication strategy that we did was a little mini campaign called 'Share Your Stories.'. . . From there we put together our blog posts . . . pushing them out onto different subnets."

The engagement strategy goes beyond mere broadcasting of information to the public. Instead, agencies are actively trying to encourage their audiences to co-create and share content in different formats with them.

Networking

Very few of the interviewed social media directors also recognized that agencies do not always have to play an active engagement role when using social media applications. At times, adopting a passive strategy of listening to and absorbing comments can provide government with valuable insights about the sentiments or interest areas of their audiences. As one of the social media directors said: "Given the opportunity, people are really excited and willing to provide fantastic insight into things that help us get closer, by listening, to the taxpayer and to the people that we serve."

The agency adopting a networking strategy provides the social media tools to facilitate conversations and "mingling" opportunities among its stakeholders. It is engaging its knowledge experts to cowrite or codesign strategic plans or policies with a knowledgeable audience. This highly

interactive and multidirectional agency responsiveness produces reciprocated feedback cycles. Although several social media directors mentioned
this objective, very few interview partners were able to point to examples.
Instead, they listed reciprocated feedback and interaction as a desirable
goal for their social media use.

Other agencies step into a relatively passive networking strategy by
allowing the public to socialize amid the content they are producing. This
strategy involves the provision of interactive content on social media channels. Citizens are then allowed to reuse, reshare, and recombine government content and actively use it for their own purposes. For example, one
social media director explained the agency's use of YouTube this way: "We
started talking about YouTube because we have quite a video library, and
we wanted to find a way to socialize and make it more easy for people to
find, make it more easy for people to share it."

A networking tactic for a social media strategy therefore not only
includes active interactions with the public but also enhanced interaction
of the public with the content an agency produces and a snowballing of
the content through individuals' social networks. This gives the public,
on the one hand, a larger responsibility and control over the content. On
the other hand, the agency itself has to come to a more generous understanding of its role and responsibility as a partner in the overall network.
It actively has to leave the conversation to the people instead of guiding,
constraining, or controlling the content.

Transactions and E-Services

The last pathway or social media tactic is least known, and government
is struggling with the actual service delivery or transactional component
of e-government (Schellong, 2008). So far, social technologies have been
used mainly to interact with the public from a communication standpoint.
At its best, government is also engaging with the public and encouraging
participation. What is least tested and therefore difficult to articulate is an
extension of e-service delivery through social technologies.

In 2011, the Office of Management and Budget (OMB) directed agencies to set service standards and use customer feedback to improve the
customer experience (The White House, 2011). Agencies and departments are currently following up with implementation plans, establishing
a customer service task force, and finding ways to use innovative technologies for the implementation (Office of Management and Budget, 2011).
Agencies have to collect feedback from citizens but also provide timely

responses. Although this pace might challenge the current standard operating procedures of providing content and in some instances also collecting
input from citizens, OMB provides additional guidance on how to ensure
that maximum quality of information provided in these exchanges (U.S.
Government Accountability Office, 2010a; Guidelines for Ensuring and
Maximizing the Quality, Objectivity, Utility, and Integrity of Information
Disseminated by Federal Agencies, 2002).

CHAPTER SEVEN

SOCIAL MEDIA METRICS

Current and Potential Measurement Techniques

Measuring the impact of social media activities in the public sector is crucial to demonstrating the value of social networking services. Existing research on e-government performance has provided limited proof of the impact the use of new technologies has had on citizen participation, engagement, or more generally, satisfaction with government activities (Rocheleau, 2007; Stowers, 2004). Social media applications have the potential to improve responsiveness, reach, efficiency, and even cost savings in government. The current Government 2.0 initiatives launched by all executive departments and agencies of the U.S. federal government in response to President Obama's transparency and open government memo show that government agencies—however slow and uneven the progress may be—are implementing social media applications as additional information and communication channels.

This chapter compares traditional e-government measurement techniques with emerging current practices for measuring social media impact in the public sector. The comparison reveals that the current standard practices rely mostly on quantitative impact measures instead of qualitative measures designed to better understand the sentiments of citizens.

Although almost every federal agency and department has set up a range of accounts on social networking sites, such as Facebook, Twitter, Flickr, and YouTube, it is unclear to what degree the use of these additional interaction channels improves an agency's reputation, effectiveness, reach, or trustworthiness. Only a handful of agencies have a large number of followers. Given that the target audience of most federal agencies and departments is "the whole U.S. population," these numbers are still comparatively small and do not offer insights into the actual reach of messages posted on any of the social media accounts. This chapter provides recommendations for alternative—qualitative—measurement techniques and describes an analysis of existing Twitter accounts using Klout—a free social media scoring tool. The different types of insights social media directors in government want to gain about their use of social media are summarized in Table 7.1, at the end of the chapter.

Existing Ways of Measuring ROI from E-Government Practices

Traditional measurement techniques for measuring return on investment (ROI) include, for example, Melitski's four-step model for evaluating to what degree an agency's website is static, interactive, transactional, or transformative (Melitski, 2003). This model helps an evaluator to understand these various dimensions of capacity of e-government performance. Other approaches measure performance of e-government activities based on input measures or intermediate, end, or ultimate outcome measures (Stowers, 2004). Although the measurement of these dimensions is helpful for outside evaluators, the mere provision of numbers about even the most transactional and transformative service does not indicate how useful citizens themselves perceive the service to be.

Some studies have found statistical significance as well as other positive outcomes of federal and local governments' use of e-government applications. For example, Tolbert and Mossberger (2006) found that providing government Internet services increases process-based trust by improving interactions with citizens and perceptions of responsiveness. Other studies declare that e-government itself is still at an early stage and has not produced many of the expected outcomes (cost savings, downsizing, and so forth) that the rhetoric of e-government has promised (Moon, 2002). West (2004) claims "the e-government revolution has fallen short of its potential to transform service delivery and public trust in government. It does, however, have the possibility of enhancing democratic responsiveness and boosting beliefs that government is effective" (p. 15). Hazlett and Hill (2003) emphasize that "although there have been examples of very creative use of electronic government in the public sector, there have also been [numerous spectacular failures; evidence is lacking] to support the claim that the use of technology in service delivery results in less bureaucracy and increased quality" (p. 445). Government agencies do not seem to be able to counteract this trend. A recent study found that only 22 percent of all U.S. citizens trusted their government in 2010—indicating that providing e-government presences alone has not made a difference by generating a positive image or allowing interaction between government agencies and citizens (Pew Research Center for the People & the Press, 2010).

These examples clearly reveal a paradox: the outcomes of e-government activities are unclear or ambiguous, and at the same time a new wave of social media tools is already making its way into government. It is therefore necessary to understand how the use of social media applications might potentially make a difference in the perceptions and sentiments of citizens toward government, help to provide more efficient access to government, or increase customer service quality.

Understanding the Transformational Impact of Social Media Use

Given federal departments' and agencies' three objectives in using social media applications (participation, collaboration, and transparency), it is important to understand whether any of the social media activities these organizations engage in are making an impact, and if they are, how they are doing it. Most agencies have no formal evaluation metrics in place. In instances where vendors have provided measurement tools, they are typically not used. The most common measures are the traditional quantitative ones. All agencies count the changes in their numbers of friends and *likes* on Facebook and their followers on Twitter and similar statistics. But these measures do not go far enough to evaluate the true effectiveness of social media efforts. Currently, any hints of the impact government agencies are making when they use social media seem to be coming from spot checks of numbers not routinely noted and random reading of citizens' comments (Figure 7.1 offers an example).

A much more important consideration is how traditional indicators of return on investment can be measured in government environments with no brand competition and only the quantitative measures produced by the social networking service providers. For example, agencies look at the raw data of their number of likes on Facebook and the number of followers they collect on their Twitter account. In an attempt to interpret these counts, some social media directors try to determine whether a connection

FIGURE 7.1. SPOT CHECK OF SOCIAL MEDIA IMPACT

Jeffrey Levy, EPA
@levyj413

Follow

Key stat: spot check shows vast majority of FB views of EPA posts are via fans' newsfeeds, not our page itself. #GovD11

Source: J. Levy, [Tweet about a key social media statistic], October 18, 2011, http://twitter.com/#!/levyj413/status/126646005386051584.

exists between a specific event and an increase in likes or followers or between the click-throughs received from information the agency posts on Facebook and the additional hits these posts generate on the agency's traditional website. For this purpose directors are using real-time analytical tools, such as the freely available Google Trends and Google Analytics. In addition, Facebook Insights—a basic analytical tool provided to Facebook members who maintain corporate accounts—provides standard demographic information such as ages or locations of Facebook members who like an agency's Facebook page.

Few social media directors have measurable evidence about the sentiments of their audiences. Some browse through comments to see if they can perceive a general positive inclination or find anecdotal evidence in random single comments.

Several agencies have reverted to traditional measurement instruments to access direct citizen feedback. They use web surveys to collect information from citizens about their information needs, demographics, and referral histories. A more sophisticated version of such data collection is IdeaScale, an instrument used to collect opinions and ideas from people in relation to a particular event or need. In the first phase, citizens submit ideas in response to a guided opinion polling process. In the second phase the public rates these ideas, and the government agency that has sought the input selects the highest rated idea for its purpose. For example, the White House Office of Science and Technology Policy (OSTP) used IdeaScale to collect ideas on how to design open government plans (see openostp.ideascale.com for more information). As one of the interview partners commented, this process has the advantage of allowing public managers to "get closer to acceptable and really desirable rules." Yet none of the other interview partners mentioned using this or an equivalent social media measurement or opinion collection software module.

One of the favorite—informal—evaluation mechanisms is the comparison among agencies. Several social media directors mentioned that they frequently compare their numbers of Facebook likes or Twitter followers with the numbers for other agencies and departments. Positive numbers are interpreted as best practice indicators and also as a rough indicator that "we are doing something right."

Clearly, all measurement techniques currently in place focus on mere headcounts or quantitative assessments of the number of clicks or click-throughs or of basic demographic data. Although this shows the limit of current measurement abilities, one social media director highlighted that these numbers do have a value for his agency: "I disagree with people who say they're useless numbers. I think if nothing else, they tell you there's significant interest [in] what you're doing in this space, whether this space is Twitter or Facebook."

It also became clear from my interviews with social media managers that the metrics put in place by third parties are of limited value. Even free tools such as Google Analytics are mostly ignored. Most interview partners stressed that they need more guidance on acceptable measures to reduce the current confusion about allowable practices.

Even though existing measurement tools based on quantitative measures give a general direction, the interviewed social media directors mentioned that their need for information interpretation is unfulfilled. The comments received still need to be interpreted by an expert who has enough knowledge about the agency's mission to be able to analyze their content: "The metrics part is definitely a very important topic that a lot of us are still grappling with. You still need a human being to evaluate that feedback and see if it is really constructive . . . and we are using the anecdotal evidence we have to show a real impact."

Strikingly, all the social media directors expressed a desire to understand the content and quality of comments better, as well as the composition, sentiments, and impact of their followers. Many of the interview partners expressed a need to measure qualitative content flowing through their network so as to gain an understanding of audience sentiment (through sentiment analyses), effects on online brand reputation (through reputation monitoring applications), and the value of the information the agency is seeking to spread (through checking whether it "goes viral"). Yet at this time there are no officially allowed or approved tools available to help social media directors in the public sector to go beyond mere quantitative counts, so their solution is to use traditional web analytics to help determine whether social media applications have increased traffic to their agency's website.

Increasing the Quality of Comments and Retweets

How can government agencies increase the number of quality contributions from those employees in the agency who have enough institutional knowledge that they could help others with "unsolvable" questions to find a solution? And how can those citizens who have innovative insights to share be incentivized to contribute those insights? In trying to find approaches to solve these two problems, Titmuss's work on human blood banks, published in the 1970s, might provide a useful way to distinguish between a mere quantitative measure of impact and qualitative contributions to understanding that impact (Titmuss, 1971). Titmuss explains in his seminal work, "The Gift Relationship: From Human Blood to Social Policy," that economic analysis has its limits when it comes to rare exchanges and gifts, such as those of human blood. In crisis situations (for example shortages of human blood) in a system where blood donors are paid, the price for blood goes up; blood banks are willing to raise the price they pay donors. This attracts those people who don't necessarily give blood for the purpose of serving a higher good (the typical donor), but those who otherwise do not donate and are attracted out of desperation by the promise of additional income. This in turn means that the new donors are people with a diet that might not include expensive whole foods but a rather high degree of processed foods and who are therefore prone to have lower blood quality and, potentially, diseases. The result in short is that the blood supply rises but the overall quality is lowered. In very similar terms having a large number of comments, followers, and retweets does not provide the insights needed by government managers. Social media lower the entry barrier to connecting to government and reduce the costs to contribute, which means that more citizens send more comments to agencies. Although there are generally no price tags associated with commenting on government websites, the comparison still holds as it shows that the number of comments is not an indicator of quality—instead each comment has to be evaluated and its content analyzed.

Government needs to look at social media metrics from a different standpoint than other industry sectors do. The impact of outreach and engagement activities can be measured only in connection with an agency's mission. Take, for example, the Centers for Disease Control and Prevention (CDC) and that agency's mission to save lives by providing accurate scientific information. During the 2009 peanut butter recall and in the years following, for instance, the CDC has provided the HTML code for product recall web buttons that other organizations can copy and paste onto their own websites (see Figure 7.2). The number of buttons for this and other health issues that other organizations are willing to use on their own websites is a much better indicator of impact than the mere number of hits the CDC receives on its own website. Buttons shared and reused highlight the

FIGURE 7.2. THE CDC'S RECALLED PRODUCTS BUTTON

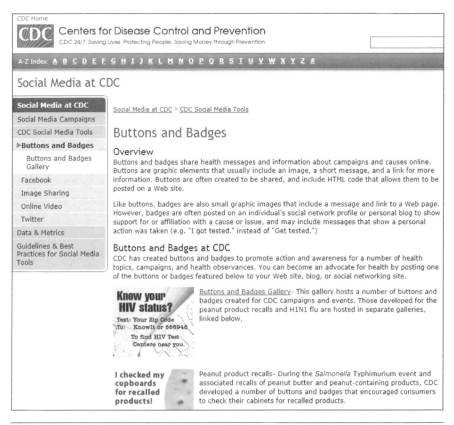

Source: Centers for Disease Control and Prevention, Social Media at CDC: Buttons and Badges Gallery, 2009, http://www.cdc.gov/socialmedia.

importance other organizations put on the information and indicate their trust in the CDC's dissemination mechanisms. Moreover, through the use of such buttons, safety information is dispensed to a highly diverse audience. Here, return on investment is not measured in dollars earned, services sold, or new customers retained; instead, in the case of government, return on investment may be measured as return on interactions or engagement, which for the CDC might directly translate into number of lives saved.

Alternatively, instead of measuring the direct impact of its own action and interactions, government can focus on measuring the motivations of citizens and employees to use agency social media sites and their levels of engagement (Hoffman & Fodor, 2010). As this chapter has discussed, traditional measurement tools do not capture the actual impact of interactions with citizens, and agencies tend to be stuck in old schemes measuring only the popularity of a specific site or, when citizens are actively seeking information on a site, indicating an apparent lack of information or additional need for information.

Marketers are measuring *conversion* rates of their communication and social media outreach activities. This is the rate at which interested visitors to a site can be converted into buyers. An analogous way of thinking might be helpful to government. For example, agencies might be measuring their rates of transforming informed citizens into peers who are willing to relay helpful information to their friends and peers in their network, which can help to lower the burden on government of information transmission. The downside is that it can also lead to transmission of misinformation, rumors, and to a certain extent, the loss of government authority over disseminated information.

The ability of information to spread through the actions of social media networks of users and potentially become viral has, in fact, cost-saving potential for government. In theory, a blog post, for example, is immediately distributed throughout the subscriber network, and government can focus its efforts on content creation and production instead of distribution. This provides a less invasive and more targeted approach to information dissemination than wide broadcasting efforts with expensive TV spots or newspaper ads can offer.

The Current State of Impact Measurement

Encouraged by the social media efforts of agencies such as the U.S. General Services Administration (GSA) and OSTP, and truly outstanding lighthouse projects such as the CDC's social media campaign to inform the public about pandemic diseases (see, for example, Centers for Disease Control and Prevention, 2009), other departments and agencies in the federal government have started to use social media applications.

At this time most social media directors in the U.S. federal government state that they do not actively measure what kind of impact their social media activities have. As one of the interview partners said: "I would call it 'Return on Ignorance' rather than 'Return on Investment'—we are not really measuring what we do right now."

The lifting of the policy restricting the use of cookies has had a clear impact on the way federal social media directors can track their audiences (Office of Management and Budget, 2010). As the Twitter update in Figure 7.3 shows, social media directors had been waiting for this opportunity.

Moreover, a majority of the interviewed social media directors are unclear about whether they are reaching the audiences their agency mission statement targets. Figure 7.4 illustrates an instance of the Federal Communications Commission reaching out through its website to survey web surfers in order to learn in what ways the FCC can use social media channels to increase citizen participation, engagement, and interaction.

FIGURE 7.3. TWEETING THE COOKIE POLICY

Source: N. Bonner, [Tweet about persistent cookies], 2010, http://twitter.com/#!/IrishPrince/status/17046809051.

FIGURE 7.4. THE FCC'S EXPERIMENT WITH SOCIAL MEDIA USE

Source: Federal Communications Commission, Featured Discussion, 2010, http://reboot.fcc.gov (the FCC's Beta website).

Changes in Web Practices and Standard Operating Procedures as Proxy Impact Indicators

Consider the following anecdotal evidence that social media use can make government operations more effective. David Carr (2011) reports the following story, which he heard from John Hagel of Deloitte, about a metropolitan transit authority providing a microblogging service to its maintenance workers:

It turned out one of the transit authority's biggest financial drains was the expense of bus maintenance and the amount of time a broken-down vehicle would be out of service. Part of the reason for the maintenance issues was that parts were scattered across different depots, with no coherent tracking mechanism. Just by providing maintenance workers a microblogging tool to post requests for parts they needed, the authority was able to speed up repairs and reduce the cost of the maintenance operation. This experience "turned out to completely transform their view of social software from an interesting marketing tool without a whole lot of specific impact" to something more game changing, Hagel said. . . . One way of identifying a good social software starting place is to start with metrics that matter and trace them back to a target business process.

These feedback cycles can also work with public feedback from citizens, and in this way information received through social media channels from citizens can have an impact in an agency. As one social media director says: "Consumer issues are becoming more and more important for us. . . . [One] of the things we created . . . for our homepage was consumer resources, a block that has rotating messages, so that people can see the latest consumer information." This director's agency has actively implemented additional functionalities based on feedback, suggestions, and requests it has received from citizens via social media channels. A similar example can be seen on the Federal Deposit Insurance Corporation's website (Figure 7.5). In response to citizen feedback, the FDIC "created a box on [its] home

FIGURE 7.5. THE FDIC'S WEBSITE AFTER INCORPORATING USER FEEDBACK

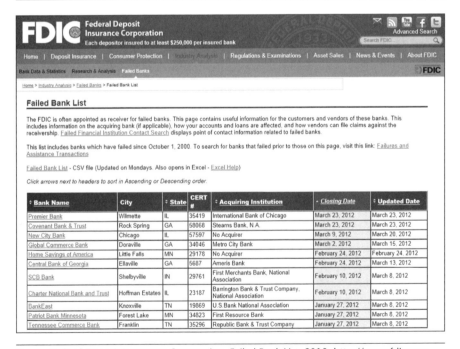

Source: Federal Deposit Insurance Corporation, Failed Bank List, 2010, http://www.fdic.gov.

page, that's actually one of the primary spots on the home page, with updated bank failure [information]."

Agencies and departments are becoming more responsive the more they interact with citizens and special audiences through social media channels. They not only push out content but also better understand the need to actively listen to conversations and discussions about their own activities—without being actively involved in the conversations. As one social media director put it: "You are already part of the conversation—if you want it or not." This highlights for him the need for his agency to be aware of the "temperature" in the sentiments citizens articulate on agency social media about either topics of interest to the agency or the agency itself.

Once they improve their listening capacity, agencies and departments can actively intervene—either by counteracting rumors or by responding directly to citizens' needs. A recent example of this responsiveness cycle is certain feedback the Transportation Security Administration (TSA) has collected through the blogosphere on its mode of operations. A post on the TSA blog (displayed in Figure 2.12 in Chapter Two) describes how TSA bloggers listened actively to sentiments posted on numerous blogs and noticed a number of legitimate complaints about TSA security screening practices. The agency analyzed the sentiments and responded by making operational changes and then by blogging that "posters on this blog have had their first official impact on our operations. That's right, less than one week since we began the blog and already you're affecting security in a very positive way." In this instance, feedback through the social media channels had the impact of actively changing standard operating procedures.

Capturing Citizen Data to Improve Operations

Social media directors in the public sector face the problem that they are first movers in a problem space and have little comparable experience. This is true for the most innovative agencies and departments in the federal government, as presented in this and earlier chapters, and also for agencies in state and local governments. Many of my interview partners expressed the need to explore and understand their audience's interactions with the technology better and integrate the lessons learned to improve their standard operating structure and ultimately improve government operations. Overall it became very clear that most current measurement techniques are hands-on approaches using freely available tools chosen and applied without any guidance from formal authorities, such as the Federal Web Managers Council or the Web Content Managers Forum.

Both formal and informal networks and their inner workings are still underexplored in the public sector literature (for a detailed discussion see Isett, Mergel, Leroux, Mischen, & Rethemeyer, 2011). Social networking services that provide new venues for highly informal interactions and networking in and with government are even less studied and understood so far, but are challenging the day-to-day management of social media directors. Although the technology itself has not changed citizens' behavior—citizens were talking about good and bad government practices with the help of other publishing media before—social media do provide a new form of publicness and openness for interactions and content sharing. Social media produce a wide range of networks and network effects, adding to earlier perspectives on networked governance.

Having tools in place that help government agencies to understand and follow themes that are developing can help social media directors to frame content delivery and form interactions. Recently, the Government of Singapore announced its first official sentiment analysis to learn how Singaporeans think about their government (Hicks, 2010). Singapore's government focuses on passive listening activities instead of merely pushing information toward the nation's citizens. Other techniques that may help social media directors to understand an agency's actual reach and the qualitative dimensions of its interactions with citizens include Twitter mood indicators (Mislove, Lehmann, Ahn, Onnela, & Rosenquist, 2010), and the analysis of an agency's Twitter network composition (Lazer et al., 2009; Naaman, Boase, & Lai, 2010).

Any measurement tool government social media directors use will fail if they do not connect online activities to their agency's mission and objectives (Figure 7.6) (Bretschneider & Mergel, 2010). Are government agencies and departments actually reaching the audiences they are promising to reach in their mission statements? The acceptance of social media among audiences that are otherwise unreachable for government and the successful distribution of government information through these highly interactive and bidirectional channels is increasingly linked to citizens' perceptions of the authenticity and vibrancy of government.

At this point in time, we are observing only the early stages of experimentation with social media applications. Federal agencies and departments need the freedom and resources to experiment with this highly disruptive and potentially transformative technology. In the corporate sector this form of experimentation is seen as part of the organization's R&D (research and development) activities, with the potential to create new services and products. Social media activities can help government to stay relevant and effective.

FIGURE 7.6. HOW SOCIAL MEDIA USE MAY SUPPORT AN AGENCY'S MISSION

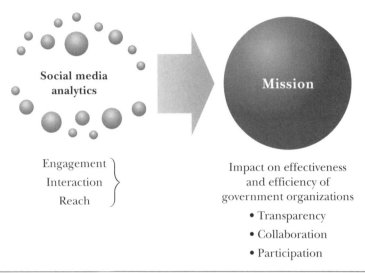

From a research perspective, the use of social media applications in the public sector opens several venues for future inquiry. As an example, it is desirable to understand how citizen interaction shapes standard operating procedures beyond the selective examples presented in this chapter. How is new knowledge created in Facebook comments extracted and used to affect the organization? Does government agencies' use of social media applications support agency missions, and are agencies becoming more transparent, accountable, participatory, and collaborative? Existing measurement instruments that might help researchers to answer such questions are rudimentary at best and need to be extended to generate more meaningful insights.

Combining Quantitative and Qualitative Social Media Measurement: Klout Scores for Federal Twitter Accounts

A relatively new—and in parts of Government 2.0 highly criticized—tool to measure social media activities on the web for free is Klout. It is currently considered the only effective free tool that allows anyone on the web to understand public social media activities.

Klout produces a score that gauges the influence of social media users, including federal agencies. The more a user posts updates, engages with other users, and reuses others' messages, the higher its Klout score will be over time. Klout aims to measure the relevance of a user's actions and interactions within the user's own network and in comparison to others in the network. The basic idea of Klout is that the mere quantitative number of Twitter followers or updates does not provide value. What Klout, in comparison to a mere follower score, measures is therefore a combination of the return on engagement, participation, interaction, and attention, but not necessarily a return on investment. One quantitative measure alone does not make a person influential in a network. But it helps government users to understand whether their updates matter and are recognized as important information by their audience. The Klout account descriptions in the following list and the Klout scores in Table 7.1 are compiled from information that was available on Klout.com in December 2011. According to Klout:

The Department of Education is a thought leader. "You are a thought leader in your industry. Your followers rely on you, not only to share the relevant news, but to give your opinion on the issues. People look to you to help them understand the day's developments. You understand what's important and your audience values that."

The Department of the Treasury is a specialist. "You may not be a celebrity, but within your area of expertise your opinion is second to none. Your content is likely focused around a specific topic or industry with a focused, highly-engaged audience."

The Centers for Disease Control and Prevention is a pundit. "You don't just share news, you create the news. As a pundit, your opinions are widespread and highly trusted. You're regularly recognized as a leader in your industry. When you speak, people listen."

The Department of Health and Human Services is a broadcaster. "You broadcast great content that spreads like wildfire. You are an essential information source in your industry. You have a large and diverse audience that values your content."

The U.S. Navy is a networker. "You know how to connect to the right people and share what's important to your audience. You generously share your network to help your followers. You have a high level of engagement and an influential audience."

FIGURE 7.7. NASA'S KLOUT SCORE

The National Aeronautics and Space Administration is a taste maker (Figure 7.7). "You know what you like and your audience likes it too. You know what's trending, but you do more than just follow the crowd. You have your own opinion that earns respect from your network."

Table 7.1 provides an overview of selected Twitter accounts in the U.S. federal government, their number of followers, and their Klout scores. For each department or agency, the table gives the number of Twitter accounts

TABLE 7.1. KLOUT SCORES OF U.S. GOVERNMENT TWITTER ACCOUNTS

Department or Agency	Twitter Accounts Being Followed	Twitter Followers[*]	Klout Score	Klout Label	Twitter Handle	Twitter URL
Department of Agriculture	159	47,453	60	Broadcaster	@USDA	http://twitter.com/#!/USDA
Department of Commerce	113	10,532	57	Specialist	@CommerceGov	http://twitter.com/#!/CommerceGov
Department of Defense	322	54,671	61	Thought Leader	@DeptofDefense	http://twitter.com/#!/DeptofDefense
Air Force	356	31,428	61	Thought Leader	@usairforce	http://twitter.com/#!/usairforce
Army	294	104,524	67	Thought Leader	@USArmy	http://twitter.com/#!/USArmy
Coast Guard	90	16,479	59	Broadcaster	@uscg	http://twitter.com/#!/uscg
Marine Corps	157	69,935	72	Thought Leader	@usmc	http://twitter.com/#!/usmc
Navy	23,474	31,093	47	Networker	@navynews	http://twitter.com/#!/navynews
Department of Education	13	76,113	64	Thought Leader	@usedgov	http://twitter.com/#!/usedgov
Department of Energy	85	33,900	59	Broadcaster	@Energy	http://twitter.com/#!/ENERGY
Health and Human Services	116	152,308	62	Broadcaster	@hhsgov	http://twitter.com/#!/hhsgov
Centers for Disease Control and Prevention	94	53,029	66	Pundit	@CDCgov	http://twitter.com/#!/CDCgov
Food and Drug Administration	8	3,268	10	Broadcaster	@us_fda	http://twitter.com/#!/US_FDA
Department of Homeland Security	176	51,220	64	Thought Leader	@DHSgov	http://twitter.com/#!/DHSgov

Agency					
Federal Emergency Management Agency	456	78,897	75	Thought Leader	@fema	http://twitter.com/#!/fema
Transportation Security Administration	190	17,182	52	Thought Leader	@TSABlogTeam	http://twitter.com/#!/TSABlogTeam
Department of Housing and Urban Development	234	17,287	50	Thought Leader	@HUDNews	http://twitter.com/#!/HUDNews
Department of the Interior	16,738	17,129	56	Specialist	@Interior	http://twitter.com/#!/Interior
Fish and Wildlife Service	586	6,831	54	Specialist	@usfwshq	http://twitter.com/#!/usfwshq
National Park Service	276	26,930	58	Thought Leader	@natlparkservice	http://twitter.com/#!/natlparkservice
Department of Justice	104	428,471	62	Broadcaster	@TheJusticeDept	http://twitter.com/#!/TheJusticeDept
Federal Bureau of Investigation	961	246,249	55	Thought Leader	@FBIPressOffice	http://twitter.com/#!/FBIPressOffice
Department of Labor	91	27,507	54	Thought Leader	@USDOL	http://twitter.com/#!/USDOL
Department of State	261	171,970	71	Thought Leader	@StateDept	http://twitter.com/#!/StateDept
Department of Transportation	875	25,065	60	Broadcaster	@RayLaHood	http://twitter.com/#!/RayLaHood
Department of the Treasury	140	25,578	52	Specialist	@ustreasurydept	http://twitter.com/#!/ustreasurydept
Department of Veterans Affairs	770	26,653	62	Thought Leader	@DeptVetAffairs	http://twitter.com/#!/DeptVetAffairs
Environmental Protection Agency	40	51,275	61	Thought Leader	@EPAgov	http://twitter.com/#!/EPAgov
Federal Communications Commission	35	450,044	66	Thought Leader	@FCC	http://twitter.com/#!/FCC

(continued)

TABLE 7.1. KLOUT SCORES OF U.S. GOVERNMENT TWITTER ACCOUNTS (*continued*)

Department or Agency	Twitter Accounts Being Followed	Twitter Followers*	Klout Score	Klout Label	Twitter Handle	Twitter URL
Federal Deposit Insurance Corporation	0	4,722	39	Specialist	@FDICgov	http://twitter.com/#!/FDICgov
General Services Administration	147	2,872	48	Specialist	@usgsa	http://twitter.com/#!/usgsa
National Aeronautics and Space Administration		1,600,478	80	Taste Maker	@nasa	http://twitter.com/#!/nasa
National Archives and Records Administration	34	8,613	53	Specialist	@USNatArchives	http://twitter.com/#!/USNatArchives
U.S. Agency for International Development	792	123,429	72	Thought Leader	@usaid	http://twitter.com/#!/USAID

*Twitter numbers as of December 2011.

the organization is following, the number of Twitter followers the organization itself has, its Klout score, and a Klout label categorizing its activities. The score is based on what Klout calls *engagement*: a combination of the number of tweets sent out, the number retweeted by others, and the number of Twitter accounts that can be reached based on the number of retweets and the number of followers in each retweeter's network.

Recommendations for Social Media Directors in the Public Sector

Given that the use of social media applications seems to be a growing trend in the public sector, what can public managers do to understand the impact that they have as a result of their online social networking activities? Based on my data analysis, here are the main recommendations for IT professionals in the public sector:

1. *Keep measuring what you are measuring.* Keep an eye on the number of followers and number of comments to see trends in interests.

2. *Gain a better understanding of the composition of your follower network.* Identify knowledge hubs and important followers to understand how to engage and activate those highly influential and networked individuals as knowledge replicators. Actively understand how content is spread through the social graph of your network.

3. *Analyze your audiences' preferred habits on social networking sites.* Part of a successful social media presence is an understanding of the blogosphere and the Twittersphere: How do citizens interact with your content on Twitter? Take the time to observe, learn, and apply best practices.

4. *Experiment with text analysis instruments.* Trace information spreading about hot topics or at least your agency's name.

5. *Listen to conversations without being actively involved in the conversation.* Do not feel the need to always be actively involved, but make an effort to hear what topics are being discussed, so that you will not be surprised when hot topics are bubbling up. Intervene when necessary—for example, when rumors are spreading false information.

6. *Create and initiate cultural change in your agency.* Socialize key personnel into the use of social media applications despite the extreme openness that might at times contradict formal bureaucratic reporting structures.

Instead, open social media accounts for multiple authors, and include specialists who can knowledgeably respond to citizen requests.

7. *Allow for multiple social media channels and the distribution of real-time information.* Learn to understand each channel instead of applying the same principles to all channels. Responsiveness and impact in a real-time, information-sharing environment might be challenging, but as soon as you start, citizens will expect this form of responsiveness cycle for future interactions with your agency.

8. *Don't ignore the knowledge citizens are willing to provide through your agency's social media channels.* Citizens can be used as authors and have the potential to create new knowledge for an agency, knowledge that the agency might otherwise have to purchase from consultants or vendors.

Summary: Social Media Metrics and Outcomes

The insights of current measurement practices are summarized in Table 7.2. For each social media goal, such as reach, audience, participation, feedback, and satisfaction, the table lists the currently available success indicators. Freely available tools to measure these indicators are also provided, as are possible outcomes—ways to understand and use indicator findings.

TABLE 7.2. MEASURING SOCIAL MEDIA PERFORMANCE

Goals	Success Metrics	Tools	Outcomes
Reach	Number of followers and *likes* or friends (change from start) Number of hashtags; number of followers on Twitter Number of retweets on Twitter Number of *unlikes* Number of unsubscribers	Raw data from social networking sites Facebook Insights, Facebook Fan Page, Twitter account Raw data from Twitter account	Is measured (per event), but no reaction offered or conclusions drawn Indicates interest and diffusion Indicates change in interest
Types of citizens	Demographic data: Ages Locations, cities	Facebook Insights or Fan Pages	Supplies insights about the target audience
Participation	Click-throughs from social media sites Number of tags	Real-time web analytics program	Supplies information that might be used in creating follow-up videos with specialists in most interesting topic area
Direct feedback	Number of times content is mentioned in other broadcasting (news) media Number of links pointing to a blog post Number of incoming links or off-line mentions	Asking direct questions (for example, using IdeaScale) Comments on Facebook	Contains useful information for shaping agency actions (allowing agency, for example, to "get closer to acceptable and really desirable rules")
Satisfaction	Sentiments of influencers	Browsing for positive (or negative) comments on blog, for informative Facebook comments, and for anecdotal evidence	Gives agency the ability to add information or other features or change practices to meet user needs and interests
Loyalty, retention, and brand awareness	Number of return visits Number of incoming links Number of referrals from trusted sites and organizations	Focusing on improving length and quality of visit (as opposed to offering event-driven, one-hit wonders)	Results in increased trust, usefulness, attention
Comparison to other agencies	Growth rates at other agencies	Raw data from Facebook and Twitter accounts	May justify the agency's choice of actions

Note: Content is based on interviews conducted with social media directors of the most innovative U.S. federal agencies in 2010.

PART TWO

SOCIAL MEDIA PRACTICES: PARTICIPATION, COLLABORATION, AND TRANSPARENCY

CHAPTER EIGHT

PARTICIPATION 2.0

Participation 2.0 refers to the use of Internet and social media technologies to engage citizens with government. Federal-level public engagement initiatives have received most of the attention, but in most cases citizens are not turning to a federal agency to discuss their concerns. Instead, most citizens are concerned about local government topics and want to be heard and included in decision-making processes in their immediate neighborhood. Therefore, this chapter highlights two forms of citizen participation: local issue reporting as well as participation in challenges at all levels of government.

Government agencies and departments have a choice of whether to offer online or in-person participation, or a mix of the two. This decision needs to be made only after consideration of numerous design issues, such as the nature of the problem, the available time and resources, and the goals, among others. In addition to producing other benefits, online participation can be seen as a tool to promote open and transparent government, increase citizen trust, encourage political efficacy, and improve the responsiveness of government to citizen needs and concerns—especially on the local government level.

Defining Participation 2.0

Online interaction between government and citizens is so far mostly conducted on a Web 1.0 level—that is, on proprietary, static, and noninteractive websites—and in accord with Government 1.0, the idea that public agencies need to develop websites to provide information to citizens. By the late 1990s and early 2000s, Web 2.0 tools were evolving (O'Reilly, 2007). Whereas Web 1.0 tools limit users to passive viewing of provided information, user-centered Web 2.0 tools facilitate collaboration through interactive information production and sharing (Bretschneider & Mergel, 2010; Cormode & Krishnamurthy, 2008; Howe, 2006). Examples of Web 2.0 approaches include web-based communities, hosted services, social networking sites, picture- and video-sharing sites, wikis, blogs, and mashups, among others. These tools are enabling the development of Government 2.0, defined as "the use of social media applications to increase participation, transparency, and interagency collaboration in the public sector" (Bretschneider & Mergel, 2010; Mergel, 2011).

In turn, Government 2.0 is giving rise to Participation 2.0. At the core of Participation 2.0 processes are the social media channels that allow bidirectional interactions among government agencies and citizens. Examples include posting comments to blogs and Facebook Fan Pages, using Twitter messages to provide breaking news and information, and allowing the use of public datasets for mashups with other applications, such as Google Maps. Government organizations are also developing websites that allow citizens to identify and alert managers to problems or deficits in their community (for example, CitySourced, www.citysourced.com). Likewise, civic hackers and enthusiasts are developing applications that make use of data released by government (for example, the London Data Store, data .london.gov.uk) or that encourage broader engagement in the community (for example, Localocracy, www.localocracy.com).

Together these government- and citizen-initiated applications have substantively changed the way public managers and citizens interact and have facilitated the emergence and development of *distributed democracy efforts* and *digital neighborhoods*. The notion of distributed democracy has its roots in the recognition that governments need greater citizen involvement to effectively address the numerous public challenges in an increasingly complex environment. As a consequence, some governments are using Participation 2.0 technologies to engage citizens in the identification, organization, prioritization, and solving of problems that government does not have the resources or knowledge to solve on its own. Responsibility is therefore distributed to citizens to create digital neighborhoods, where citizens can actively take on some of the problems of government and help to enhance the civic life of their communities. In some cases, citizens are even organizing to take over noncritical tasks and responsibilities that were traditionally in the hands of government. A recent example on the island of Kauai, Hawaii, is illustrative: businessowners and residents joined forces to repair an access road to a state park, a repair for which the State Department of Land and Natural Resources did not have the finances (Simon, 2009).

Following categories developed and used for engagement events by America Speaks and the Deliberative Democracy forum, Participation 2.0 can be divided into the following activities: inform, consult, include or incorporate, collaborate, and empower (Leighninger, 2011; Lukensmeyer, 2010). Each activity is described in the following sections, including the use of social technologies and their applications in the public sector to these activities.

Inform

In terms of information sharing, the strengths of the Internet and social media tools are their ability to allow immediate, multidirectional exchanges between citizens and government. When used in conjunction with mobile phones, social media tools can instantly reach citizens wherever they are. A number of instances exist of local governments using Internet and social media technologies to inform citizens. For example, the overwhelming majority of local governments use Web 1.0 tools on websites to inform citizens about various events such as public meetings, decisions, and community activities, among a wealth of other types of information. Many of these websites offer social technologies to encourage interactive information production and sharing through mechanisms such as events postings, blogs, and discussion boards. In addition to websites, many local governments and their individual agencies use Facebook or other social networking sites to provide citizens with information. Similarly, many local governments use Twitter, the microblogging service, which can be accessed via the Internet or mobile phone, to provide information to citizens. In some cases governments use Twitter simply for updates and to direct citizens back to websites for more information, and citizens use it to report problems and ask questions (as with, for example, the City and County of San Francisco's 311 service, sftwitter.sfgov.org/twitter). In other cases Twitter is used to supply breaking news or other critical information (for example, evacuation routes or shelter locations in emergency and natural disaster situations) as quickly as possible to all constituencies. Another example is the use of Twitter to issue Amber Alerts for missing children (twitter.com/ AMBER_Alert). The informing category basically allows government to broadcast information widely to citizens who prefer to receive their information through social media channels.

Consult

Social media technologies are increasing the ability of local governments to consult with citizens. Consulting can include the receipt of and response to comments, concerns, requests, and complaints. A case in point is SeeClickFix (www.SeeClickFix.com), an application based on FixMyStreet, fixmystreet.com, which is used in the United Kingdom). These innovative web applications allow both citizens and public managers to collaborate asynchronously on nonemergency issues in their community. The idea harnesses the willingness of citizens to report issues, such as potholes, trash problems, or other nuisances, on a central platform by uploading pictures (taken with a cell phone) along with a short explanation. The participating government agencies, public works departments, or community groups can then log in and give these citizens feedback and progress reports, such as "work process started" or "issue resolved."

A similar project, called Love Lewisham (www.lovelewisham.org), is being used in Lewisham, a district in southeast London. The project allows residents to photograph and report environmental issues, such as graffiti, trash, and abandoned vehicles, by text message or MMS to the local authority, along with the GPS location of the problem. The local authority responds to the complaint, and informs residents via the website about the actions taken to address the issue. Finally, the City of Boston is using an iPhone application called Citizens Connect for citizen-to-city transactions (www.cityofboston.gov/mis/apps/iphone.asp; status updates are provided at mayors24.boston.gov/selfservice/CoB_Case_Statis.htm). The application is a gateway that allows citizens to report issues to the city's citizen relationship management (CRM) system.

Include or Incorporate

Other local governments use Participation 2.0 technologies to engage the public in information processing and to give citizens more influence over decision making. Wikis, the software platforms that allow nontechnical, interactive online content creation, have emerged as an important and commonly used tool in such cases. With the aid of a simple text editor window, wiki users are easily able to collaborate and produce joint outcomes, and they do not need web programming skills (Goodnoe, 2005).

An example is the Wikiplanning™ project in San Jose, California (www
.wikiplanning.org), which uses a wiki to conduct a *virtual charrette* in order
to solicit information from citizens, city planners, vendors, and others. The
goal is to "create a new and better avenue for citizens to provide input on
the city's future" (Veen, 2009) by defusing confrontational attitudes common in planning and development and by constructing joint ownership of
solutions. This form of participation mostly solicits input from the public—
making citizens feel more engaged and a part of the overall process.

Collaborate

Participation 2.0 technologies allow for government to partner with the
public throughout the decision-making process, from the identification of
the problem to the development of alternatives and the identification
of preferred solutions. An emerging example, which uses both in-person
and online participation, is the virtual ward panels in London. As part of its
policing effort, London created safer neighborhood ward panels, groups of
neighborhood residents who hold public meetings to collect information
on area crime and safety and report that information to their area police
department. To supplement this effort, the Westminster City Council
has launched a pilot project, called Virtual Ward Panels, which will use
Participation 2.0 technologies such as blogs and discussion forums, along
with online surveys and voting tools, to engage a broader, more diverse
set of residents in the work of creating safer neighborhoods. The goals
are to engage citizens and give them a say in developing and selecting the
policing priorities and strategies for the area in which they live. This effort
goes beyond the inclusion step, making the participation process and specifically its outcomes more transparent. Citizens directly interact with the
submitted solutions, see how others have voted, and are thereby part of
the final decision making.

Empower

Participation 2.0 technologies can also be used to empower citizens, that is,
to place decision-making authority in their hands—the highest level of citizen participation. No cases at the federal level have been made public that
truly fit into this category, where citizens are engaged beyond the collaborative level, though it is likely that some exist. At the state level, however,
citizen empowerment is occurring, at least to some degree, in the Virginia
Idea Forum (www.ideas.virginia.gov). After logging into the website, citizens

TABLE 8.1. TYPES OF PUBLIC INVOLVEMENT IN DECISION MAKING

Level and Goal of Involvement	Examples of Participation 2.0
Inform: provide the public with balanced and objective information to assist them in understanding the problem, alternatives, opportunities, and solutions.	Interactive websites Facebook and social networking sites Twitter
Consult: receive and respond to citizen comments, requests, and complaints, and obtain public feedback on analysis, alternatives, and decisions.	SeeClickFix FixMyStreet Love Lewisham Citizens Connect (citizen-to-city transactions)
Include or incorporate: work directly with the public throughout the process to ensure that public concerns and aspirations are consistently understood by staff and the public and are considered.	Wikiplanning™
Collaborate: partner with the public in each aspect of the decision including the development of alternatives and the identification of the preferred solution.	Virtual ward panels
Empower: place final decision-making authority in the hands of citizens.	Virginia Idea Forum
Multiple levels of involvement.	Redbridge i Harringay Online

Source: T. Nabatchi and I. Mergel, *Participation 2.0: Using Internet and Social Media Technologies to Promote Distributed Democracy and Create Digital Neighborhoods* (Phoenix, AZ: Alliance for Innovation, 2010); adapted from C. Lukensmeyer and L. Torres, *Public Deliberation: A Manager's Guide to Citizen Engagement* (Washington, DC: IBM Center for The Business of Government, 2006), p. 7, table 1.

submit their ideas about improvements for state government. Together, citizens discuss the ideas and collaborate to develop and enhance them. These ideas are then rated by users, and the ideas with the highest ratings receive an official response from a representative of the state. The premise of this state-level example could be applied easily to local government endeavors. Table 8.1 provides a summary of types of citizen engagement and participation, including examples on all levels of government.

Case Study: SeeClickFix—Online Distributed Democracy

This case study highlights one part of the growing Government 2.0 ecosystem in the United States of America. SeeClickFix (SCF) is a web-based service designed to help citizens report nonemergency issues in their neighborhoods. The reports can be submitted via a web interface; by means of iPhone, Blackberry, or Android reporting apps; or though a Facebook application. Local government officials receive alerts about submitted issues and then can track progress on these issues via the *Watch Area* the officials are responsible for. The platform allows direct feedback mechanisms. Local government officials assign a work order number to each issue and can change the status of the repair (from open to in progress or fixed). Citizens are automatically informed about changes in the status of their reported issues, which establishes a full feedback cycle. The service is integrated into the social networking services Twitter and Facebook and provides map-based reporting widgets for government and newspaper websites.

Ben Berkowitz, the cofounder and CEO of SeeClickFix, had the initial idea for the service in 2007 and officially launched the platform in 2008. In his words, the motivation to create the service was the lack of responsiveness of his own local government in New Haven, Connecticut:

> So there was graffiti in my neighbor's building next door to my house, and when I went to talk to my neighbor I had some trouble approaching him to remove it. And when I tried to call local government here in New Haven, Connecticut, I had some trouble getting a response from them. And so while waiting on hold for a city employee I thought, you know, I bet that other people have documented the same issue as me, by calling into this black box in City Hall, and there's no record of it, and it'd be great if we could make this public. And so we [my cofounder(s) and I] sat down at the weekend, we spent four hours and we made a little Google map that'll ask people to publicly document issues in their community. And then we went and created a tool called the Watch Area which was the ability for governments and others to receive alerts on the things that were happening within their geography.

Citizen Needs

As Ben Berkowitz described in discussing his motivation, the main need that is met by SeeClickFix is to alert local government about issues that need to be fixed in the community. These issues may be potholes; graffiti; broken infrastructure such as problems with roads, street lights, or sidewalks; flooding; needs for improvements around pedestrian, cycling, or transportation infrastructure; or beautification projects around parks, but also issues with trash removal, parking in bike lanes, and the like.

Although reporting and alerting local government about nonemergency issues is an established communication channel in the United States, it is done mostly via direct phone calls or e-mail submission forms on a local government website. Most of the time, government does not send a response back to citizens, and it is oftentimes unclear whether an issue has been take care of or is still open. This disconnect—between citizen needs and government action—results in one-way reporting, with no feedback mechanisms. That is why many citizens describe issue reporting as a *black box*. SeeClickFix set out to open up this black box, to depict reported issues in a transparent way on a Google Map mashup (Figure 8.1). Beyond reporting, SCF also allows local government officials to report fixed issues, with the goal of potentially increasing their own accountability and responsiveness. Moreover, SCF helps governments to integrate their work order system with SCF's reporting system on the backend (a service available only for Pro users, a distinction discussed later in this chapter).

FIGURE 8.1. HOW SEECLICKFIX WORKS: FLOWCHART

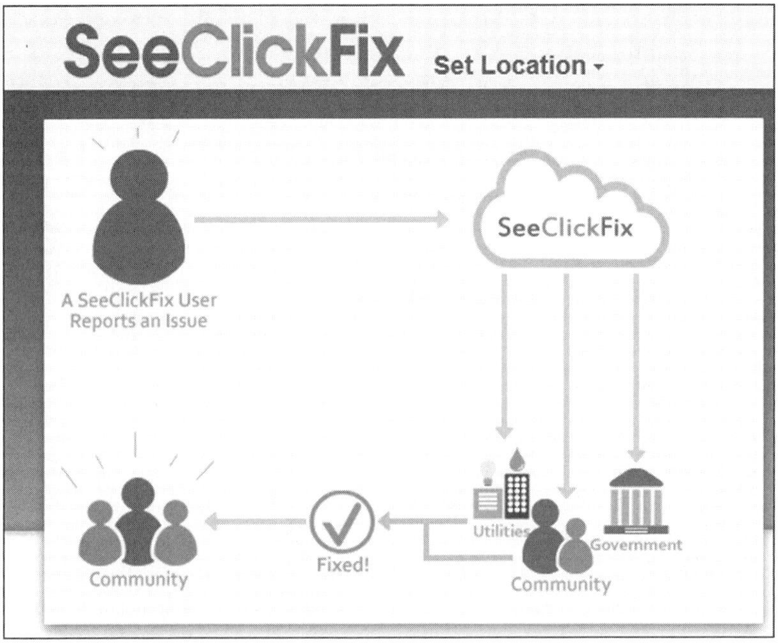

Source: SeeClickFix. Used with permission.

Inspiration for the Project and Comparable Services

The initial idea was developed by Ben Berkowitz and his cofounder. "We looked at FixMyStreet [in the United Kingdom] after we got the idea," Berkowitz said, "because we heard that they were doing similar things to what we wanted to do. And we looked at the code and decided we were going to just do it on our own, and base it on top of Google Maps. Difference to FixMyStreet: alerts can be sent to anybody so it's not just governments that are helping us fix problems on SeeClickFix."

The *New York Times* reported that "SeeClickFix is not unique in its hyperlocal focus. Other sites, like EveryBlock.com and CrimeReports.com, post data from government organizations and news outlets. FixMyStreet .com features discussion between residents and government officials, but only in Britain" (Slotnick, 2010). Nevertheless, SCF does have the unique ability to provide updates, based on zip codes, on a Google Map, and this ability is not restricted to the United States. Users can set customizable Watch Areas (such as the zip code area marked by the lines in the center of the map in Figure 8.2).

FIGURE 8.2. A SEECLICKFIX WATCH AREA DEFINED BY A ZIP CODE

Source: SeeClickFix. Used with permission.

How Does It Work?

The main reporting tool is a web interface, accessible via www.SeeClickFix .com. Citizens enter their zip code and are directed to a map for their neighborhood that has a list of already reported issues, including current status and the number of votes to fix an issue received from other users. Figure 8.3, for example, displays a map for zip code 13210, in Syracuse, New York.

Ben Berkowitz explains the core functionalities of the platform: "The reporting function and the listening function are really the two core pieces of the SeeClickFix platform that all of the tools fit around. The tools that we've developed that have fit around there are a website, where people can do both reporting and receiving of alerts, as well as voting and commenting on other people's publicly documented issues. We also created a mobile website and three applications: one on the iPhone, one on the Blackberry,

FIGURE 8.3. ISSUES REPORTED BY ZIP CODE ON SEECLICKFIX

Source: SeeClickFix. Used with permission.

and one on the Android, which enable camera and GPS functionality for documenting issues."

Citizens Create an Issue Report

Reporting an issue is made easy and citizens can report issues they come across from "where they are." They can take pictures with their cell phones or regular cameras, upload them to SCF, highlight the geographical location, select the type of the issue, add a short description explaining the issue, and submit it. Local government receives a standardized e-mail report and can (if it chooses to) submit the issue to the responsible department to start a work order. Other citizens can vote and comment on the reported issues ("Fixing a Pothole with Your iPhone," 2010). They can vote an issue up or down in importance and receive *civic points* for their participation. Figure 8.4 displays an example of using the recently launched

FIGURE 8.4. USING THE SEECLICKFIX ISSUE REPORTING PROCESS ON FACEBOOK

Source: SeeClickFix. Used with permission.

SCF Facebook application for a report (Crosseau, 2011). Figure 8.5 shows several screens from the iPhone application.

Role of Government in the Reporting Process

As outlined previously, SeeClickFix is a private initiative of its cofounders. It was not initiated by government, and it does not mash up existing government data. SeeClickFix has harvested over 16,000 e-mail addresses from local governments so that an alert can be submitted to the appropriate government as soon as a citizen reports an issue. Almost all American cities have a destination on SCF. Governments can chose to opt in or even to opt out. Many have updated their e-mail accounts, asking SCF to use a new e-mail address where they can actively monitor complaints. Some, however, have actively opted out of receiving e-mail alerts—stating that their existing citizen reporting systems are providing a valid channel for their citizens to submit reports. Moreover, *citizens can sign up their local governments*, as Berkowitz explains: "You know, citizens could sign up their government. But we had a ton of governments sign themselves up as well, when they heard about the service, because they were looking for a more open way to communicate . . . and certainly enabling the media partners [such as local newspapers] with the tools was a great way to get on the ground."

Once an issue is reported, public officials can respond directly to the submitted issue. SeeClickFix provides local governments with tools that can be directly connected to their existing work process system and

FIGURE 8.5. USING THE SEECLICKFIX ISSUE REPORTING PROCESS ON A MOBILE PHONE

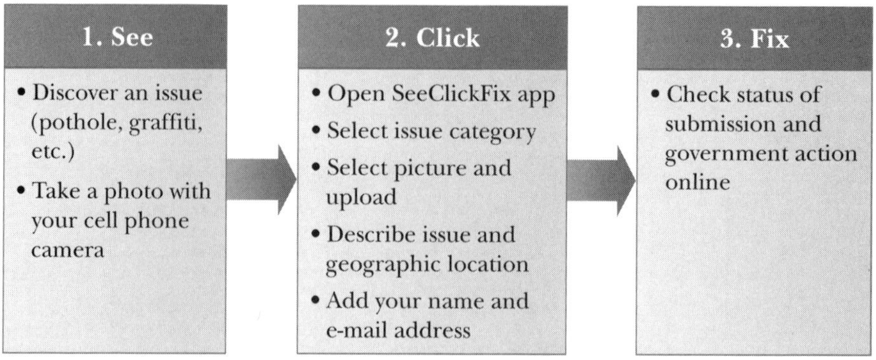

1. See	2. Click	3. Fix
• Discover an issue (pothole, graffiti, etc.) • Take a photo with your cell phone camera	• Open SeeClickFix app • Select issue category • Select picture and upload • Describe issue and geographic location • Add your name and e-mail address	• Check status of submission and government action online

individualized by department (that is, public works, parks and recreation, police, and so on). As soon as the status of an issue is officially changed by a public servant, notifications are sent out to all the watchers in the community. "The tool really does work for actually solving problems, not just voicing your concerns. And for the most part has been set favorably in the eyes of government," says Berkowitz. "[There are] certainly governments that are frustrated, that think that SeeClickFix is a duplicate of their black box web system, where it's clearly not. It's a social platform that ties into government, and if they want to consume, look at it, they can. And if not, we'll just send them an e-mail."

The City of New Haven, Connecticut, where SCF was founded, has adopted the tool and is its first Pro user. The city's current chief administrative officer, Robert Smuts, describes the decision-making process when the city chose a new reporting tool:

> We did have something before, but it didn't really take off on either capacity. SeeClickFix meanwhile, after it started up, residents really took to it, and . . . without us really doing anything, you had a huge amount of residents in New Haven who started using this tool. There's the free application where you set up a Watch Area, and do a key word, and you get the e-mail sent to you. We then set [SCF] up for several of our departments . . . [and] to funnel the e-mails to us for potholes, tree branches, or graffiti, whatever the issue was. . . . [The cofounders] approached us and convinced us to set [SCF] up for ourselves. And so we started getting all of these e-mails and reporting issues. Meanwhile, as time's ticking by, some of our departments started looking for a better work order system, the backend of this. And we settled on a company. Transportation Traffic and Parking was our first department, and now we're rolling [the work order system] out to other departments. Department of Public Works is pretty much live on Cityworks as our work order system. And so on the front end the volume of SeeClickFix [alerts] kept increasing, and it got to the point where getting the e-mail from SeeClickFix is easier for us to process than getting just a citizen e-mail, because it's formatted in a consistent way. And it's a lot easier for us to process than a phone call. It still, if you get enough volume, can be a little overwhelming. So particularly departments like Public Works and Transportation Traffic and Parking were getting a large volume of SeeClickFix e-mails. And so we were talking with the company about how to better manage that, and they came up with two different ideas. One is the dashboard product that they have, which is something you can pay a monthly subscription for, and the

FIGURE 8.6. RICHMONDGOV'S CITIZENS' REQUEST PAGE

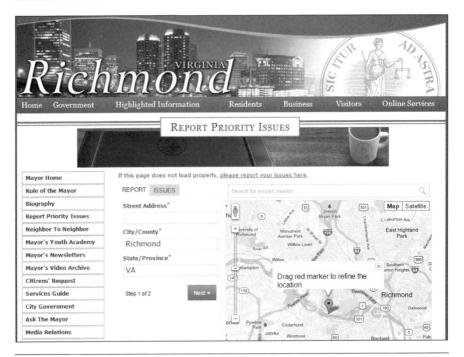

Source: RichmondGov, Citizens' Request, 2011, http://www.richmondgov.com.

other—we actually pursued both—the other is to pay to integrate their SeeClickFix frontend onto our backend system, Cityworks. So we paid them to do that and both of the companies figured out how to talk to each other. And now they're integrated.

Another SCF adopter is the City of Richmond, Virginia, which created an issue submission page on its official government website, thereby maintaining the look and feel of the official site for this process. Citizens are not directly taken to the SCF website; instead the city provides a seamless integration, as shown in Figure 8.6.

Figure 8.7 shows a snapshot of Richmond's issue statistics for a month, providing government officials with an overview of newly opened issues, closed issues, and the overall number of reported issues during this reporting period.

FIGURE 8.7. CITY OF RICHMOND ISSUE STATISTICS FROM SEECLICKFIX

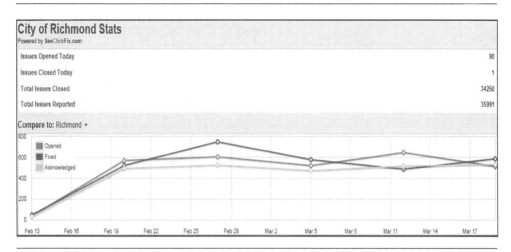

Source: SeeClickFix. Used with permission.

Business Model

SeeClickFix was founded as a corner-of-the-desk project and without any initial funding. Over time the cofounders won several contests, prizes, and angel funding. As Berkowitz described it in 2011:

> We got a contract with the City of Houston to help them with mobile reporting for a one-year pilot project, for the Public Works and Engineering team. We won the WeMedia competition, which was a small business competition. I went full time from that, the combination of those two revenue streams. And then we went to some friends and family for an angel investment run, so that we could bring on a few more people. And we started generating more revenue on our ad network for the course of the years 2009 and 2010. We started to bring on more government clients. And then we decided that once we kind of got into a break-even point, that we wanted to grow, and we took a series A investment from . . . [O'Reilly AlphaTech Ventures] and Omidyar Network to grow the team. Now we're growing about five people up. We'll be at ten people hopefully in the next month.

The basic SCF e-mail delivery service is free for participating cities. Over time, SCF has introduced a pricing model for the Pro, Plus, and Connect categories. The categories differ in the extent of services provided. A Pro

FIGURE 8.8. 2011 SEECLICKFIX PRICING SYSTEM

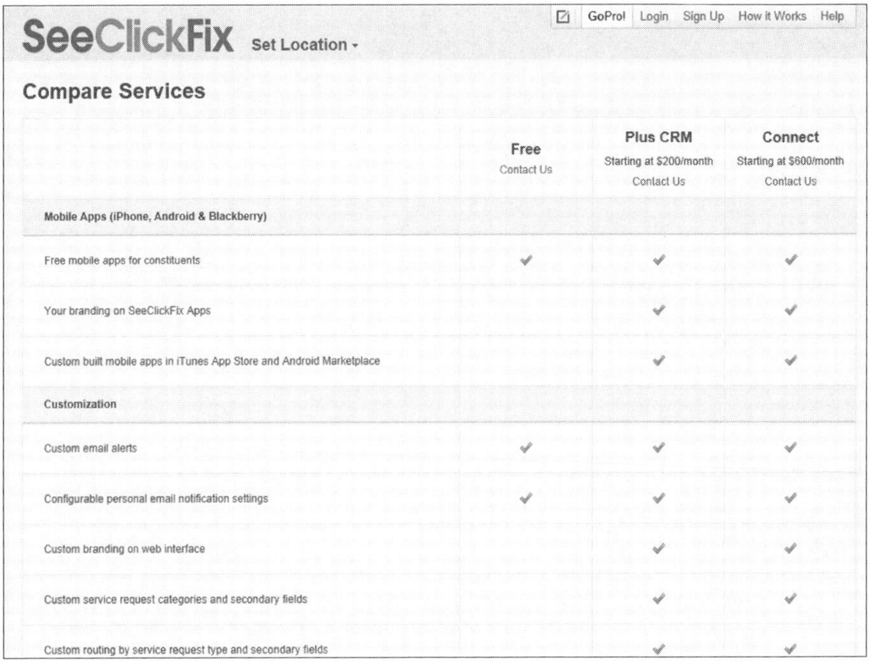

	Free Contact Us	Plus CRM Starting at $200/month Contact Us	Connect Starting at $600/month Contact Us
Mobile Apps (iPhone, Android & Blackberry)			
Free mobile apps for constituents	✓	✓	✓
Your branding on SeeClickFix Apps		✓	✓
Custom built mobile apps in iTunes App Store and Android Marketplace		✓	✓
Customization			
Custom email alerts	✓	✓	✓
Configurable personal email notification settings	✓	✓	✓
Custom branding on web interface		✓	✓
Custom service request categories and secondary fields		✓	✓
Custom routing by service request type and secondary fields		✓	✓

Source: SeeClickFix. Used with permission.

user can customize and brand the interface for $40 a month. A Plus user can customize smartphone apps and the reporting tool for $100 a month. A Connect user receives an enterprise integration into the government's existing CRM system in addition to the previous two services (Figure 8.8).

Berkowitz reported in 2011, "Yes, we're generating revenue. I mean, you know, not humungous revenue, but we're generating enough revenue now to probably support about five of us I would say. We're not at break-even anymore, so we've hired more: five people plus the office and it's rather extensive, it's pretty good."

Number of Users and Reported Issues

So far the SeeClickFix web service has several hundred thousand users, not all of whom are actively submitting issues—many are using the page to track issues and observe other users' behavior. In May 2011, the service marked its one hundred thousandth submitted issue (Figure 8.9).

FIGURE 8.9. 100,000 ISSUES REPORTED ON SEECLICKFIX, MAY 9, 2011

Source: Ben Berkowitz, Facebook update. Used with permission.

For example, in the City of New Haven the volume of issues reported through SCF is far greater than the volume the city receives from citizen phone calls or other means. Although it is not possible at this point to draw a direct correlation between the number of issues submitted through either of the existing channels, city managers interviewed for this case stated that their anecdotal evidence shows that New Haven's citizens take more to the easy-to-use online service than to the traditional channels of citizen-government interaction. By the end of 2011, over 20,000 issues were reported in New Haven alone.

User Profile

The user profile obviously varies across communities and local governments, depending on ease of access to the service, population, and distribution of users. What is obvious, says Berkowitz, is that "there's way more people that come to the site than actually contribute: maybe like 10 percent of the people that view the data contribute. There are a lot of people that are just interested in what's going on in their neighborhood, and that's a good thing too. . . . It's pretty well mixed." SeeClickFix therefore did not only develop into its main reporting service but also offers a way to observe how responsive government is to valid issues that are reported in its community. Figure 8.10 shows the U.S. cities that are the top performers in responding to citizens.

According to Berkowitz, there is a slight tendency for users to be women over thirty, who seem to report more issues than all other contributors. However, SCF's targets include all user groups, and by providing a wide range of channels to access the service, it tries to be highly inclusive.

FIGURE 8.10. TOP-PERFORMING CITIES IN CITIZEN
RESPONSIVENESS

HOW'S YOUR CITY DOING?

Top Performing Cities

We run global analyses to see how cities are
responding to their citizens. How does your city
compare?

- **La Plata County, CO - City Score
  111**
- **Elk Grove - City Score 109**
- **Cofer, VA - City Score 106**
- **Davee Gardens, VA - City Score 105**
- **Omaha, NE - City Score 105**

Source: SeeClickFix. Used with permission.

The cofounders, Berkowitz says, would like "everybody to use it." They have
observed that "socioeconomically, it does tend to start in wealthier communities," although "that's not always true, and it tends to spread quickly
to less wealthy communities . . . which are pretty evenly distributed . . . in
the city."

Dissemination Channels

SeeClickFix does not actively advertise its service; instead the initiative
follows a unique *distribution model.* It offers a small web widget that can
be embedded on local newspaper sites, local television sites, local neighborhood group sites, and Ning sites—Ning is a social networking service
that allows its users to create their own niche social networking platform. Using local newspapers as a distribution channel allows citizens to
report issues from their local news hub—pages they visit on a daily basis.
Berkowitz explains the reason for this approach: "We've started with some
real thought leaders in local news press, like the *Boston Globe,* and the word
traveled through that press. Then we go to conferences and talk to local

[journalists about] . . . how these kind of issues can really be [a] subject for journalistic endeavors."

As a result many online newspapers and government technology magazines are directly linking to SeeClickFix or are using the web widget, including Soft Company, *Inc.* magazine, *Huffington Post, TechCrunch, ReadWriteWeb,* the *New York Times,* the *Wall Street Journal, Business Insider, BusinessWeek,* and Forester, and also Philly.com, *SFGate,* the *Tennessean,* and other regional online papers. Figure 8.11 displays the SeeClickFix widget as it appears on the *Boston Globe*'s website.

Other forms of cross-pollination include informal collaborations with nongovernmental organizations: for example, Idle Free Philly, an anti-idling campaign in Philadelphia. Another Philadelphia-based initiative is running a competition for the most civic points on SeeClickFix. Moreover, many bicycling groups—such as the Atlanta Bicycling Coalition in Atlanta and also groups in New Haven, Lansing, Philadelphia, and other parts of the country—are linking to SeeClickFix. Finally, groups that are interested in parks and recreation are directly linking to the SCF service.

Drivers of Success for SeeClickFix

The popularity of SeeClickFix cannot be pinpointed to one exclusive driver, although Ben Berkowitz puts his finger on one aspect that will not go away in the future: there are "a lot of potholes in the world. A lot of broken things that need to be fixed." Citizens will always have the need to report issues in their communities, and with the ongoing budget crunches in governments around the world, an easy-to-use, low-cost product supports this need to talk about things that go wrong in a neighborhood. Here are three more drivers for SCF.

It Meets a Real Need
The service fits a real need that has not been met previously by local governments: for very low setup costs, local governments can now connect to citizens in an immediate way. Governments can now respond to individual complaints directly and build relationships with citizens and use a channel that citizens have chosen to use—instead of using a one-way push strategy that has not been well accepted by citizens.

Moreover, many local governments, either lacking a system or dissatisfied with their current approach, are in the process of searching for the right citizen customer relationship management tool. SCF again fits their needs and is easy to adopt, and the company works with local government professionals to adapt to their needs.

FIGURE 8.11. NEWSPAPERS AS DISSEMINATION CHANNELS: SEECLICKFIX ON THE *BOSTON GLOBE* ONLINE

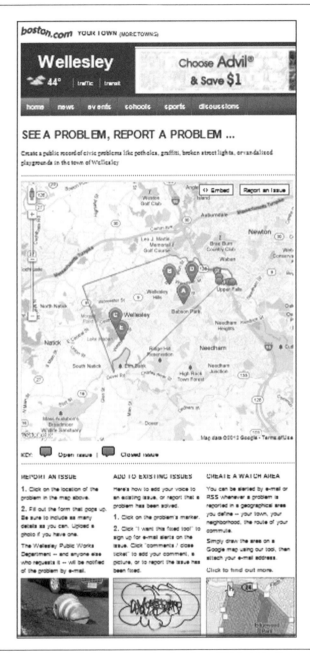

Source: Boston Globe, See a Problem, Report a Problem, 2011, http://www.boston.com/yourtown/wellesley/seeclickfix.

It Fits the Government 2.0 Era

E-services are popular in the Government 2.0 era. Online submission services, such as SeeClickFix, fit the current Government 2.0 trend of citizens becoming willing to take over responsibilities to help improve their environments. Independent of the kind of online service local governments are willing to adopt, a large percentage of citizens' concerns are coming to governments through web submission services instead of traditional channels such as phone calls or even e-mail forms. Take for example one instant analysis one city manager offered to me: "Now let me tell you, I just was looking at this. For [this one] month's time, there were 838 instances [of citizen reports] recorded in our system. Let me see the status on those. Out of those, [for] 593 the problem has been solved; others are in process of being worked on. Three were taken by phone calls. It looks like 302 came in on the website, and then we have a couple other applications that feed into that. So, see, the website's bringing in a lot of these, because people can get on any time, day or night."

The trend at this time is clear: even local governments that are non-adopters in other ways are providing online submission platforms that fulfill the immediate need and offer convenience of access for their constituencies. As one representative of a local government considering adding a mobile application says, he believes ease of use is what drives acceptance and adoption of the web service: "I think it's because people have to go to a website and enter it. So that's what's so attractive about having a mobile application, because everybody has their cell phone with them. And I think we would get more usage if somebody who was driving through their neighborhood and saw a tree falling into the road, or a pothole, or a sign that's been tweaked by weather, snow, and they [could] snap a picture and submit the request right then and there. I think we'll get a higher participation rate. That's what so attractive about these mobile apps." What this comment also shows is that local government professionals are more and more willing to share responsibilities that were traditionally only in the hands of governments. Distributing observations to neighborhood watchers can increase effectiveness and efficiency in government by, in effect, putting more "inspectors" of public services on the job around the clock.

The multichannel approach with its multiple points of entry might defuse some of the *digital divide* concerns. Providing access to the SCF service not only on expensive smartphones but also on the websites of newspapers and community and nonprofit organizations and on Facebook might increase inclusiveness. When asked whether adding another access point was likely to present a problem for anyone, one local government professional responded: "No, I think it's a good thing. I mean it's just another access point. If we were only using mobile phones, that would be a problem." And he went on to note that in fact "most of our issues come through the widgets and not the phones."

Even though most of government managers' motivation to at least pay attention to citizens' submissions on SeeClickFix is involuntarily driven by citizen crowdsourcing efforts, we can also observe a lot of personal commitment and an immense sense of *civic duty* among public managers. Take for example Raleigh, North Carolina, councilman Bonner Gaylord's use of SeeClickFix. Gaylord started the use of SCF for his constituencies and then brought his fellow council members, the mayor, and at the end the city government on board. A local announcement tells more of the story: "The local news site WRAL was so excited by the prospect of enabling open communication between citizens and their governments that they agreed to front the $400/month cost for the City's use of the professional issue tracking and customized smartphone and reporting features." For his initiative, Gaylord received an Outstanding Public Servant award from the 2011 Spectrum of Democracy Awards (North Carolina Center for Voter Education, 2011). Figure 8.12 shows how Gaylord incorporates SCF into his city council website.

One of Its Founders Has a Public Presence

The cofounder and current CEO of SeeClickFix, Ben Berkowitz, has truly become the face of the company (Howard, 2010). He is the one speaking to journalists, and he is known in the government technology press and within the broader Government 2.0 movement as the face of SeeClickFix (Fretwell, 2010; Kamenetz, 2010). This fact might come with disadvantages, but at the moment it looks as though it is helping the organization move toward the goal of securing funding and scaling up its activities to increase service access and sustainability. Berkowitz himself says, "I don't know if I'm helping or hurting."

Ultimately, the real driver is an overwhelming use of the service among citizens. With additional funding sources SCF might be able to advertise its service directly in those neighborhoods that might be underserved or reach out to more local government officials. One clear signal that will make the business case for the adoption of this service in local government comes from SCF's first Pro user, the City of New Haven: Berkowitz reports, that "there was one survey done in New Haven around happiness, satisfaction with government, and I think the end result was that citizens

FIGURE 8.12. SEECLICKFIX ACCESS THROUGH AN ELECTED OFFICIAL'S WEBSITE

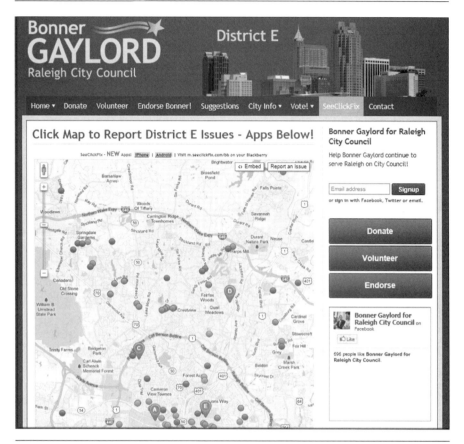

Source: B. Gaylord, [City council website for Bonner Gaylord], 2011, http://www.bonnergaylord
.com/section/report-problems.

who use SeeClickFix are 15 or 20 percent more likely to be happy with their government."

Other interview partners have reported that they have no way of surveying their citizens and therefore do not know if the service makes a difference. Others have reported that anecdotal evidence suggests SCF has made a difference in the way that citizens perceive the interactions with their local government. The degree of citizen satisfaction might stay unclear until we have comparable studies and results telling us the exact correlation between the factors of uptake of the service, responsiveness of government, and effectiveness and efficiency of service provision on the one hand and increased satisfaction with government transparency, accountability, and responsiveness on the other.

Barriers to the Adoption of SeeClickFix

SeeClickFix does face some criticism and some reluctance on the side of government. Issue reporting, or "complaining," is a dicey issue, and town hall meetings especially oftentimes drift into repeated discussions about the same issues ("you have your frequent flyers," says one of the interviewed city managers). This can lead to a them versus us attitude or support a general belief that citizens contact government only to complain (Kennedy, 2010). SCF has tried to counter this tendency by providing a voting and commenting function for each submission, making it easier for government to understand where truly pressing issues occur.

Nevertheless, many local governments were surprised when they received unsolicited, standardized SCF e-mails with citizen reports. Some tried to change the e-mail address that was harvested by SCF and inserted into the system without official verification, so that issues would directly go to the correct corresponding e-mail address. Others tried to opt out of the service by contacting SCF and asking the company to remove their e-mail addresses from the system. Especially in the early days of the service, it appears that SCF was unable to accommodate these requests, which resulted in some negative sentiments being expressed by local government officials: for example, "You know, it's unfortunate, because you would like for something like that to really partner with the cities to work together."

Other local governments' officials responded to SeeClickFix's early focus on citizens instead of on a collaborative partnership with local governments in even stronger terms. In some localities the report e-mails go to e-mail accounts that are not monitored or the reports are ignored or marked as spam. The result is that citizens perceive their local governments as unresponsive and in turn public servants are surprised as they hear about all their citizens' complaints. The service is seen among some nonadopters as a guerrilla tactic. One of the nonadopters and critics of SeeClickFix states:

> You can't just throw up a system like that. . . . Because what it looks like he's doing is trying to make us look bad. On purpose. Where, in fact, we had a system very similar to that already out there for our citizens. And I think it's OK for him to do this; I think it's great to have something that anybody anywhere can get on and report. But what's not great is

if you haven't let them [governments] know that you've done that, so that then we can tie it into the systems we already have. And the other side of that is—once we find out about it, and we try to e-mail you [the company] and contact you, and you don't call us back—it very much looks to us like you're someone who's just trying to cause trouble and not really offer something of value to people. . . . And so what that does is it makes the appearance that [our city] . . . does not care. When in fact we do.

All my interview partners in local governments stated that they are in the process of exploring a new citizen relationship management system and perceive SCF as the best that is out there, even though they criticize some of the initial tactics. They do wish to connect their existing or future services with the SCF submission system and to integrate the complaints into their public works system.

SeeClickFix—in the business of providing a valuable public service for citizens—sees a main barrier as governments' communication style and lack of knowledge: "Governments that didn't want to communicate [with their citizens and with SCF] were a big barrier. You know, you have to take it with a grain of salt when governments get upset with you that you're doing something that they wish they had done."

Measuring the Success of the Initiative

The early success of a start-up initiative is usually evaluated with statistics, such as increased numbers of contributors. As mentioned earlier in this case study, SCF has just recently reached over 100,000 reported issues, submitted by about 10 percent of website visitors. Beyond the number of issues reported, the website's success needs to also be measured on the extent to which governments are responding to issues and how many issues are fixed—and reported on SeeClickFix as fixed by government. That means that success is not just the responsiveness of starting a work process and filling a pothole but also letting citizens know that their complaints were heard and that government is willing to create a bidirectional relationship with its constituencies. SCF's success will ultimately be a sign that governments understand the necessity of an active responsiveness cycle and that they are willing to respond to citizens who are using the SCF web platform. As Berkowitz states: "We're sending alerts to 16,000 governments, I think. Probably a thousand of them are pretty responsive. The number is definitely growing."

Another important indicator of success for the service is its influence on the Open311 movement in the United States. Berkowitz comments:

> I think we've definitely been an influence on Open311, which is that standard for open communication. Because one of the chief complaints from governments is, "You're sending us e-mail," and we'll say, "Yes, but that is one of the ways you've asked to be communicated with. We're just making people actually use that instead of the phone." And they quickly said that they would like that connectedness in their CRM and work orders. We're providing cheaper solutions for work orders—or issue tracking as well—so we're affecting the way governments can bridge their software also.

Outlook

SeeClickFix is on its way to establishing itself as an independent company. The initial angel funding will help to fund the existing service and support ongoing innovation. In Berkowitz's words, these are some of the additional services that are planned to improve SeeClickFix:

> I think we're just going to keep doing a lot more of the same. We're going to start doing phone reporting, and we hope to integrate a lot more phone, meaning that someone can report a pothole by voice, and they'll go into the system. We're going to keep improving the tools and building more tools that help neighbors help each other out. That could mean helping pay for a project, through citizens, or answering questions they might have about their community, or just better connecting people to each other around the public sphere. We will try to keep making our prices easy for them to do that, and we're building tools that make it easy to integrate. We will keep working with vendors to hopefully get them to open up and enable Open311 or a connection with SeeClickFix.

SeeClickFix seems to attract enough citizens to build a critical mass from which governments can receive remarkable input that cannot be ignored. In 2011, the Government 2.0 movement in the United States was just in its second year, and so far many initiatives have focused mainly on federal projects begun as part of the Open Government Initiative. With more citizens forcing governments to respond to their requests online, the ultimate success of SeeClickFix will be local governments' responsiveness and acceptance of the service as a valid channel of information exchange and a trusted feedback mechanism between citizens and local governments.

Case Study: Incubating and Harvesting Knowledge from Citizens

Harnessing the knowledge citizens and government employees are willing to share on social media applications in the public sector is one of the most difficult tasks facing government agencies in the era of Government 2.0. Every day thousands of citizens are commenting on government Facebook posts and blog entries or resharing information published on Twitter. Rarely, however, has government taken the opportunity to harvest innovative ideas and knowledge that is published through these channels. The main reason for many agencies to set up an organizational account is still "to be where the people are." Recently open innovation platforms have started to address this disconnect and are providing easy access to participating in making government cool again.

Opening Government to Crowdsourced Ideas

Social media tools are great channels for encouraging and collecting citizens' insights on the issues and plans of government. Unfortunately, today's standard social networking services do not have the capability to automatically extract and collate new knowledge or ideas from content that citizens are submitting through the existing commenting channels. In some cases the sheer volume of comments makes proper analysis very difficult. The challenge is to extract new ideas or valuable insights from the influx of comments in a productive and efficient way. Dashboard solutions, such as Radian6 (www.radian6.com; a commercial application for social media measurement) can help to provide a general overview by reporting the "temperature" of audiences retweeting and commenting on issues government is concerned about. It is far more challenging, however, to actually curate content and extract new ideas and innovative knowledge out of the steady flow of information that comes into government with every tweet or comment.

Open innovation platforms are designed to fill this gap (Chesbrough, 2003). With these platforms, government can take a crowdsourcing approach and issue an open call to a large, usually undefined group of people (all citizens, potential contractors or industry representatives, citizen programmers, and so on), so that many different people can contribute to the solution of a complex government task. The platform then helps to direct and coordinate the input received from citizens (or application developers, knowledge matter experts, companies, and so on), input that would be unsorted and overwhelming on social media channels. These open innovation mechanisms for crowdsourcing solutions are useful for issues where expert knowledge might not be available or is too expensive to access. They also improve the participation and engagement of citizens. Crowdsourcing provides a means for governments to engage citizens directly with the decision-making process.

Virtually any topic can be crowdsourced by government, meaning that agencies can post an issue in the form of a *challenge* and ask for the submission of solutions. The focus is on innovation, creativity, and the generation of new ideas from stakeholders or subject matter experts. In some cases the open innovation platform allows participants not only to submit their ideas but also to provide additional information on how their ideas can be executed, and every participant can comment on all other submitted ideas. The agency will select the best solution or set of solutions, and those whose ideas are selected are often compensated in some way. This approach is more cost effective than the traditional requests for proposals, which are often time consuming to create and evaluate and have specific design criteria and solutions in mind. A challenge opens the conversation and allows the "crowd" to come up with the solution, often without the agency having to set rigid requirements.

Open innovation platforms at the federal level are designed to coordinate and streamline the submission and influx of innovative ideas. Local governments are also using open innovation platforms in a similar fashion. New York City's open innovation platform, NYC Simplicity, is used to generate cost-saving ideas from employees. The iMesa program of the City of Mesa, Arizona, is a response to the economic downturn, designed to collect citizens' ideas to save money. The Idea Factory of Harford County, Maryland, also solicits ideas from constituents designed to stimulate new ideas and innovation. Some of these platforms allow citizens to vote on each other's ideas and earn points for every online activity they perform on the platform. In some localities these virtual points can be traded in for real-life products, such as a ride with the police chief for a day in the City of Manor, Texas (see www.cityofmanor.org/labs).

Platforms and the ways they are used differ depending on the goals and needs of each agency. Some platforms, such as NYC Simplicity, are used for internal purposes only. City employees are asked to help the city be more innovative and save costs during major budget crunches. Other platforms are mostly used to crowdsource citizen ideas on how to innovate government operations, such as Harford County's innovation portal (Figure 8.13).

FIGURE 8.13. HARFORD COUNTY'S INNOVATION PORTAL

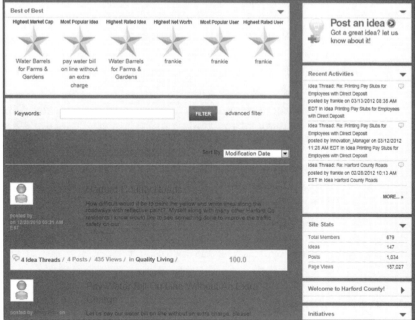

Source: Harford County Government, Featured Challenge, n.d., harfordcountymd.spigit.com/ Page/Home.

Designing Challenges

When we observe only the first lighthouse projects and experiments with open innovation platforms, designing challenges appears relatively easy. The U.S. General Services Administration's Challenge.gov, for example, provides an open innovation platform for free to all federal agencies, and challenge administrators can follow a relatively straightforward process.

The devil lies in the details. Here are a few lessons learned by open innovation administrators while experimenting with local government platforms:

- Start by carefully crafting the problem statement you want your employees or citizens to solve. The challenge has to be posed in plain language so that nonexperts immediately understand the problem.

- Experiment with challenges in-house first, before opening the floodgates to the public. Your internal sandbox can provide valuable insights for streamlining the process for public challenges.

- Design participation incentives. Think about monetary and nonmonetary giveaways that no one else offers and make it worth participating in the challenge. Showcasing submitted solutions on your website can be an incentive for some citizens to participate; others might want a monetary return on their ideas and their time invested in helping government.

- Set a time limit. Close your challenge after a predefined time and make sure that you communicate the duration and the elapsed time to your participants. Having that one-time opportunity to submit an idea can also serve as an incentive for participants.

- Create a transparent evaluation process. Post the evaluation steps and the experts involved in judging the submitted solutions prominently on your website.

- Communicate how you plan to implement the chosen solution. Throughout the implementation process make sure to show the value of the crowdsourced solution: How much money was saved? Why are government operations now running smoother than before?

Table 8.2 provides an overview of current open innovation platforms on all levels of government.

Challenges and prizes for innovation in government have the potential to reinvigorate government operations and to inject new ideas into government that would otherwise need to be purchased from vendors and consultants. On the one hand, a side effect of open innovation platforms

TABLE 8.2. LOCAL, STATE, AND FEDERAL OPEN INNOVATION PLATFORMS

Agency Name	Platform Name	Platform Open to	
		Employee Idea Generation	Citizen Idea Generation
Local government			
New York City	NYC Simplicity	✔	
Mesa, AZ	iMesa	✔	✔
Maricopa County, AZ	Idea Factory for "Rewarding Ideas"		✔
Manor, TX	Manor Labs		✔
Harford County, MD	Harford County innovation portal		✔
State government			
State of Washington	Transforming Washington's Budget		✔
State of Vermont	BroadbandVT.org		✔
Federal government			
Department of Veterans Affairs	VAi2: Veterans Affairs Innovation Initiative	✔	✔
NASA	NASA Idea Central	✔	
GSA	Challenge.gov		✔

can be an increased perception of government transparency. On the other hand, none of the existing challenges has shown that citizen satisfaction increased as a result or has been able to articulate how the information provided by challenge participants was then integrated into government decision making, resulted in changes of the standard operating procedures, or led to new policies.

Lessons for Using Participation 2.0 Technologies

Participation 2.0—the use of social media applications to engage citizens—has become a major focus of all open government initiatives. In many cases federal open government plans even collapse the collaboration and participation dimensions into one stream of activities, instead of distinguishing between different types of goals and outcomes. The challenge for public administration in general is to distinguish between the needs of citizens, the foci of government, and the location of interactions between government and citizens. On the federal level, oftentimes, citizen engagement is not taking place. It is at the local level that most citizens have concerns and get involved in government issues that directly affect them, and where they feel they have a legitimate incentive to spend their time in order to improve their community's situation.

Public managers need to address several important issues before embarking on a Participation 2.0 endeavor. First and foremost, they must decide what processes they can support with the use of social technologies and how they can support the mission of their own organization.

Then they must determine at what level they wish to involve citizens— do they simply want to inform citizens, or do they want to consult, include, collaborate with, or even empower citizens? This requires an analysis of mandates and political realities, as well as an examination of financial, human, technological, and other constraints. Moreover, public managers must provide a clear explanation to citizens about how their input will be used in government decision making. This requires public managers to think about and address ways to visualize, inform, distribute, and implement feedback mechanisms so that citizens feel their input has been received and is being processed.

Once the decision to launch a Participation 2.0 project has been made, public managers need to consider how to overcome several challenges. Some of the challenges of using Participation 2.0 are similar to the challenges of using traditional forms of public participation: for example, managers may need to address issues of low engagement and turnout. There are some interesting examples of addressing such issues by using online contests, such as Apps For Democracy (www.appsfordemocracy.org) or the Centers for Disease Control and Prevention's 2009 Flu Prevention PSA Contest (www.flu.gov/psa/psacontest1.html).

Other challenges emerge specifically from the nature of Participation 2.0 tools. From the perspective of citizens, issues of access and digital literacy have to be addressed (Mergel, 2010). Participation 2.0 technologies cannot be used by those who do not have access to them and may exclude those who are unfamiliar with them. Thus public managers must consider means for addressing these issues. Some communities are working to lower access barriers by providing computers with Internet access at public libraries and community centers. Others have to provide alternative channels of access to interactive platforms to ensure the highest possible degree of inclusion.

From the perspective of government, information overload has become a huge issue. Participation 2.0 technologies increase the amount of information received, which requires more work for processing, analysis, and verification. Thus public managers must consider how to establish the necessary back office systems for information processing and analysis. Protocols and procedures need to be devised for collecting, processing, synthesizing, and evaluating information, and otherwise translating and transforming citizen comments in ways that make this material easily digestible and useful for public managers, elected officials, and other audiences.

Finally, there is the challenge of co-optation. Although Participation 2.0 opens access to a greater number of users, there is the chance that organized users and groups could overwhelm an interaction system with their opinions and ideas. A recent example is the manipulation of President Obama's first online town hall meeting, where the number one issue discussed was the question of legalizing marijuana. This is not the most pressing issue for the majority of Americans; however, the marijuana legalization lobby is so strongly organized that it was able to dominate the discussion (National Public Radio, 2010). Thus public managers need to consider issues of recruitment and participation to reduce the likelihood of co-optation. Moreover, public managers need to establish guidelines and protocols for online engagement (that is, the rules by which participants share and respond to opinions) and mechanisms for monitoring and handling violators. What is therefore needed on all open innovation platforms is rigorous monitoring and the willingness to intervene in the event that participants are violating the terms of use or the accepted netiquette.

CHAPTER NINE

COLLABORATION 2.0

Knowledge sharing in the public sector is mostly regulated through rules, a clear sense of hierarchy with fixed reporting structures, standard operating procedures, and laws, all of which tend to restrict the free flow of information across organizational boundaries (Mergel, 2011). The result is that information produced in one agency might not be available to agencies or other entities in other corners of the overall system. This can and often does lead to reinventing the wheel and to innovative knowledge being bound up in knowledge silos (Noveck, 2009). Consequently, ideas that might meet knowledge needs of several similar stakeholders in government are prevented from spreading through the whole system.

Collaboration 2.0: A New Form of Information Sharing

As this book demonstrates, social media tools are challenging this traditional, need-to-know information-sharing paradigm (Dawes, Cresswell, & Pardo, 2009) and are increasing the degree of participation of all stakeholders in the process of creating, maintaining, sourcing, and sharing knowledge. The resulting—partially informal—emerging interactions between the public and government are creating opportunities for increased transparency, accountability, participation, and collaboration (Office of Management and Budget, 2009). Moreover, as I and others have argued, social media tools are potentially disruptive and may have transformative effects on knowledge sharing that have not been fully covered in the public administration literature (Mergel, Schweik, & Fountain, 2009).

In the public sector, people and organizations are usually operating within traditional bureaucratic interactions bound to defined federal, state, and local levels and also department or even team boundaries and with very clearly divided tasks and reporting structures. The nature of the tasks to be accomplished is usually so complex that they need to be divided into fine-grained and independent components that can be treated separately while still contributing to the overall objective of the task: service delivery to the public (Simon, 1976/1982, p. 69). As Blau and Scott (1962) point out, "the larger the group and the more complex the task it seeks to accomplish, the greater are the pressures to become explicitly organized" (p. 7). This bureaucratization has led to very elaborate rules and regulations that every member of the organization has to follow. Free sharing of information is restricted, and legal and policy constraints regulate the distribution, storage, and usage of information.

Hierarchies have proven to be inefficient in many ways when it comes to searching for information. Hierarchical structures restrict vertical information sharing to defined categories within single entities in the traditional service delivery model (Blau & Scott, 1962, p. 16; Eggers, 2005). Everything that goes beyond structured information and that is not systematically covered disrupts regulated information flows and needs to be absorbed by other information-sharing mechanisms, such as informal networks or market mechanisms (Powell, 1990) or even ad hoc bazaars without any rules at all (Demil & Lecocq, 2006). From the management literature, we know that not all the knowledge that is needed to perform certain tasks and to solve problems that government actors are confronted with is readily available within a single organization. On the contrary, knowledge may be codified to a certain extent—and not everything that an organization knows is searchable in databases, handbooks, manuals, or standard operating procedures or known by experts within an agency (Anand, Glick, & Manz, 2002; Grant, 1996). Especially when it comes to knowledge—that is, information that is relevant, actionable, and in part based on experience—transfer is difficult and flows mostly through informal processes such as socialization and internalization (Morrison, 2002; Nonaka & Takeuchi, 1995, 1996).

Prior research on knowledge sharing and advice seeking has shown that seeking knowledge from others has clear informational benefits, such as access to solutions, meta-knowledge, problem reformulation, validation, and legitimation (Cross, Borgatti, & Parker, 2001). That is in part the reason why members of an organization often rely on knowledge from external third parties and have to reach out to their informal network contacts (Anand et al., 2002). Along with formal networks, informal networks of professionals help people to access knowledge that is not accessible in codified form due to its highly intangible and tacit nature but that is needed to conduct the tasks within a professional environment (Cross, Rice, & Parker, 2001; Kram & Isabella, 1985; Morrison, 2002). Social media tools can help to break up knowledge silos and can support both horizontal and vertical information-sharing needs.

Collaborative Networking Approaches

Networks in government can either be formal or informal (Krackhardt & Hanson, 1993; Mergel, 2010). Formal networks are built on collaboration agreements, sometimes accompanied by a memorandum of understanding that states what each network member contributes to the agreed outcome. Informal networks are based on personal interactions and contacts that usually bridge hierarchical reporting structures and allow the informal social or professional exchanges that might help each network member fulfill the mission of his or her local departments. Given the bureaucratic restrictions on information sharing just described, informal networks have proven helpful for knowledge sharing in the public sector. To support the use of informal social networking elements in government, more and more federal government agencies and departments are using in-house social networking sites to allow their employees to network with each other.

Most of the time, not all knowledge that is needed to fulfill the mission is readily available in each and every agency, and government has to hire additional human capital—contractors, consultants, or external vendors—to temporarily add what is needed. When the project is done the social and human capital and slack capacity leaves the agency and is no longer obtainable for similar knowledge needs.

A prominent example of the lack of knowledge sharing that has been widely reported is the Intelligence Community's inability to "connect the dots" in the months leading up to the 9/11 catastrophe. Knowledge created on vertical as well as horizontal levels across multiple government agencies was not integrated; it never escaped the knowledge silos and so was not available to build a basis for improved and better informed decision making. Figure 9.1 shows how knowledge acquisition processes are traditionally organized along hierarchical boundaries. A request for information has to go through the hierarchical steps in the requester's own organization and

FIGURE 9.1. HIERARCHICAL KNOWLEDGE ACQUISITION

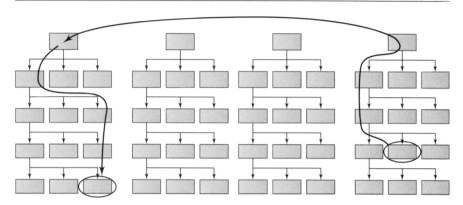

get supervisors on different levels involved, and then, once it is prepared or released, the information travels the same way in reverse, back to the person who requested the knowledge.

This has led to the creation of an information-sharing environment supported by a host of so-called Web 2.0 applications, such as video-sharing tools, blogs, shared document and collaboration spaces, and photo galleries. Prominent examples are wikis such as Diplopedia in the State Department and DoDTechipedia in the Department of Defense. U.S. Army soldiers in combat have implemented wiki technology to speed up the collection of peer-to-peer information about battlefield conditions. Figure 9.2 shows how a shared wiki can help to break up knowledge silos in government and allow simultaneous reading, creation, and sharing of government knowledge.

These examples of increased collaboration in unlikely environments, such as the highly regulated and compartmentalized command-and-control culture of the Intelligence Community, can serve as a model for other cross-organizational collaboration and government networking activities. In addition, they have the potential to move government from a need-to-know to a need-to-share information paradigm.

A-Space—also called Facebook for Spies—is together with Intellipedia part of a wider range of tools used in the information-sharing environment of the Intelligence Community. A-Space—where "A" stands for *analyst* and *analytic*—was launched in 2008 as the social network for the Intelligence Community, by the Office of the Director of National Intelligence, to

FIGURE 9.2. DISTRIBUTED KNOWLEDGE SHARING USING A WIKI

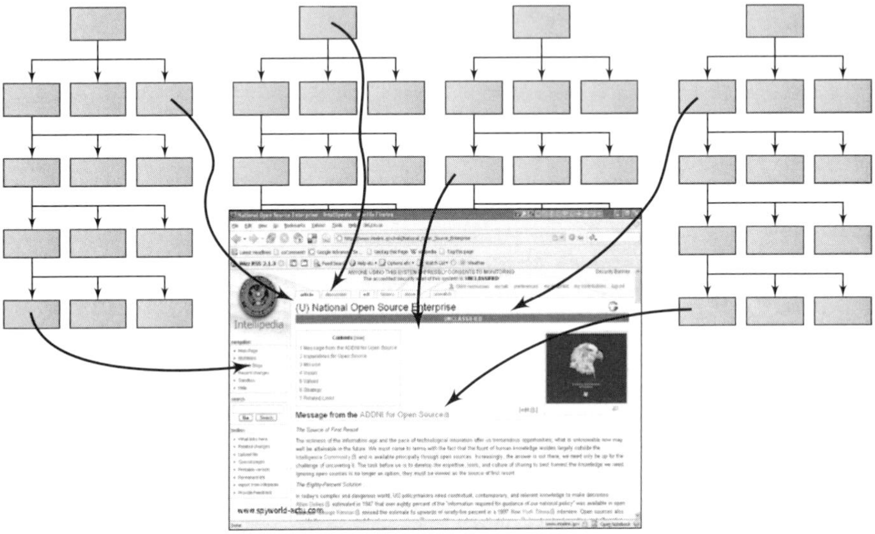

Source: Copyright © 2012 by Ines Mergel. All rights reserved.

coordinate foreign and domestic security efforts. A-Space was developed specifically for prominent intelligence organizations such as the Central Intelligence Agency (CIA), Federal Bureau of Investigation, and the National Security Agency. It aims to improve the way that intelligence agents communicate with each other and helps them to gather information on topics that might be spread across sixteen different intelligence agencies. Participation is largely voluntary and based on word-of-mouth stories of success. Intelligence officers have to ask for access, and the introduction to the tool has become part of the initial training of new employees. The goal is to break down some of the physical communication silos in the Intelligence Community, where most exchanges have traditionally been restricted by strict firewall settings. As a consequence, analysts worked in parallel on similar intelligence data collection and analysis problems without knowing of each other's solutions and interpretations of the problems. The result was that analysts did not know about conflicting opinions and interpretations of critical intelligence information and might have made misleading recommendations. A-Space allows its members to search classified and unclassified sources simultaneously and also offers web-based messaging and collaboration tools. The goal is to enhance the quality of the final analytical product in order to manage the mission more effectively at a community level and to build more integrated analytical operations across the sixteen intelligence agencies.

A similar effort, called Spacebook, has been designed in the National Aeronautic and Space Administration (NASA) as a professional network with the aim of connecting the heterogeneous groups of employees at NASA. The more diverse a network is, the more likely connections and conversations are to lead to new ideas and innovation. The intention is to give NASA employees a way to connect, to share their information and resources, to trade questions and ideas, to collaborate, and ultimately to innovate. Spacebook provides user profiles, forums, groups, and social tagging. Employees can create their own pages where they can publish a status update, share files, connect with others, follow others' activities, and join communities of interest and collaborate in protected spaces on an intranet. The functions are simple and user friendly and can be used to set up virtual teams of NASA subdivisions across the world. The intended outcome is to give NASA employees access to diverse and potentially conflicting viewpoints on a specific subject and to encourage collaboration beyond the local team to create innovations. Moreover, the ability to access and reuse information that has already been created in other parts of the agency can potentially reduce duplication of effort and ultimately save taxpayers money.

Yet another similar initiative is the Department of State's Diplopedia social networking site, located in the DOS Office of eDiplomacy. Originally an initiative of Condoleezza Rice's *transformational diplomacy*, Diplopedia has the goal of providing information for U.S. foreign affairs specialists, whether located domestically or abroad, in one central space. Diplopedia today also includes a set of social media tools, such as blogs, communities, and virtual work environments for teams. (This wiki is described in more detail in a case study later in this chapter.)

Owing to the success stories of A-Space and Spacebook, the U.S. General Services Administration (GSA), through its Office of Citizen Services, has received a mandate to create a government-wide network called FedSpace. President Obama's transparency and open government memorandum (Obama, 2009) and the Open Government Directive from the Office of Management and Budget (2009) directed federal agencies to increase collaboration within and among themselves and to optimize the use of information technology. In January 2010, discussions about how to do this across the entire federal government began. FedSpace was inspired by successful federal efforts—such as Intellipedia, Spacebook, and the

MAX Federal Community—as well as projects of commercial and nonprofit organizations that have obtained value from similar collaborative efforts.

FedSpace is a secure intranet and collaboration workspace for federal employees and contractors and is designed to be "for Feds by Feds." This online social network for government allows access only to public managers with a dot-gov e-mail address. The goal is to enable government employees to work collaboratively across agencies, through the use of Web 2.0 technologies such as file sharing, wikis, a government-wide employee directory, shared workspaces, blogs, other social media tools, and search mechanisms that have not existed before.

FedSpace has the goal of bringing together civilian agencies working on similar topics and making information sharing easier through a single platform. Federal employees can share ideas, best practices, and knowledge when FedSpace makes it easier for them to connect to each other and collaborate across agencies. Although some federal agencies already have a few collaboration tools in place, most of these tools are agency specific. Intellipedia for example is limited to the Intelligence Community and to other agencies via its highly restricted channels. By contrast, FedSpace is designed to improve the availability and the accessibility of information across all agencies. Moreover, users can create their own content on the common intranet and can post news or links to resources that might be of use for the federal community as a whole. At the center of FedSpace is the creation and maintenance of professional and instrumental relationships and also informal team-building and collaboration opportunities. Some of the problems FedSpace aims to solve are finding collaboration partners, that is, other federal employees who have worked on similar problems before; locating specific contacts in other federal agencies; and generally supporting federal employees in the conduct of their daily tasks.

An international example is GCConnex, a government-wide social networking platform used by the Government of Canada that has already implemented the vision FedSpace is trying to accomplish. GCConnex is part of GCPedia, the internal wiki of the Government of Canada. This wiki environment is open to all government employees in Canada and is designed as a proof of concept for collaboration and knowledge sharing across all levels of government. GCPedia is only accessible via the Government of Canada network, and contributors must be on a computer on that network to be able to access it. GCConnex is a new initiative within GCPedia. Similar to A-Space or Spacebook, it provides government employees with the opportunity to set up their own profile page, post their biographical information, connect to existing contacts, and create new contacts as a way to network with government employees who are working on similar tasks but who would otherwise not have the opportunity to connect to each other. The goal is to replace inefficient, exclusive point-to-point conversations on e-mail with a centralized workspace.

Another informal social networking site, GovLoop, was started in 2009, an effort led by Steve Ressler, a former employee at the Department of Homeland Security. Ressler saw the need for government employees to share information outside their restricted hierarchies and started this social networking site using an existing service, the Ning platform. This free social networking environment allows its users to create their own niche social networking sites. Users can create a profile page, write a personal blog, connect with other members, and comment on each other's blog posts.

GovLoop is designed to provide an informal online network for public sector employees at all levels of government and also allows unrestricted access to journalists, vendors, consultants, academics, students, and others. The result is a collaborative space that fosters free-flowing discussions and networking opportunities among parties who otherwise do not have the opportunity to connect with each other except at conferences or through formal contractual exchange relationships. GovLoop grew its membership within a year to over 30,000 members by word of mouth, some media coverage in practitioner technology publications, and tweets and posts on Twitter and blogs. GovLoop's success can be attributed to technology that provides a basis for multilevel interactions with various audiences and through various channels, and a high degree of informal information sharing with otherwise disconnected parties.

Most collaboration activities will come with a steep learning curve. Restricted knowledge-sharing cultures, top-down hierarchies, and strict regulations about report structures are contradicting the openness and free culture of knowledge sharing that these innovative government networks promote. This cultural change needs to be well prepared and supported by top management to move an agency from secret and protected government information hoarding to an open, sharing culture. The benefit of this change is that government networks support the creation of professional connections among federal employees with similar experiences or needs for knowledge and the opportunity to staff projects with existing expertise available in government without hiring expensive external knowledge on a temporary basis. At this point there is no quantitative evidence on the extent to which collaboration is possible when it is not mandated, and other than anecdotally, it is unclear to what extent this form of informal knowledge sharing and networking leads to improved outcomes.

Recent failures to connect the information dots in the public sector and President Obama's call for a more collaborative government suggest a need for new ways of information sharing in government. Using data from interviews with IT professionals and managers in public sector organizations, this chapter now turns to shedding light on the managerial, cultural, behavioral, and technological issues they face when using wikis. It can serve as a day-to-day guide to managing wikis as collaborative tools in the public sector, providing practical examples and hands-on tips.

Wikis as Collaboration 2.0 Platforms

In this section I show how wikis, as collaborative technologies, can be used in government to improve information creation and sharing capacities across organizational boundaries and hierarchies (Chang & Kannan, 2008). Although wikis are traditionally used as collaborative websites on which to create and edit other hyperlinked websites, in the public sector they may also be used as creative tools for community-building sites or corporate intranets, and they have the capacity to replace siloed knowledge management systems within restricted department environments (Guy, 2006; Trkman & Trkman, 2009).

Wikis are websites that can be modified by their users. Users can collaboratively create content, edit and change existing content, and discuss content with each other. The word *wiki* is a Hawaiian word meaning "quick," and it highlights the fact that wikis are easy and fast to edit.

Wikis are used to facilitate interaction and project collaboration. The most prominent wiki is Wikipedia, known as the world's online encyclopedia, founded in 2001 by Jimmy Wales. Content authors can quickly create entries and then edit and revise information on every term they want to define. They can create a page on a specific topic and then publish a draft to the public; the draft is then open to the whole world for edits and changes—and even deletion.

The original Wikipedia article page is structured with *hyperlinks,* which connect keywords used in that article to definitions provided in other articles. Definitions or other content should not be replicated from other original articles. Instead, new articles should link to those original articles to show readers previously published materials.

Software that operates on the WYSIWYG principle (*what you see is what you get*) makes editing simple and easy. The formatting possibilities are reduced to a minimum set of functions and pages are not flashy or highly decorated, with the result that the content of the page is the focus of its authors and readers. Every registered user can edit content with a simple mouse click.

Disputes between authors can be discussed and tracked using the *discussion page*. Especially with high-profile articles that are constantly monitored by their authors, I would suggest that any new author or editor explain why he or she is making changes and provide an original source to support the changes and defend them against other authors. In the event that multiple authors cannot agree on changes made by another author, the article can be reverted to the previous version—once created and edited content is not lost. Therefore content that is considered *off-topic* can be easily excluded from an article. An author can also suggest that content needs to be reviewed by the wiki administrators, merged with other existing articles, or if it is of particular value, moved to its own article page.

The original Wikipedia idea was to give editorial rights to every single person in the world, making Wikipedia a "democratic" content production site. Over time the community has evolved into a hierarchical editorial system with several levels of access. In addition, an informal culture has evolved in which some users perceive themselves as article owners, reacting immediately to even the smallest changes random Internet surfers are making to their articles and correcting mistakes within minutes or even seconds.

It has become clear over time that the fear of vandalism—seemingly a possibility owing to the site's open community structure and editorial system—is unsubstantiated. Although so-called Internet trolls who might try to vandalize an article do exist, the community is very quick in responding to errors or in reverting an article to its previously agreed-upon status. Overall, the number of authors contributing is following a *power-law distribution*: a few authors contribute a very high number of articles, but the majority of the authors make only incremental changes.

A 2005 study published in *Nature* showed that Wikipedia comes close to the *Encyclopaedia Britannica* in terms of the accuracy of its science entries. Their error rates are comparable; however, the mistake elimination process shows a remarkable difference between the online and printed encyclopedias. Until the 2012 decision to stop producing a print edition of the *Encyclopaedia Britannica*, it had been updated and reprinted about every four years, whereas Wikipedia authors are able to detect errors within four minutes on average and thus can eliminate errors almost immediately (Terdiman, 2005).

As mentioned earlier, Wikipedia is built on wiki software called MediaWiki. Recently a host of other free wiki applications have emerged, such as PBworks, Socialtext, Wikia, Wetpaint, and Wikispaces. All of these freely available tools are similarly easy to navigate and to maintain. Each can be used as an open wiki or as a closed system with restricted user access. Some wiki software applications offer an instant messaging service among the authors, blogging features, and other extensions helpful for wiki use in the public sector.

Wikis can be used for a variety of purposes. They may offer open information creation environments, such as Wikipedia, in which everyone can freely create collaborative content. Or they can be dedicated to a specific purpose, in which case authorship rights might be limited to specific authorized users. Some users might have a wiki for personal note-taking purposes; others might integrate a wiki into a corporate intranet as a full-fledged knowledge management system.

Wikis are highly interactive tools. They allow single authorship, joint authorship, bidirectional exchanges, and interactivity with the content once it has been produced. In the current open government environment, they can be used as externally facing tools to share content with stakeholders and will therefore potentially contribute to increasing the transparency of processes, decision making, and information sharing. In addition, they can allow, for example, citizens to interact with the content or to contribute their own content and discuss the current content—a way to increase public participation in the public sector. Lastly, they can be used as collaborative technology to support intra-, inter-, and extraorganizational collaboration and coordination of projects.

Wiki Use in the Public Sector

In the public sector too, wikis can have several purposes. They can be used for intraorganizational information sharing. In such cases they are intended purely for internal knowledge creation and sharing. Outsiders do not have access, and these wikis constitute a parallel structure to existing information-sharing applications. Wikis can also be used for information sharing across organizational units in government. In these cases they help government agencies to provide a collaboration and information-sharing environment for a number of different agencies whose intranets are not connected. Finally, wikis can be used for public interaction and for information sharing and collaboration purposes with citizens, including citizens involved in idea generation and policy definition processes. Table 9.1 provides an overview of the most prominent wikis in the public sector. The remainder of this section presents case studies of six of these wikis.

TABLE 9.1. PROMINENT WIKIS IN GOVERNMENT

Type	Case	Goal	Sector	Maturity or Duration	Access
Intra-organizational wikis	Diplopedia	Intraorganizational knowledge creation and sharing	Federal government: DOS	Launched in 2006	Only DOS access
	DoDTechipedia		Federal government: DOD	Launched in 2008	Only DOD access
Inter-organizational wikis	Intellipedia	Interorganizational knowledge sharing	Federal government	Launched in 2006	For members of U.S. Intelligence Community, by invitation
	GCPedia (Canada)		All levels of Canadian government	Launched in 2010	For individuals with dot-gov e-mail address
Public wikis	BetterBuy wiki (GSA)	Inclusion of stakeholders across government, industry, and public	Federal government and external users	Launched in 2010	Public access; anonymous postings allowed; log-in required
	Watershed Central wiki (EPA)	Bringing experts together in joint information-sharing environment	Federal government and external experts on all levels; serving local watershed conversations	Launched in 2009	Only preapproved access
	CrisisCommons	Collaborative, interorganizational emergency relief, project management	Worldwide: private and public actors	Launched in 2010	Open access
	Future of Melbourne wiki	Citizen-government interaction	Local government	Time-bound: open only for specific time frames	Open access for citizens and other stakeholders
	San Jose Wikiplanning™	Citizen-Government interaction	Local government	Time-bound: open only for specific time frames	
	Manor, Texas, wiki	Citizen-government interaction	Local government	Launched in 2010	

Source: Adapted from I. Mergel, *Using Wikis in Government: A Guide for Public Managers*, 2011, http://www.businessofgovernment.org/report/using-wikis-government-guide-public-managers.

Intraorganizational Wikis

Case Study 1: Diplopedia

Diplopedia, launched in 2006, was one of the first wikis used in the federal government. Created to be the U.S. Department of State's wiki, Diplopedia is operated on MediaWiki software (as Wikipedia is) and managed from the DOS Office of eDiplomacy (www.state.gov/m/irm/ediplomacy) (Anderson, 2010; Cohen, 2008). With its more than 10,000 pages of content, Diplopedia is intended to provide information for U.S. foreign affairs specialists, stationed both at home and abroad, in one central space.

Diplopedia's goal is to connect foreign affairs officers who have similar or complementary experiences and knowledge and to enable horizontal sharing of analytical information (Bronk & Smith, 2010). For example, a diplomat with an assignment to a foreign country can connect with current personnel abroad, read their blogs, interact directly with them, ask questions, gain access to existing local knowledge, and therefore prepare for the upcoming assignment in a more efficient way than he or she could without these connections. In turn, personnel who have specialized experience and knowledge about a specific region can chime in and help to solve problems.

Access to Diplopedia is granted only with the appropriate Department of State ID and clearance (U.S. Department of State, 2009). Editing is allowed only with correct attribution—unlike in Wikipedia where anonymous contributions are allowed. A neutral panel of knowledge experts is called in cases where conflicting information has been provided and the discrepancy cannot be resolved by the authors. Moreover, articles are seen as *rolling documents*, that is, as documents that are continuously updated and linked to original sources, and not as authoritative final products. Some wiki pages are edited by the Diplopedia administrator to ensure that the data provided have an enduring value for the whole department.

As with all wiki examples, measuring exact outcomes of collaborative experiments is very difficult. The standard operating structures are still in place at the DOS and are used in parallel with innovative tools such as Diplopedia. Nevertheless, there is some evidence that the use of this wiki can increase the speed of report creation and the accuracy and inclusiveness of the report itself. As an example, now multiple embassies around the world can easily contribute their information to a report, as one interviewee said, "instead of e-mailing it to a person whose inbox is all clogged up." (Figure 9.3 shows the Diplopedia welcome page.)

FIGURE 9.3. DIPLOPEDIA

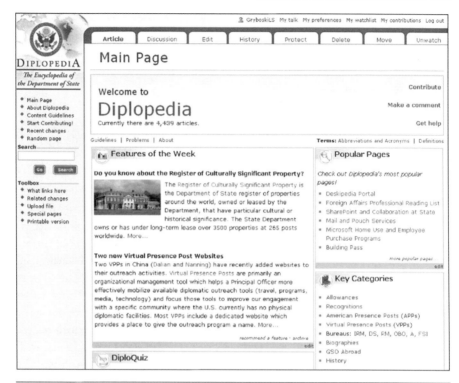

Source: U.S. Department of State, [Diplopedia welcome page], n.d., http://en.wikipedia.org/wiki/Diplopedia.

Case Study 2: DoDTechipedia

DoDTechipedia was created in response to the Defense Authorization Bill of the U.S. Congress in 2008. It was designed as an internal tool (www.dtic.mil/dtic/announcements/DoDtechipedia.html) to help science- and technology-related employees to create a community inside the Department of Defense in order to start sharing information better.

The goal is to support employees inside the Department of Defense who are interested in research and development, science, and technology in sharing their information and expertise on each area and start matching them up with knowledge gaps by identifying their needs. Access is granted to all DOD employees with a common access card and to DOD contractors. In addition, anybody in government who has a valid interest in the exchanges can apply for access through an internal registration process.

DoDTechipedia is run and managed by the Defense Technical Information Center, a team of people, including developers, administrators, and community managers, who help to spread the word about the tool and to get people up to speed so they can become contributors. In addition, marketers—called *evangelists*—distribute brochures and do road shows where they inform and train people in various organizations on how to use this wiki tool.

DoDTechipedia is used to support a crowdsourcing process for all science- and technology-related problems in the department. Anyone with a valid ID can contribute a problem description, and all participants can then suggest solutions. The process starts out with the collection of coalescing information on the state of practice for each of the technology areas and with descriptions of what other sections in DOD are already doing with their projects. The wiki is tied to a library of technical research documents at the Defense Technical Information Center that helps participants with information on industry direction and available core capabilities and also provides articles sorted by specific technology areas. The wiki itself is used to support crowdsourcing processes and to help people with a need for a specific technology to think through their local problems, to search for available solutions, and to refine problem statements to the point where they might receive funding. The best solution is then funded.

So far the wiki has recorded about 400,000 page views and the creation of about 9,000 pages; more than 20,000 DOD employees have been signed up as users, and the editorial team consists of twenty-four *gardeners*—people who review documents and, when necessary, merge them with other existing documents or suggest other connections. (Figure 9.4 shows a DoDTechipedia page.)

Interorganizational Wikis

Case Study 3: Intellipedia

Intellipedia is one of the most prominent examples of interorganizational knowledge creation and sharing using social media applications in the public sector. It was started in 2005 with a pilot project and was officially launched in 2006 (Andrus, 2005; Calabresi, 2009; Lawlor, 2008). Today Intellipedia stands as a brand name for a range of tools to help the Intelligence Community improve the way it captures and manages information. Intellipedia encompasses a whole host of interactive Web 2.0 applications used among the agencies and departments within the Intelligence Community. The wiki element is based on an idea initially described in a

FIGURE 9.4. DODTECHIPEDIA

Source: U.S. Department of Defense, About DoDTechipedia, n.d., http://www.dtic.mil/dtic/
announcements/DoDtechipedia.html.

seminal article by Cal Andrus (2005) called the "The Wiki and the Blog,"
which received the Intelligence Community's internal Galileo award.
Andrus's core idea was that the Intelligence Community needs to have
access to the diverse set of information resources that can be collected on
each problem and needs also to have the flexibility to discuss and write
freely about these problems within the community.

The goal of Intellipedia is to provide new ways of capturing "what the
Intelligence Community knows about various topics." The wiki approach
is designed to improve the current operating procedures. As one of the
Intellipedia evangelists says, "What we do right now is buried in e-mails

[and] attachments and [shared] occasionally at conferences." The same MediaWiki application used to host Wikipedia allows linkages between a prospect or an idea and the people who are interested in it. This information-sharing environment can reveal where, across all the agencies that are part of the Intelligence Community, people are working on similar issues and might be able to contribute to the overall organizational knowledge base. Content provided on the wiki is directly linked to specific people using the *breadcrumb concept*—an approach that allows deep knowledge discovery even when content is classified and the searcher's security clearance does not permit full access to the whole content (Rasmussen, 2009). Access to Intellipedia is organized along different security levels, allowing for gradual access from an "open" (to the community) portion of the content to full access with the highest security clearance. Links to the initial authors' and contributors' contact information permit people to find others who are working on similar problems. As one of the Intellipedia managers says, Intellipedia allows "connections of the who with the what and the what with the who" (Burke, 2008). Therefore authors and contributors are encouraged to use the breadcrumb approach and directly connect to authors and analysts to start off-line conversations. Instead of deleting content without explanation, analysts are encouraged to contact each other directly, call each other on the phone, and explain changes to show that they are sincere. As a by-product of this activity, analysts can establish off-line contacts through their online interactions.

The key guidance for content creation is the principle of "governance through gardening." As soon as content pages are made accessible to the Intelligence Community, every reader needs to *garden* the space; the initial author does not "own" the content anymore. Instead, as with Wikipedia, as soon as readers discover errors or can provide information that is complementary with or—more important—contradictory to the original article, these differing viewpoints can be posted and the existing article can be amended or discussed in the *discussion* area of the wiki page. As one of the Intellipedia managers emphasized, the most interesting content and extensions of the initial ideas are being discovered in the ongoing discussions and provide value to the community and those tasked to analyze overlapping issues.

Content is organized topically instead of organizationally, in order to break up knowledge silos. As part of their gardening efforts, editors are encouraged to merge content when different agencies are creating pages on the same topic, so that content is not replicated and consistent information sharing is provided in a single location.

One goal of Intellipedia is to make discoverable information that is organized in shared hard drives, e-mail lists, or internal memos in the form of Word documents and that has previously been provided only to a limited list of recipients. This too can break down organizational silos—and help to change the culture to make the responsible sharing of information the new normal. Participating in and contributing to Intellipedia are voluntary and so rely mostly on altruism. Contributors need to actively decide that they want to use the wiki to capture their knowledge—even though contributions might not be rewarded immediately. Information accuracy is secured by the so-called gardeners, each of whom tends to a series of pages and helps to confirm the accuracy of the content posted.

Outcomes are difficult to evaluate, as contribution is still on a voluntary basis and impact on individual knowledge sourcing and sharing activities is relatively difficult to evaluate. Most of the evidence so far is anecdotal—or not being shared outside the Intelligence Community. One anecdote that shows the strengths of a wiki approach comes from an analyst who was looking for particular information about improvised explosive devices in Iraq. He created an Intellipedia page asking intelligence officers and others in the field to collect evidence: "Twenty-three people at eighteen or nineteen locations around the world chimed in on this thing, and we got a perfectly serviceable set of instructions in two days. Nobody called a meeting, there was no elaborate gotta go back and check with Mom to see if this is the view of my organization." This shows that the use of Intellipedia can shorten the times needed to access information and support the mission of providing accurate information—and by extension, save lives.

The Intelligence Community is making efforts to change from a need-to-know to a need-to-share collaborative culture, which is one of the most challenging tasks to accomplish for any government organization. The Intelligence Community itself is a large conglomerate of independent organizations, all of which were trained to safeguard proprietary information. Therefore adoption of innovative processes without changing the standard operating procedures is a time-consuming task. Innovation does not happen overnight and cultural changes will take time. (Figure 9.5 displays an Intellipedia screenshot.)

Beyond the core wiki for information aggregation, the Intellipedia platform consists of Intelink blogs, for communication and discussion of topics; Tag/Connect, for tagging content; Inteldocs, shared drives and a document management system; Gallery, a photo-sharing application, also known as CIA Flickr; and iVideo, a video-sharing application similar to YouTube.

FIGURE 9.5. INTELLIPEDIA

Source: Intellipedia, [Intellipedia web page], n.d., http://en.wikipedia.org/wiki/Intellipedia.

Case Study 4: GCPedia (Government of Canada)

In 2008, the Government of Canada launched a government-wide wiki modeled after Intellipedia and called GCPedia. It is located under the authority of the chief information officer in the Treasury Board Office and was launched with the goal of increasing intraorganizational knowledge sharing and collaboration efforts. In 2009, a report by the Privy Council stated that the Canadian public service needed to adopt Web 2.0 tools and explicitly mentioned GCPedia as one of the tools that should be applied. In addition, GCPedia received attention in 2010, when the clerk of the Privy Council, Wayne G. Wouters, the most senior Canadian public servant, joined GCPedia by creating his personal user page and started to invite ideas from Canadian government employees.

GCPedia was created for several reasons. Public sector employees had articulated the need for a collaborative space in which to share knowledge. As in governments everywhere, knowledge was mainly stored and archived in a collection of knowledge silos (silos within silos) that made it difficult to identify what knowledge was available where. The general sense was that government organizations were not communicating what knowledge they possessed and government employees were therefore constantly reinventing the wheel. GCPedia provides an open collaboration space with the support of various departmental chief information officers and individuals who work together, share their knowledge, coproduce material, and make it available for comments. The number one business reason for the creation of GCPedia was therefore to share and reuse existing knowledge in order to increase the efficiency and effectiveness of government work.

Moreover, the hope is that those employees who are searching for knowledge will spend less time re-creating things that have already been done somewhere else in an agency. The goal is to be more efficient and improve existing knowledge, as opposed to re-creating knowledge. Ultimately, the goal is to create a national inventory of the Canadian government's knowledge base.

GCPedia started as an "off the corner of our desks" project. In the early *seeding phase*, students created 300 to 400 pages documenting the wiki project, a charter of project plans, the architecture, the rules for managing and using the wiki, the assurances that essential policies would be complied with, the training needed, and initial ideas on how to generate value by using the wiki. Contributions to GCPedia can be made only by government employees with an official dot-gov e-mail address. Only attributable contributions are allowed, to establish a high level of transparency and accountability. So far there are no compartmentalized security levels, and all contributions are open to all contributors. The rule of thumb for the type of information that is allowable is, "if you can e-mail it, it can go on GCPedia."

Knowledge sharing is defined very broadly, and currently the initiators are mostly letting the contributors use the platform for their own purposes and are observing the emerging patterns of collaboration. One area where an apparent need was met was the coordination of classified documents, a pattern revealed when policy groups began using GCPedia to coordinate their efforts.

The general approach follows a simple rule, "You don't need permission to do your job"—and part of a government employee's job is collaboration and knowledge sharing. The use of this innovative collaborative tool therefore also follows the rule, "You don't need permission to use a word processor." Few incentives for contributions are given. Individuals' adoption of GCPedia is occurring mainly through word-of-mouth advice.

According to some of the most active contributors and GCPedia evangelists in the Government of Canada, collaboration among and across government employees is mostly organized through formal e-mail lists, and the results of this process are sent by e-mail to the supervisors. In those cases where the formal knowledge-sharing process does not give an employee access to the knowledge needed, he or she may revert to informally sharing knowledge via external channels, such as Yahoo groups. There is some GCPedia evidence that public servants have started to share information and collect feedback on specific projects. Some have started to build collaborative and interdepartmental communities of practice (Janelle, 2009). Efforts are being put forward to train more and more public servants in order to increase their knowledge about the GCPedia tools and make them more aware of potential benefits from the use of collaborative technologies. (Figure 9.6 shows an introductory page from GCPedia.)

FIGURE 9.6. GCPEDIA

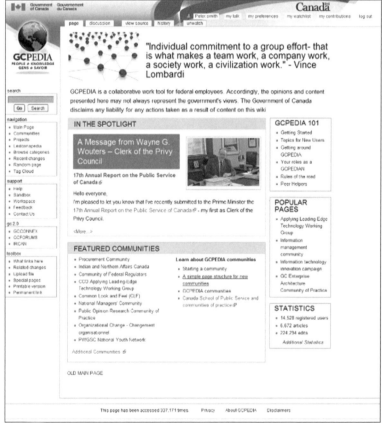

Source: Government of Canada, [GCPedia web page], n.d., http://www.gcpedia.gc.ca.

Public Wikis

Case Study 5: The CrisisCommons Wiki

The CrisisCommons wiki is a project and knowledge management wiki that supports and coordinates geographically distributed technology projects for emergency relief situations. CrisisCommons was founded by Noel Dickover and Heather Blanchard, after initial discussions at the first Government 2.0 Barcamp and Transparency Camp, both held in 2009. The founders were envisioning an open forum for practitioners, first responders, humanitarian aid workers, IT professionals, academics, and the private sector (Brewer, 2010; Goetz, 2010). The goal of this network is to use the IT skills of volunteers who want to help out in a disaster situation but are not able to be on-site. The first project was initiated in response to the 2010 earthquake in Haiti, and tools and learned practices from that project were reused during the earthquake in Chile later that same year. The group found early support through the Department of State, the World Bank, and National Public Radio (NPR), and recently also received a prestigious grant from the Alfred P. Sloan Foundation.

The initial CrisisCommons meeting attracted over 400 participants who then started their own local CrisisCamps in the United States on both the East and West Coasts. The concept was quickly picked up in several international locations, providing a context and meeting platform for so-called civic hackers. The initial meeting included conversations with representatives of Google, Yahoo, and Microsoft and resulted in the formation of a partnership with the World Bank, called Random Hacks of Kindness (Goetz, 2010). The decentralized groups all work on a volunteer basis, and there is no one specific task or joint goal that they all have to agree on or work toward. The relative openness of the meetings leads in turn to idea creation and an entrepreneurial culture among the participants.

CrisisCommons coordinates activities and outcomes through a host of social media applications: a Twitter account (@crisiscamp); a Facebook group (www.facebook.com/pages/crisis-commons); a blog feed (crisiscom mons.org/feed); and Eventbrite, a tool for scheduling events. Members of local teams use their own WordPress blogs to share information.

The CrisisCommons wiki provides mostly a project and knowledge management platform to collect and coordinate project ideas emerging from the diverse and decentralized locations across the United States and all global initiatives. The wiki provides a workspace where local project teams can coordinate their own projects. The content is evolving with emerging project ideas and is described by CrisisCommons cofounder Noel Dickover as "pure chaos at times." The projects are self-selecting; once initiated they evolve into larger projects that are supported by several project members or they are dropped after a while. If they continue to grow, they attract more supporters and result in applications that are actively in use during crisis relief situations. The CrisisCommons administrators intervene only so far as to make suggestions on how to merge projects or consolidate wiki pages.

Incentives for participation are not provided. In contrast to some other knowledge management systems, being part of a larger movement and providing help from the corner of one's desk seems to be incentive enough to participate.

A host of technological applications have arisen out of the emergent collaboration among the CrisisCommons participants and their interactions on the wiki platform. With open source tools, such as situational awareness tools and OpenStreetMaps, applications for obtaining real-time information have been created. Examples include the Haiti hospital capacity finder and the Haiti Diaspora for collecting stories of how people survived the earthquake. The wiki serves as a coordination platform to track the maturity of each project and to find volunteers. In an ongoing project the lessons learned from large-scale responses, such as those in Haiti and Chile, have been applied to local contexts as well. Using the Twitter hashtag #eastsnow, volunteers are tracking how social media applications were used by citizens and government agencies to connect with each other and share information during the snowstorms of the 2011 to 2012 winter season (see, for example, wiki.crisiscommons.org/wiki/East_Coast_Snow_AAR). (Figure 9.7 shows the welcome page for the CrisisCommons wiki.)

Case Study 6: Wikiplanning™ in San José

The Wikiplanning project of the City of San José, California, is part of the city's online solution to the problem of improving civic engagement in urban planning initiatives. The project team describes the Wikiplanning project as a *virtual charrette* for city planning. The city used a wiki platform to invite all concerned parties in the city to help design the city's Envision 2040 general plan. It served both as a new citizen engagement tool and internally as a planning and aggregation instrument to work through the submitted suggestions for the final plan.

The wiki was set up with the goal of incorporating the values of the community into decisions about major changes in the city's architecture and to ensure that the city was reflecting the values of the community in the plan that was developed. In general the wiki approach allowed the city to reach out to different neighborhood groups, businesses, and other

FIGURE 9.7. THE CRISISCOMMONS WIKI

Source: CrisisCommons, [CrisisCommons wiki], n.d., http://wiki.crisiscommons.org/wiki/Main_PageCrisisCommons.

stakeholders and to ask people to post information in the form of photographs or comments on a message board and also to allow people to ask and answer questions.

At the beginning of the project an initial survey asked citizens fifteen questions. The results of the survey were then used to direct the policies, actions, and goals that were ultimately incorporated into the plan.

In a next step a collaborative session on the wiki was initiated in which a group of designers drafted solutions to the city design problems. Citizens were then asked to discuss the drafts in multiple online sessions in which the participants divided into subgroups (or charrettes). Each subgroup prepared material for future dialogue. This form of citizen deliberation helps to form solutions that carry the values of the citizens and integrate all interest groups. Throughout all the steps of the deliberation, intermediary results were posted on the wiki, and citizens were allowed to leave comments and questions—these contributions could be anonymous or attributable to a specific citizen. Overall the process is described by the project team as consisting of the following steps: "teach, discuss; gather input; and build consensus."

In addition to the deliberation results, other multimedia content and events were constantly provided and posted to the wiki to support the decision-making process: multimedia learning sessions, online chat events, message boards, surveys, and podcasts. In addition, plans, status of the discussion in the community, and background information for citizens, especially those not engaged in the process, were posted.

The major outcome of this charrette-like planning process can be seen in its high degree of inclusiveness. All feedback from the community was

FIGURE 9.8. WIKIPLANNING™

Source: Wikiplanning™, [Wikiplanning™ welcome page], n.d., http://www.wikiplanning.org.

considered for incorporation into the new city plans, and the results were posted and then presented and discussed at public meetings and task force meetings. All information collected was maintained and presented on the publicly facing side of the Wikiplanning project. (Figure 9.8 shows the Wikiplanning welcome page.)

Overall, the outcomes of the Wikiplanning process included

- A high degree of support for the final solutions
- The integration of the values and interests of all stakeholders
- The inclusion of the younger generations, who usually do not take part in public meetings or any kind of policymaking processes
- Convenience of access and the ability to participate during off-hours

Considerations for the Use of Wikis in the Public Sector

Although wikis seem to present many challenges on the surface, wiki managers report several remedies for these issues and have also described how they found effective ways to communicate and dissolve some of the "social media myths" people may subscribe to.

Legal Aspects

Oftentimes public managers are hesitant to jump on the social media bandwagon, so it is not a surprise that there is also hesitation to start using wikis. As one of the wiki managers said, "It's still an uphill struggle to do it." Part of this struggle involves legal issues, and to help managers deal with them, the GSA has developed model contracts with a series of social media vendors that can be easily adapted to each agency and department in the U.S. government (Aitoro, 2009; U.S. General Services Administration, 2010).

For example, many public managers fear that social media tools—and among them wikis—are not compliant with Section 508 of the Rehabilitation Act (Bretschneider & Mergel, 2010). This section is relevant to the use of wikis by both internal and external users. It requires the federal government to purchase and maintain information technologies that meet the accessibility standards of the Rehabilitation Act and to make online information and services fully available to all Americans who have disabilities.

Another element of access concerns *multilingual inclusiveness*. Especially in areas with substantial use of languages besides English, translations into

Spanish and other languages have to be considered to comply with Executive Order 13166, Improving Access to Services for People with Limited English Proficiency. This effort might in turn increase inclusiveness.

Privacy

Besides inclusiveness concerns, privacy concerns increase the pressure on public managers who want to adopt a wiki approach in government. One remedy here is to actively mitigate the risks of leaks or accidental exposure of proprietary information: work with your legislative staff and lawyers to avoid the risk of involuntarily exposing proprietary information. Moreover, it is important to set up an information-vetting process to address all privacy concerns. For in-house wikis, remind people that these are internal applications that run only on the firewall-protected intranet—data on these wikis should in theory not be accessible to anybody outside government unless someone deliberately moves those data. Every leak is therefore considered criminal behavior and should be prosecuted accordingly.

Digital Literacy

Among the reasons why hesitation to use wikis has set in is the problem that individuals have varying degrees of digital literacy. This can be an issue for both publicly facing wikis and those intended purely for in-house use. For public wikis, being inclusive is one of the most important elements. Citizens can easily be excluded when they lack digital skills, especially when there is no alternative source for information collaboratively collected, commented on, and reengineered on a wiki. The interactivity with other citizens who are contributing and collaborating solely on the wiki is lost for those potential contributors who are not able to access the wiki. A remedy for this is to also use other submission tools, such as e-mails, phone calls, or other means of surveying public participants.

Moreover, digital literacy or a low acceptance rate of new technological solutions is also a problem among employees. Innovation takes time to spread. My suggestion is therefore to use a wiki approach in-house first. Select a group or topic that lends itself to a collaborative approach. After you have made your first steps in-house with a friendly group of participants who are willing to help you work out the technological and cultural challenges, open the wiki to other departments. The last step should be to include citizens and make the wiki publicly available—where appropriate.

Information Accuracy

Public managers also face the challenge of responding to the myths of information overload and loss of control over information contributions. As one of the wiki administrators puts it, "I think the bigger barrier to entry is that people think the minute they put something out there, people will jump all over it and mess it up."

In most cases this is a relatively unnecessary fear because most people mainly search for information on Wikipedia or on other publicly available but more specialized wikis. They mostly consume the content of their search results, instead of actively contributing new content. People rarely leave comments or actively edit content on the web. But even when they do, it might not detract from the original content. The good news, derived from the experiences of wiki administrators, is that people are usually adding value, and they almost never vandalize the existing content. In a recent interview the manager of the U.S. Coast Guard's CG-LIMS acquisition wiki recalled that he has had to ban just one user, because that user was pushing his own agenda instead of adding value to the designated content areas.

A remedy for the fear of losing control over content once it is created is to establish clear guidelines and to communicate your policy. Explain in detail how wikis work, that there is always a way to revert back to previous versions, and that content is never lost—even though it might look at first view as though it has been—and help your coworkers understand the logic of the technology. This will raise their awareness of and confidence in the tool itself.

Incentivizing Participation in a Collaborative Wiki Approach

The most difficult-to-address challenge is creating a collaborative culture that respects the existing hierarchical knowledge-sharing culture deeply established in any government organization (Massey, 2009). The traditional forms of collaboration, networking, knowledge sourcing, and information sharing are very much organized along clear reporting structures and usually flow from the bottom up. The emancipated and open knowledge creation and sharing approach of a wiki environment is, on the surface, challenging, and it presents a paradox for public sector organizations that needs to be addressed. This is the paradox. Especially at the beginning the benefits of using new technology (or any kind of innovation) will not be visible right away; instead improvements might set in only in the long run.

There might even be an increased workload at the beginning when systems have to be in place in parallel and when getting familiar with the wiki requires extra time from people. In addition, especially in environments where knowledge comes prepackaged through the hierarchical reporting structure or is embedded in clear, standard operating procedures, people might not perceive the need to collaborate. Without an existing off-line collaboration culture, it is difficult to make the case for online collaboration.

Moving to an open collaboration format will be challenging—no matter what the context. One means of addressing this challenge is to highlight how a wiki environment can improve the organization's methods for reaching everyone potentially interested in contributing—for moving toward a true crowdsourcing element in knowledge sharing in the public sector. People might also be reminded that it will be possible to find ways to inform the public and stakeholders so that they are not excluded from new collaborative tools.

It might also be helpful to highlight that existing processes are expensive and time consuming for all involved stakeholders. A wiki environment can eventually make existing processes more efficient. A recommendation that seasoned wiki administrators have is to start, where appropriate, with closed collaboration spaces. Help people get into the groove of working collaboratively online just within their team, so that they get used to the unknown environment. After a while the team might decide to move its results into the open space and share them with a broader audience.

Allowing for and incentivizing online participation is one of the toughest goals to accomplish, especially in the public sector. There are a lot of myths surrounding the extent to which people want to share or "overshare" their knowledge online. The main challenge is finding approaches to get smart people involved and to incentivize them to share their knowledge and also finding ways to avoid contributions from those people who do not actively contribute valuable knowledge to the project.

Take, for example, contributions to the online encyclopedia Wikipedia. Recall that they follow a power-law distribution—that is, a few users are creating large amounts of information whereas a majority of the users are making only incremental changes (such as correcting typos and the like) (Hindman, 2008). In turn this means that every new wiki project might also experience mainly these two types: those who are willing to overshare and those who make only small contributions. What you really want to accomplish is having as many people as possible willing to contribute something substantive to this new form of organizational knowledge base, rather than contributing only the smallest possible unit, lurking, or not contributing at all. It is therefore important to understand what incentives public sector employees might respond to that can encourage them to change their current organizational knowledge search and sharing habits, accept a new medium, and make valuable contributions.

One way to understand what is needed and what can be asked of contributors is to start using the tool yourself. Create the energy and vibrancy in the tool that will lead others to start finding value in it. Share the value and provide useful knowledge that make it worthwhile for your agency's employees to come back on a regular basis. It will help them to incorporate the wiki into their day-to-day routines. Ultimately, you need to create an environment that others want to join. As one of the wiki managers I interviewed said, "Create the part everyone wants to join. No one wants to be the first or the last one at a party. Create a very basic, joyful construct [that] social creatures want to be involved in."

For specific tasks—such as public ideation processes using Wikiplanning—a time limit for public contributions increases the likelihood of contributing. People may feel that this is their one shot at participating. Allow brief windows of opportunity and publicly announce these participation events. Promoting the project in newspaper articles or during face-to-face forums increases the likelihood of online participation. Indeed, one wiki manager reported that "engagement seemed to [be] incentive enough."

Another essential tactic is to actively keep the platform free from trolls, sometimes also referred to as *noisy idiots*, who are following their own agenda but are not contributing on topic. An easy way to do this is to allow only directly attributable contributions made by users who have registered with a confirmed e-mail address. Do not allow anonymous contributions in a wiki environment where a sense of online discipline and netiquette is necessary to make the majority comfortable. This will help to increase the value of contributions and avoid chasing away potential contributors. Some industry contributors might be concerned about revealing too many insights that are attributable to their companies—in those cases the wiki administrator might post the information on their behalf without direct attribution. In addition, industry contributions need to be vetted by an internal editorial team to avoid pushing a specific agenda that might not serve government's purposes.

At the beginning, the already existing material on a wiki needs to be easy to read and accessible but not too perfect. Potential contributors should find it easy to comment on articles so that they can get over the first bump of their writing and contribution anxieties. People feel more comfortable at first making minimal contributions, such as correcting typing errors and making other small corrections to the material, before they might be willing to contribute whole pages of new content. Contributions need to be manageable for both contributors and the editorial team, so that they do not lead to information overload and early frustrations.

A reference group whose members are highly regarded in the organization can help to strongly support the project. They will be the champions that bring more people on board—as they show their commitment they might encourage others to follow. Political bodies might need to step back to allow free, open, and creative knowledge sharing. Bringing in high-profile people, who lead by example, can also help to convince laggards to share their knowledge.

Actively thank contributors. People need to feel satisfaction that their contribution made it into the formal part of the adopted final document, the vision of the new city, or the new policy, or that their idea was endorsed by the city council. At the end, contributors generally need to feel that they are being heard and that the time they spent on their contributions made a difference. Other forms of recognition may also be appropriate, such as giving out badges or thanking people by name.

CHAPTER TEN

TRANSPARENCY 2.0

Transparency 2.0—or the use of social technologies to increase transparency and accountability in government—can be interpreted along many different dimensions. Traditionally, transparency of government operations is connected with issues such as requesting information from government through the Freedom of Information Act. Others interpret transparency as a function of oversight of and insight into government processes, such as clearly observable and communicated decision-making processes and outcomes. Throughout the previous chapters, examples of the use of social technologies to increase transparency of government operations have been highlighted: government agencies are using social media tools, such as Twitter, blogs, and Facebook, to publish more information to those audiences that might not otherwise have access or are not interested in having access to government information in other ways.

Especially during the Obama administration, the concepts and actions of open government have been reinterpreted, and they now include the explicit mandate to publish public sector information in accessible and reusable formats for public consumption. O'Reilly (2010) has labeled such efforts as the launching of the data-publishing platform Data.gov or the online publishing of the White House visitor schedule *government as platform*—moving away from Kettl's notion of government providing services like a vending machine (Kettl, 2008).

Government agencies collect vast amounts of data in many areas. The government is now making these raw datasets accessible so that people and organizations, *civic hackers*, can reuse these data to create purposeful applications that are of value to the public. This chapter focuses on one specific initiative, Data.gov, a data-sharing platform. Federal agencies are mandated to upload their public datasets to Data.gov. Remarkable initiatives now exist for reusing these data, and this chapter looks at some of them as well as at best practices for citizen engagement and citizen customer service and the barriers to and challenges in the reuse of public sector information.

Data.gov: A Foundation for Open Government and the Reuse of Government Data

Data.gov is a new platform that is foundational for the reuse of government-produced data. It is one of the Open Government Initiative's flagship projects, and its stated purpose is "to increase public access to high value, machine readable datasets generated by the Executive Branch of the Federal Government" (Data.gov, n.d.).

It supports the notion of running government as a platform, instead of as a full-fledged service provider. Government is seen as a preparer and provider of government-related information, but it leaves the generation of the creative solutions and the reuse of government data up to citizens, corporate programmers, and civil society organizations. The underlying thought is that government cannot provide all the creative solutions its citizens need—however, it can display facts and figures in datasets and make them easily accessible on a platform, where citizens can then download them in machine readable form and reuse them for their own purposes. On this platform each dataset is accompanied by a short description, metadata, information on how to access the data, and sometimes visualization tools with which to slice and dice the data.

In contrast to most other government sources of data, Data.gov presents a rare opportunity to access government data without applying for the release of that information. Traditionally, citizens' requests for government data have been submitted under the Freedom of Information Act (FOIA). Under that Act, agencies and departments have a limited time to respond to such requests and need to provide the data within sixty days. Much government-produced data is not available in digital format, so the burden on the agencies is steep and access is therefore limited. In setting up Data .gov the current administration is following a proactive approach, with the goal of increasing transparency and ultimately accountability and trust in government operations.

Besides its data platform, Data.gov also provides a platform through which communities can connect with discussions about different categories of data (such as health, law, or energy), an area called Open Government that provides real-time updates about ongoing events (such as the recent tsunami in Japan), a developers' corner for programmers to connect and exchange ideas (Figure 10.1), and a subpage called Learn in which educators can exchange ideas about how to use Data.gov in the classroom (see, for example, a list of university syllabi that give Data.gov as a resource: www .data.gov/story/datagov-in-the-classroom).

FIGURE 10.1. DATA.GOV

Source: Data.gov, [Web page], n.d., http://www.data.gov.

Data.Gov and the Reuse of Public Information

Data.gov would not have become a success as a destination without incentives from the government to citizens to start creating applications. The government ran contests and challenges that incentivized the participation of third parties, such as citizen developers, private organizations, consultants, students, and so on, and encouraged them to program smartphone applications that made use of the data provided on Data.gov. These contests are publicly announced and open to everyone. They apply crowdsourcing mechanisms and invite the public to contribute innovative ideas for mobile phone applications. The most innovative solutions are then featured on Data.gov. Some contests, such as those run on Challenge.gov, are incentivized with small prizes (see, for example, the recently concluded Open Internet Apps challenge run by the Federal Communications Commission [FCC], at challenge.gov/FCC/114-fcc-open-internet-apps-challenge). This is the incentive structure the FCC employed to encourage participation: "Winners will have their apps and research featured on the FCC's website and social media outlets. Authorized travel expenses will be reimbursed by the FCC (up to $500 per individual, or up to $1,500 per team). Honorable mentions may also be awarded in this category at the discretion of the FCC."

Here are some other important contests to reuse public data by creating applications for smartphones and other devices:

- Apps for Democracy, which includes a free, downloadable how-to guide for running your own contest (www.appsfordemocracy.org)
- Apps for Communities, which challenged developers to create mobile-friendly apps for smaller communities (appsforcommunities .challenge.gov)
- Open311, which was founded in order to coordinate a standardized, open access, read-write application with which citizens could report non-emergency issues (open311.org/about)

The result of these varied (and still ongoing) challenges is summarized in Figure 10.2. To date, Data.gov as a platform and the contests have resulted in almost 400,000 raw datasets being accessed, over one thousand smartphone applications that rely on government data being created, and over 170 agencies and subagencies participating in this process. The Data.gov site displays a selection of the applications created; however, the actual number of applications that could be based on Data.gov is practically unlimited.

FIGURE 10.2. DATA AND APPS

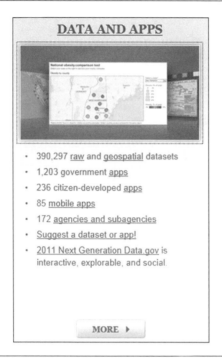

Source: Data.gov, Data and Apps, n.d., http://www.data.gov/metric.

As of May 2012, government has officially approved and featured over 236 mobile applications that rely on datasets provided on Data.gov and that are available for free. The showcased applications displayed in Figure 10.3 are winners of the contests and challenges described earlier and were chosen because they did such an outstanding job of putting the data extracted from large machine readable datasets in Excel or XML formats into practical contexts where many people could benefit from them.

One prominent example of a winning application is the FlyOnTime open source data site (Figure 10.4). The developers explain that

FlyOnTime.us is a free resource for air travelers and anyone else interested in the on-time performance of the commercial air system in the United States. The flight and weather information presented on this website is derived from data provided by the United States federal

FIGURE 10.3. APPS SHOWCASE ON DATA.GOV

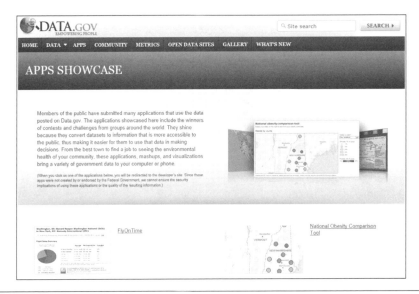

Source: Data.gov, Apps Showcase, n.d., https://explore.data.gov/catalog/apps.

FIGURE 10.4. THE FLYONTIME APPLICATION

Source: FlyOnTime, [Web page], n.d., http://flyontime.us.

government, while the security line times are submitted by visitors like you. This website has four goals:

1. Help American air travelers find the most on-time flights.
2. Help the American public understand the data from government sources by presenting it in interesting and attractive ways. . . .
3. Tap the wisdom of crowds to collect data on airport security line delays.
4. Allow developers to access flight on-time data in a simple, programmatic way [FlyOnTime.us/about, n.d.].

The site also allows travelers to contribute their own data while they are waiting in line at the airport. FlyOnTime was recently discussed in the *New York Times* as an outstanding example of the practical use of online government data (Thaler, 2011).

Another high-profile initiative for the reuse of public information is run by the U.S. Department of Health and Human Services (HHS). The Health 2.0 initiative invited developers to create mobile applications that make use of data publicly available in the health data warehouse at HHS (Figure 10.5). Although there were some privacy concerns, especially ones connected to individual-level health data, the initiative was well received overall and had a direct impact on the reuse of data by public health professionals. Microsoft's search engine, Bing, for instance, is reusing public health data that can be sorted by geographical location and is displaying the results on health maps. Moreover, citizens can add their information to the official government information and review hospitals and private sector health providers.

Winning mobile applications that are reusing public or government information are also featured on USA.gov—a website run by the U.S. General Services Administration (GSA), the core agency responsible for citizen engagement and mobile applications (Figure 10.6).

Best Practices for Mobile Applications That Reuse Public Information

Most applications available from government agencies are designed for purely informational or educational purposes. That means that government provides mashups of existing raw data with geolocations or other existing data to create informative displays. Very few of these applications are designed for *transactions* between government and citizens—where citizens can access government services or directly interact with government.

FIGURE 10.5.   HEALTH DATA APPLICATIONS

Source: Health 2.0, Technology Guide, n.d., http://health2apps.com.

FIGURE 10.6. MOBILE APPS TO ACCESS GOVERNMENT INFORMATION

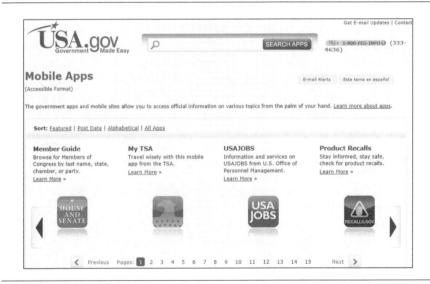

Source: U.S. General Services Administration, Mobile Apps, n.d., http://apps.usa.gov.

As of May 2012, eighty-five official government mobile phone applications were displayed and described on the GSA's apps page (apps.usa.gov). All these apps are provided through Apple's iTunes store but are free to users. Most of these apps do not allow government access to the personal information of their users, but the apps page suggests checking individual terms of service agreements.

Educational and Informational Applications

At this point only a handful of government agencies are actively developing and using mobile phone applications to display some of their content or to allow citizens to actively interact with agency data and among each other. Agencies such as the Library of Congress, the Smithsonian, NASA, and the Environmental Protection Agency (EPA) are using mobile phone applications for educational purposes. For example, the NASA Visualization Explorer app (Figure 10.7) provides current mission information, images, videos, satellite tracking, and more (National Aeronautics and Space Administration, n.d.).

Another helpful information application, this one from the Health Resources and Services Administration of the U.S. Department of Health and

FIGURE 10.7. THE NASA IPHONE APP

Source: National Aeronautics and Space Administration, [NASA app screen shot], n.d., http://apps.usa.gov/nasa-app.shtml.

Human Services (HHS), is the Find a Health Center iPhone application, which displays health centers by zip code (Figure 10.8).

As mentioned earlier, health-related government data may also be displayed in the form of a map, as in Figure 10.9. For example, HHS has partnered with Microsoft's new search engine, Bing, to display government health information whenever individuals actively search for public health information. Search results display not only direct links to suggested pages but also an informational overview of data derived from the HHS health dataset. For example, Bing will display official reviews of public health providers and listings of local hospitals with their rankings; it also allows citizens to submit their own reviews.

Utah is one of the most innovative U.S. states and has recently redesigned its state portal with a dedicated subpage for informational iPhone applications (Figure 10.10), such as the Utah State Park Field Guide, Professional License Lookup, real-time reports about skiing and avalanche conditions, and weather updates. However, this state portal also offers apps for interactional and transactional services, such as Salt Lake City 311, a free iPhone application for initiating work orders.

FIGURE 10.8. THE FIND A HEALTH CENTER APP

Source: Health Resources and Services Administration, Find a Health Center, n.d., http://www .hrsa.gov/mobile/map.html.

FIGURE 10.9. BING HEALTH MAPS MERGE HHS DATA WITH GEOLOCATION DATA

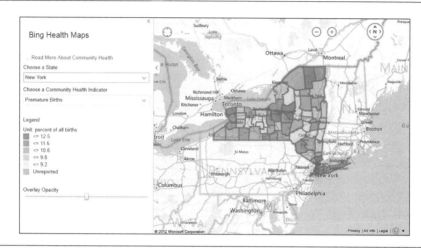

Source: Bing, Bing Health Maps, n.d., http://www.bing.com/community/site_blogs/b/maps/archive/2010/06/02/new-bing-map-app-bing-health-maps.aspx.

FIGURE 10.10. STATE OF UTAH'S IPHONE AND IPAD APPLICATIONS

Source: State of Utah, Utah iPhone and iPad Applications, n.d., http://www.utah.gov/connect/mobile.html.

Transactional Applications

Transactional applications, through which citizens can directly interact with government, are the exception right now. Most applications display information but rarely let citizens directly interact with government in real time nor do they offer interactive feedback cycles.

One exception is SeeClickFix. As previously described, in Chapter Eight, the SeeClickFix application allows citizens to report nonemergency issues they discover (*see*) in their neighborhoods. Moreover, beyond allowing citizens to create a text entry to describe an issue, the application provides a way to include a picture and to report the issue (*click*)—together with description, picture, and geolocation of the user—directly to the local public works department. Governments that are using the service can then start a work order and report fixed issues in real time (*fix*) (Figure 10.11).

Table 10.1 lists a selection of government smartphone applications available on the local, state, and federal levels, and also applications developed

FIGURE 10.11. USING THE SEECLICKFIX APPLICATION

Source: SeeClickFix. Used with permission.

TABLE 10.1. PUBLIC SECTOR INFORMATION REUSE INITIATIVES

Level	Initiative or Application	Description	Access
Federal	Applications for mobile phones	The GSA offers a selection on a USA.gov page.	http://www.apps.usa.gov
	Challenge.gov	A GSA platform that all other federal agencies can use to run challenges and contests.	http://www.Challenge.gov
State	Utah mobile applications	State of Utah smartphone application collection for citizen services, government-to-government, and government-to-business purposes.	http://utah.gov/connect/mobile.html
	CrimeReports	Police departments compile crimes reported by citizens and allow mashups with Google Maps.	http://www.crimereports.com
Local	SeeClickFix, for mobile phones and other devices	Citizens report nonemergency situations in their neighborhoods by uploading a description, location, and picture to SeeClickFix. Local government starts the work process and reports back.	http://www.seeclickfix.com
Civil society and individual citizens	CrisisCommons	Civil society collaborates with civic hackers, public radio, the World Bank, and governments to create applications for emergency response support.	http://www.crisiscommons.org
Corporate sector	Weather.com for mobile phones and other devices	Data collected by the National Oceanic and Atmospheric Administration power this app.	http://www.weather.com
	Health maps from Bing	Data collected by the HHS Community Health Data Initiative are used to create interactive health maps on Bing (and Google).	http://www.hhs.gov/open/plan/opengovernmentplan/initiatives/initiative.html

in collaboration with government and nonprofits in order to increase transparency.

Drivers for Reusing Public Information

Multiple incentives, or drivers, exist for reusing government data in ways that increase government transparency. Some of these drivers are incentivizing data use from within government, while other drivers have arisen outside government. And some government agencies have taken a relatively reactionary stand when it comes to these drivers. Both types are discussed in the following paragraphs. Owing to the interest in delivering government data by means of mobile phone applications, the subject of mobile availability and cost is at issue in any discussion of drivers and, especially, barriers.

Driver 1: innovation mandated by the Open Government Initiative of the current administration. The open government and transparency memorandum, published a day after President Obama's inauguration in January 2009, clearly mandates innovativeness. All executive departments in the federal government have had to come up with open government plans showing how they will share and reuse public sector information in innovative ways. Although a few open government efforts were already under way at the time the memo was issued, the president's message clearly forced all agencies to go public with their plans.

Driver 2: the low costs of crowdsourced solutions in a time of economic downturn and decreasing budgets. The open data and open government movement does not require just government innovations but also innovations that are crowdsourced among citizens or civic hackers. Government 2.0 Barcamps, or unconferences, have helped to organize this citizens' movement and have resulted in initiatives such as CrisisCommons. The movement has also presented start-up opportunities for services, such as SeeClickFix, to engage citizens in community issues. As described earlier, these examples show that Government 2.0 has developed from a "Wild West" in the use of open data and social media applications to an organized movement and even a convergence and consolidation with tangible outcomes, such as public services, with value for all citizens. Some of these crowdsourcing initiatives include Government 2.0 Barcamps, Open311 Barcamps, Transportation Barcamps, Random Hacks of Kindness, and CrisisCommons developers' camps. When government agencies attempt crowdsourcing to resolve problems, the solutions are not predesigned by the agencies; instead, an issue or problem that challenges government is posed, and members of the public are asked for innovative solutions. Payments as incentives are relatively low and in some cases cover only the expense of having to travel to present a solution.

Driver 3: the low risk, given that applications are evaluated by practitioners and government officials and that most applications are nontransactional and purely for informational purposes. Most open data applications that are reusing public sector information are purely for informational or educational purposes. Content authority stays with government and therefore seeking such applications poses a low risk for government agencies. The upside is potentially more interesting for government. Citizens' use of mobile applications might increase government transparency and accountability.

Driver 4: high visibility, which might in turn lead to higher transparency, accountability, and ultimately trust in government operations. The open data flagship initiative Data.gov has received immense press coverage, and its success has increased the visibility of the White House Open Government Initiative. Even though many datasets were previously available in one form or another, the centralized storage of a wide variety of datasets has triggered a bandwagon effect. Moreover, the developments arising from the U.S. Open Government Initiative have spread globally. By 2011, more than fifty countries had joined the Open Government Partnership (www .opengovpartnership.org)—a global initiative to extend these ideas of open government and open data (Mergel, 2012). Many other governments also have their own data platforms now (see, for example, the United Kingdom's data.gov.uk). Although there are currently no citizen reports or surveys that support what I am about to say, it seems highly plausible that the more data that are available and the more experimentation with the existing open data that citizen hackers and developers can do, the more likely it is that useful applications will emerge and ultimately lead to higher transparency and accountability of government.

Driver 5: increased cell phone and smartphone diffusion. The open data movement in the United States is possible at this point in time because of the increasing numbers of people who are taking up smartphones. A recent report by Roger Entner (2011) on the blog *Nielsen Wire* shows that in 2011 about 90 percent of Americans were cell phone users, and Entner projected that by the end of 2011 about 50 percent would be using smartphones—that is nearly 80 million users. At the time of Entner's report, iPhones, Blackberries, Droids, and smartphones in general had about 40 percent of the U.S. mobile market. This technology is a major factor in increasing the reuse of public sector data.

Driver 6: increased use of social networking sites and connectivity. Accompanying the trend of growing smartphone use, we also see a new trend toward sharing and reusing data and information in general. A recent study by the Pew Internet & American Life Project shows that about 65 percent of all American adults are using social networking services to access information (Madden & Zickuhr, 2011). This has led to an increase in online connectivity, in time spent on social networking services, and in the importance of news feeds. For example, one out of four American adults checks health information through his or her social networking sites, social media applications, or other online resources. For the U.S. Department of Health and Human Services this fact implies that HHS will be able to reach citizens through social networking services and that citizens are more likely to be inclined to access government information through these services.

Driver 7: technological and social innovations. Technological innovations are driven mainly by unexpected citizen interests and behaviors. Innovating government agencies as well as platform providers are usually responding to an external innovative use. An example is the innovative use of Twitter for emergency response or the role of the social media in uprisings such as during the Arab Spring or the London riots. Social behavior is only observable by governments and results in ad hoc responses. Similarly, local governments were surprised when citizens began using SeeClickFix for the reporting of nonemergency issues, and governments had to adopt the platform to respond to the citizen demands.

Driver 8: a low degree of internal innovativeness and a high receptiveness to external innovation. Governments in the United States are confronted with ever larger mandates, increasingly complex tasks, and large budget cuts. Some local governments even have budget freezes and therefore have little or no capacity to innovate. In the past, governments were able to hire additional consultants or other external experts to introduce innovations into their operations. Their inability to do this now has established a context for a greater willingness to allow free innovations to flow into government agencies from outside. Governments have therefore become more receptive to innovation from external sources, such as SeeClickFix.

Driver 9: the "coolness" factor. The general climate in the United States toward government is relatively negative. As noted before, 69 percent of U.S. citizens do not trust their government (Pew Research Center for the People & the Press, 2010). The current administration has therefore explicitly called for an effort to "make government cool again" (Mergel, 2011; Stern, 2009). In many subsequent talks and speeches President Obama has called for the public and for government to accept innovative ideas and has asked students to look among themselves for the next founder of a Google or a Facebook. This again increases the incentives for government to be innovative and generally allows for a climate of innovation and openness.

Driver 10: Generation Next expectations. Hand in hand with the coolness factor and a generally innovative climate in government go the anticipations of the next generation of government employees. The incoming cohort of young government employees is expected to be more tech savvy than any generation before. Therefore government has to employ current social networking services and mobile phone applications that will encourage these future employees to be interested in government and consider that public service could fulfill their needs. Job opportunities in government have to be competitive with private or nonprofit sector job opportunities if government agencies are to win the war for talent.

Barriers to Reusing Public Information

Government agencies engaging in transparency efforts—especially in the highly innovative environment of social media—face multiple barriers on the organizational front and also among citizens.

Barrier 1: diffusion and affordability of smartphones among Americans. The acceptance and diffusion of smartphones in the United States is predicted to improve during the next few years, but at this point in time smartphones and especially the subscriptions to data plans are very expensive and that is limiting their use. Recent predictions suggest that toward the end of 2011 about 50 percent of all cell phone users will have access to a cell phone with wireless Internet access (Entner, 2011), which will allow all these users to download applications, including those that rely on public sector information. Nevertheless, the cost of purchasing a smartphone is relatively high (between $100 and $400), and more important, the monthly service fee can range up to $100. These costs can prevent parts of the population from purchasing a smartphone and could lead to an even wider digital divide. In addition, wide geographical areas in the United States are not covered by cell phone towers, so connectivity is mostly available in urban areas.

Barrier 2: diffusion of broadband access. One major barrier to the use of any advanced mobile applications, such as the ones described in this book, is that citizens first need access to broadband in their communities. Even though some of the telecom providers paint a positive picture, independent research institutes find that broadband access rates in the United States are relatively low compared to those in some other developed nations, with the United States ranking about fifteenth in the world in terms of broadband diffusion among citizens (Meinrath & Losey, 2010). Currently about two-thirds of U.S. citizens have access to broadband Internet, making it relatively inconvenient to access government information online for those who do not have such access.

Broadband access also comes with a high monthly subscription rate. According to the Federal Communications Commission, lack of broadband access is one of the main barriers to downloading advanced content. The national broadband plan details how the U.S. government plans to connect all U.S. citizens with affordable broadband access (see www.broadband .gov for more information). Wide broadband access was mandated by the U.S. Congress in 2009 to ensure that every U.S. citizen has access to broadband capability in order to advance "consumer welfare, civic participation, public safety and homeland security, community development, health care delivery, energy independence and efficiency, education, employee training, private sector investment, entrepreneurial activity, job creation and economic growth, and other national purposes" (Federal Communications Commission, 2011).

Barrier 3: low use of smartphone applications. In 2011, about 90 percent of adults in the United States owned a cell phone, but only 9 percent of them reported that they have at least one mobile phone application on their smartphone. Acceptance and use of mobile applications is taking off, but slowly. This may have to do with the fact that data plans are still very expensive or with the possibilities that citizens may have no interest in accessing government information, that they may not trust online information and may prefer off-line contact, or that the information that is currently provided is not of use to them.

Barrier 4: the digital divide, which means differential levels of digital literacy and awareness and different perceptions of usefulness. A result of barriers 1, 2, and 3 is a clear digital divide along the lines of education, race, location, and so forth, in the United States. The digital divide is defined as dichotomous access—either citizens have access or they do not have access. Although many argue that access is a matter of convenience, in many parts of the country and among parts of the population access is an issue of far more than mere convenience. Very few communities have Internet access in their libraries, community centers, or other public places. Internet cafés are rarely available.

All activities that government conducts online have to be compliant with Section 508 of the Rehabilitation Act, which covers access to electronic and information technology procured by federal agencies. All information that is made available on the web or on a smartphone application also needs to be accessible for those parts of the population who do not have access to the technology. Governments usually operate with limited resources and do whatever they can to cater to the majority of citizens, and at times there might not be enough resources to fund solutions for minorities.

Barrier 5: the government as a laggard. In comparison to other sectors, governments are relatively slow in adopting innovations. Especially when it comes to innovations such as social media, Web 2.0 applications, or innovative mobile phone applications, a long internal vetting process is necessary to make sure that the new processes are covered by existing rules and regulations. Existing standards and policies are written for the use of e-mail in government or the use of websites, but do not extend to third-party web services. It is therefore no surprise that there is a relative inertia among government agencies and employees when it comes to adopting mobile applications or social networking tools.

Barrier 6: resistance to the perceived threat of cloud computing initiatives. In a recent statement the former (and first) chief information officer of the United States, Vivek Kundra (2011), remarked that despite all the intense top-down efforts, there is still a perceived resistance in the U.S. government to using cloud computing services. Although there are clear cost-cutting and budget incentives, it became clear during Kundra's time in office that other CIOs, especially in the federal government, did not share his enthusiasm and that they feared a loss of control over processes—and also their data.

Barrier 7: budgetary disincentives. Government agencies rarely have any incentive to save a portion of their budget or spend less. Instead, there is an incentive to show that the money budgeted for specific initiatives has been spent and that future spending has to be increased. Therefore existing IT projects that are already in the budget are pushed forward, and there are no incentives for reassigning budget categories and switching to off-the-shelf, free, third-party applications. Take for example the SeeClickFix application that is free for governments to use in its basic form. Integrating it into the existing work order process costs $100 per month for every 100,000 citizens. A new work order web system, in comparison, starts at $500K, plus the cost of numerous additions and updates.

Barrier 8: a need-to-know mentality and FOIA tradition. In the United States, government agencies are "trained" to protect information from public access. What is often known as the need-to-know mentality is slowly changing to a need-to-share practice (Dawes, 1996; Dawes, Cresswell, & Pardo, 2009). This shift is slow, however, and takes a lot of cultural change. Recent incidents around the whistle-blowing platform WikiLeaks made a lot of government employees even more cautious about what their agency should publicly share. The Freedom of Information Act (FOIA) outlines the exact steps that people have to pursue to access government data they are interested in. Every new piece of information that is produced in government therefore has to be evaluated to assess its security level. Gaining acceptance of a need-to-share culture, one that allows the use of social media and mobile applications, will be one of the major barriers.

Barrier 9: privacy concerns. Whereas the government may be concerned with security and secrecy, citizens may be concerned for their personal privacy. Recently the ban on using online cookies to track user statistics for websites has been lifted for government agencies, and so they are slowly starting to track information about their users. Mobile phone applications and all other Web 2.0 applications that are reusing public sector information will have access to private information saved with IP addresses, cell phone numbers, or social media accounts.

Take for example the use of the geotagging service Foursquare by the National Archives and Records Administration (NARA). NARA is using Foursquare to let citizens check in with their smartphones at specific historic locations around the country or in museums and to provide tips to citizens about the historical background of specific government documents. The application also lets citizens provide tips that other users may access. With every check-in, government tracks not only the personal information of that individual, but also his or her geographical location.

Barrier 10: a political climate in which big government is seen as a threat. Yet another barrier has to do with the current political climate in the United States. Republicans and Libertarians especially are criticizing the current administration as having too much influence, making too many decisions on behalf of its citizens. This fear of so-called *big government* results in perceiving government as too large, inefficient, and too much involved in the lives of its citizens. The movement calls on government to let go of operations that the private sector can conduct in more efficient ways and that are not necessary or crucial to fulfilling government's core mission.

Future Challenges

The evaluation of federal agencies' progress toward fulfilling President Obama's commitment "to creating an unprecedented level of openness in Government" in order to "strengthen our democracy and promote efficiency and effectiveness in Government" (Obama, 2009) is ongoing.

The open government and transparency memo requires each agency to provide the public with information about how the agency currently handles and maintains information, and with a road map for how and when the agency will make itself more transparent, participatory, and collaborative. The level of detail required can be used to hold federal agencies accountable and to evaluate the extent to which they have made public sector information publicly accessible.

Most of the agencies that produced substantive open government plans have made significant improvements to their plans since their initial release. However, the many plans that did not meet the minimal requirements of open government or the release of public sector information show a lot of weaknesses. The current political climate might slow down progress in this area even further.

Many of the ongoing initiatives are only scraping the surface of what might be done, or they constitute early experimentation. Information is still not easily available, and few agencies have revised their websites to let the public know how they can access information.

Data.gov, the flagship initiative intended to provide a central access point for the reuse of public sector information, has been harshly criticized as a facade instead of a true innovation. At this time there are no incentives for agencies to provide, or penalties for their not providing, public sector information in the form of datasets. Changing the culture to move from a need-to-know mentality to a need-to-share mentality will be a crucial challenge. Meeting it will lead toward new initiatives and an increase in the quality of existing initiatives to reuse public sector information.

CHAPTER ELEVEN

FUTURE DEVELOPMENT IN SOCIAL TECHNOLOGIES IN GOVERNMENT

The use of social technologies in government is at an early stage of implementation, and in many areas there is still an immense amount of experimentation and testing rather than productive progress involved. Like e-government applications, social media have not yet proven themselves. Performance metrics to predict cost savings are difficult to evaluate—for both waves of technology use in government (Mergel, 2012; Moon, 2002).

As the 2011 protests and revolutions in the Middle East, now known as the Arab Spring, have shown, social media have the potential to enhance democratic responsiveness (Wasik, 2011). The protesters—collectively named *Time* magazine's person of the year in 2011—used Facebook to organize their protests, Twitter to coordinate locations and spread information, and YouTube to inform the whole world (Andersen, 2011). What the effectiveness of these social media–supported revolutions has shown is that the use of social technologies among citizens challenges governments around the world. Public managers are increasingly facing their own imperfections in social awareness and struggling to understand the directions citizens want their governments to pursue. Indeed, at the outset of the Arab Spring movement, government officials in the affected nations were unaware that citizens were using Facebook to coordinate their protest actions.

The focus of all open government initiatives so far has been mostly on participation and transparency improvements, rarely on the third dimension, collaboration. This book has highlighted some of the lighthouse projects that are observable and that are under way to make government more effective. At this point it is still unclear whether investments into, experimentation with, and early presentation of social media projects truly have the potential to transform service delivery, support the mission of individual government agencies, and increase public trust in government. In many instances, highly creative uses of social technologies in the public sector have been overshadowed by dramatic failures in the use of social media in this sector, failures that have undercut the claim that using social technologies truly results in less bureaucracy and an increase in service and information quality (Hazlett & Hill, 2003).

Innovative information and communication technologies can always improve communication between government and its diverse audiences through additional and broader channels, but at the same time they are increasing the complexity for government of dealing with the influx of new and diverse information. The examples shown in the book highlight the use of social technologies to increase the potential for both individual and organizational communication across organizational and even sectoral boundaries.

Social technologies, invented and hosted by third-party providers, have decreased the costs for public investments in technology. Development and improvement of these tools is in effect outsourced, and related costs for human capital, operations, and maintenance are distributed to social media providers, who are funded by advertisers—and therefore indirectly through citizens' purchasing preferences.

In the agencies that do have increased interactions with citizens, these interactions have increased the demands for timely responses and reflexive feedback cycles, and there is constant pressure to produce and procure relevant online content—content that goes beyond standard press releases. Beyond the new content creation processes, other organizational demands occur. For example, nine-to-five office hours clash with the always-on expectations of the 24/7 social media world. New schedules and responsibilities need to emerge, and people's personal and professional activities might blur together, creating higher and higher demands for information sharing around the clock.

Even though regulations and policies follow the apparent changing demands for secure risk mitigation in the use of social media, social media adoption in the federal government diffused slowly. In the aftermath of the 9/11 terror attacks, a series of laws emerged that have shifted the current information paradigm from the need-to-know mentality of the Cold War era to a need-to-share information paradigm (Dawes, Cresswell, & Pardo, 2009). This has already resulted in legal and regulatory actions such as improvements to the Freedom of Information Act (U.S. Department of State, 2008), the information-sharing strategy of the Intelligence Community (Director of National Intelligence, 2008), and the Army's knowledge management principles (U.S. Army, 2008). Such changes have encouraged information sharing across organizational boundaries—especially among federal departments and among state and local government organizations.

In other ways, policies for the safe and secure use of social technologies among government employees have followed the apparent need and actual use at a very slow pace. For example, social technologies and the ways that citizens and government employees are using them have forced government administrators to rethink how to store and share information and also how to define online records and their management. While implementing some procedures and allowing social media tools to be applied within hierarchical and bureaucratic command-and-control organizations, government agencies also find that they quickly bump up against various organizational boundaries and that they have to be sensitive toward structural and institutional challenges as well as legal and cultural constraints.

At the same time, the increased use of social technologies in combination with the creation of data repositories, such as Data.gov, has resulted in increased data sharing by government officials. This development has the potential to lead to higher degrees of transparency and accountability. Nevertheless, at this point in time citizens still have had to file a Freedom of Information Act request to get access to information government agencies are producing. The Open Government Initiative of the Obama administration has led to several new transparency applications, including the tracking of stimulus package money on recovery.gov and the sharing of nonsensitive data produced in government agencies on Data.gov. Large-scale citizen reviews will prove whether or not citizens perceive that their governments are more accountable and more transparent because of their innovative use of technology and repositories.

Other initiatives include the online contests Apps for Democracy in Washington, DC, and Apps for America (Sunlight Foundation, 2009), both intended to create innovative social media applications using the data provided on both contest websites. For example, one application submitted to the Apps for Democracy contest accessed city contracts and displayed their dollar values to various vendors. This example shows the potential for increased accountability in government. As more and more citizens gain access to information and communication technology at all times, that increases the demand for access to government-held data. It also increases the need for information security and protection of privacy rights.

The mere display of raw data does not increase transparency and will not move us toward a true, collaborative, information-sharing environment in government. At this point, acceptance of and accountability for social technologies and data-sharing efforts is at a standstill and all too often does not provide additional insights to the general public—beyond columns of numbers in Excel spreadsheets. To change this situation, government agencies need to think about innovative ways to display and reuse their data. An excellent example is the World Bank's Open Data Initiative (data .worldbank.org). The bank has developed data visualization tools to help users understand data through attractive formats that go beyond machine readable datasets (Figure 11.1). Another exemplar for government data visualization is the kind of highly useful display and visualization found in Google's Flu Trends (Google.org, 2008). Third parties such as Google and other information service organizations, including nongovernmental organizations, will also fuel the increased demand for well-presented data as they work to track and report public information.

The public sector still has to increase its use of innovative social technologies to improve collaboration in government as required by the Open Government Initiative. In order to accomplish this goal, government organizations need to continue to *improve their organizational communication and information sharing both within and across organizational boundaries.* The example of Intellipedia (discussed in Chapter Nine) has shown that these changes will increase intra- and interorganizational collaboration, with a simultaneous increase in coordination and governance efforts. Intellipedia—a wiki platform for sharing intelligence information across all U.S. intelligence agencies—was created to reduce the costs of parallel data processing and to break up the knowledge silos that develop when information is stored and shared only through selected e-mail lists, shared hard drives, or paper documents. The prerequisite is to understand which agency is performing which tasks and also to understand information needs as well as information creation at various levels of government. One downside to any increases in cross-organizational communication is the accompanying requirement to manage increased complexity, to improve coordination, and to educate public sector employees about collaborative practices. Knowledge-sharing trends compete with the existing

FIGURE 11.1. A WORLD BANK DATA VISUALIZATION

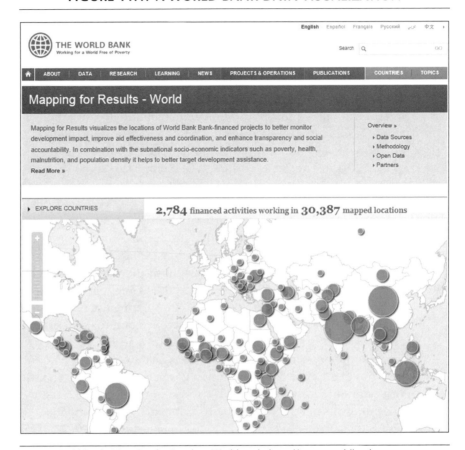

Source: World Bank, Mapping for Results—World, n.d., http://maps.worldbank.org.

bureaucratic structures and highly regulated forms of information sharing and official channels of information retrieval.

It needs to be proved that social technologies can be used in ways that support mission-specific information sharing and collaboration across agencies and with citizens. Only when these tools have proven to be more effective than the existing, formal information and communication technology (ICT) structures will they be successfully adopted on a broader basis and gain acceptance. One example of effective use of social media is the recurring and highly effective Centers for Disease Control and Prevention (CDC) campaigns that employ social media and networking tools during public health emergencies, such as the swine flu outbreak and the recall of salmonella-contaminated peanut butter. The CDC campaigns were able to harness the power of social technologies to reach citizens and particularly endangered parts of society "where they are" (Nagesh, 2009). Individuals then reused the government data provided by the CDC, in order to spread the information via their own Facebook and Twitter newsfeeds and to update their friends. Of course these campaigns are event driven and so do not exemplify an ongoing stream of voluntary sharing among networks. Viral messages get started only when an event engages wide parts of the population. The challenge for government is to move from a mode in which people are interacting with government only during an extreme event to a mode in which people are turning to government for information and news on a routine basis because that meets their everyday needs.

The current examples of social software use in Government 2.0 initiatives show surprising side effects that will ultimately have to lead to procedural and organizational changes. One major result of the use of social technologies is a set of problems associated with *information overload.* The standard response to information overload is to filter information, and individuals typically have specific processes for assessing the accuracy and quality of information in order to separate what is useful from what is not. In order to determine the quality and accuracy of the information created in different social media channels, information that might then be replicated and reposted more broadly, government has to create updated information-warranting processes, to ensure its own reputation and trustworthiness. This suggests that not only government but also society in general will need to develop new forms of *reading and writing literacy* for the vast amounts of information that could be produced using social media in the public sector. While citizens are validating information, double-checking its accuracy through their friendship networks, government's challenge is its highly centralized organization, a cultural and historical legacy that tends to leave groups relying on a sole authority to judge accuracy and make decisions. Internal mechanisms need to be developed not only to trust preferred sources but also to verify online information. Besides reading ability, appropriate writing skills need to be developed. The Plain Writing Act of 2010 is one effort to push government in the right direction, as agencies rethink the format in which they display information. Moreover, individual social media account holders posting on behalf of government need to learn to publish and write for the web just as private citizens have to develop this capacity. These newly defined official (and also personal) warranting processes need to be refined to establish a writing literacy that protects individuals and public sector employees from future costs related to personal and professional reputation loss. A prominent current example is former Congressman Anthony Weiner, who posted inappropriate messages and pictures to his public Twitter account, but costs also occur less dramatically when government officials trying to act quickly end up posting incorrect information and then have to send out corrections (Oliphant, 2011).

The innovative use of social technologies in the public sector also *increases the volatility of information and the need for more specific information targeting*. The example mentioned earlier of swine flu misinformation going viral has shown that government and citizens have an increased need for information warranting. But to what extent does government have to increase its role in setting standards, rules, and regulations? Can government outsource some of these processes to citizens and the wisdom of the crowds? The answer today has to be no: government is held accountable and needs to lead by example, controlling the quality and standards of its information-sharing processes before it allows access to the public.

Nevertheless, government departments and agencies clearly see both advantages and drawbacks in employing social technologies. The managerial challenges are being slowly mastered—with the help of top-down guidance from the White House and the U.S. General Services Administration's Center for Excellence in Digital Government. The cultural challenges that stand in the way of achieving the open, collaborative, sharing environment that social media tools mandate have to be resolved, and even though solutions are showcased in so-called lighthouse projects, they do not represent the reality across all levels of government. Going forward it is critical for government to understand how the emergent behavior among citizens, and also among innovative public sector employees, necessarily affects government operations and demands. Public administration as a discipline still needs to catch up with the new realities and create evaluation measures that look further than e-service delivery and that reveal both the positive and negative impacts of social technologies.

The Government 2.0 bundle of new information and communication technology applications has the potential to change the way government creates and shares information. These new applications might also lead to increased transparency and accountability in public authority. The broader range of communication and interaction channels resulting from these new information technologies may lead to increased inclusion and public participation. Responses to public participation, especially when it comes to mission-specific information, may therefore lead to increased reaction speed and might enhance governmental effectiveness. As mentioned earlier, limited effectiveness and performance measures are available for the now traditional e-government applications, so it is difficult to predict and evaluate the actual impact of new media tools. Specifically, very successful organizations using existing IT systems might encounter managerial and cultural challenges in adopting an additional Government 2.0 strategy. The current changes and innovations in IT can therefore create a more volatile (that is, with higher degrees of variation over time) political environment for organizations, which might threaten the status quo of the established information-sharing culture and organizational capacity. Bureaucratic organizational processes and existing infrastructure might have to be reevaluated to harness the power of social media in the public sector. Though existing organizational and political environments will mediate such changes, there is an increasing need for researchers to understand the managerial, cultural, and technological factors during new technology implementation and adoption phases.

The biggest challenge is not the new technologies themselves but the adaptation of those technologies to the given political and bureaucratic situations and institutional barriers. The bureaucratic, top-down, information-reporting strategies still exist, but are now being complemented and only partially replaced by a more horizontal information-sharing approach—with unpredictable consequences. The new technology enables a greater diversity in organizational structure, to support the parallel set of new communication channels within and across government and reaching out to citizens, but the impact of this change will depend mostly on how these new channels become embedded in the preexisting, institutionalized structures.

Other issues, such as cyber security, protecting individuals' identity, intellectual property rights, and online records management, are still open and have to be tackled in the future. Recent cyber attacks, such as the attack of the hacker group Anonymous on Stratfor, a government contractor, show how vulnerable government data are (Mello, 2011). Government has to rely on private contractors—it cannot accomplish all its responsibilities internally—but it has to protect data from unintended access. The more government agencies rely on external platforms, providers, and tools, the more vulnerable they will become and the higher the likelihood of unintended access or information glitches.

The digital divide among government organizations themselves has widened. On the federal government level much centralized effort and many resources have been invested to help agencies build effective social media presences. There has been an unprecedented level of technological innovation on the federal government level when it comes to Web

2.0 applications (as outlined throughout this book), with some spillover effects to the state level (see, for example, Utah.gov [utah.gov/index .html] for a Web 2.0–style state portal designed with the help of the citizens). On the local municipal level the situation is vastly different: budget crunches and local problems of capacity and resource limitations have slowed municipalities' progress, and fewer innovations are observable than on federal government websites and social media accounts. The digital divide also becomes evident in cases where government organizations either do not have Internet connections in their agencies or restrict web access and publishing due to limited resources (Mergel, Lazer, & Binz-Scharf, 2008). As noted earlier, it is likely that eventually even the smallest government unit will have a web presence, but capacity issues are likely to prevent most of these smaller government organizations from developing any meaningful applications involving two-way communication or social networking.

Embedded in each of these trends are some significant potential problems, particularly for government organizations. Problems of *standardization* and *integration* occur as market-driven diffusion of social technologies generates significant heterogeneity in hardware, software applications, and communication protocols. Unlike private firms, government cannot target groups of citizens but rather has to serve all individuals. Thus government agencies will face higher variation than any business in simply providing access or services. *Security* is a problem across all these areas as well. *Privacy* issues faced by government are also more complex, as in most cases agencies must work within statutes and rules not faced by business.

Another major problem faced by these new arrangements is best defined as increased *volatility in attitudes and preferences* of citizens. Constant and immediate access to information can lead to rapid but short-term changes in attitudes and behavior that can be problematic (Baird & Fisher, 2005–2006). As mentioned, the 2009 swine flu outbreak provides an example of how misinformation is spread as easily as information in the online environment (Sutter, 2009; Wildstrom, 2009). Such effects are well known and at times systematically exploited to manipulate opinions and attitudes. Another problem that derives from this new environment is increased *fractionalization of groups* into smaller and smaller subdivisions on the basis of their preferences in public goods and services. This process increases the transaction costs required for generating equilibrium solutions over which public goods are to be provided. It also opens the Internet as a platform for mobilization and activism for even the smallest and most radical groups (Chen, Thoms, & Fu, 2008)—as well as presidential campaigns (Noyes, 2007).

As mentioned earlier, research and evaluation on traditional e-service delivery performance have provided limited proof for the successful diffusion of e-government applications. The extent to which online services are improving responsiveness, reach, efficiency, and cost savings remains unclear. The current Government 2.0 initiatives are driven less by conscious top-down strategies of the agencies themselves and more by a response that is looking to the successful use of social networking services outside of government. Cross-jurisdictional, hierarchical, and vertical studies are needed to understand this new phenomenon and its implications for managerial, cultural, procedural, and informational aspects of diffusion and their overall impacts.

From a public administration research perspective, social technologies enable researchers to generate massive amounts of data. The current discussion on *big data* highlights the potential insights researchers can draw from large streams of Twitter data, blog comments, and links, in combination with mobile phone interactions and other data generated through social interactions online. In order to analyze these enormous datasets and draw conclusions about the impact of technology on use patterns and on social behavior, more research that can capture observations of passive behavioral data is necessary (Lazer et al., 2009). This research could include, for example, not only analysis of blog contents or the linkage structures of blogs, but also content analysis and natural language processing of large amounts of Facebook comments and Twitter retweets and responses in ways that go beyond mere numerical counts of followers or of *likes* on Facebook. The insights gained from this type of research will help government agencies understand how their online interactions improve their service, what impressions citizens have about government trustworthiness and accountability, and also government's own levels of effectiveness and efficiency.

One of the critical problems concerns the *aggregation of preferences.* Preferences for private goods and services are separable, so they are easily aggregated, but this is not true for preferences for public goods and services. An individual may highly value both national defense and the environment but be faced with choosing from among a small set of political representatives, none of whom has preferences that match those of the individual, leading to compromised choices. Breaking individuals into smaller and smaller groups compounds the problems of political aggregation of preferences and makes equilibrium harder to find and less stable over time.

Finally, all technological innovations need to prove themselves in the context of political and administrative realities over time. The institutionalization and formalization of social media use in government is still in a fragile state. Social media providers evolve, disappear, or change their vision for their platforms and user preferences too change over time. The relatively quick pace of change in the platforms, the potential for catastrophic events, and the ongoing changes in user behavior make it difficult to predict the future effects of social technology. Government agencies can only be in a reactive mode in relation to social media—or alternatively, choose not to participate in the evolution that social technologies have shown in the past five to seven years.

The crucial next step is therefore to develop measurement mechanisms that can show whether government use of social media is truly making an impact on participation, collaboration, and transparency activities in government.

OVERVIEW OF SOCIAL MEDIA ACCOUNTS IN THE U.S. FEDERAL GOVERNMENT

TABLE A.1. USE OF FACEBOOK BY FEDERAL AGENCIES AND DEPARTMENTS, 2010–2011

Department or Agency	Facebook Data 2010 and 2011					
	2011: Number of Users Who "like this"	2010: Number of Users Who "like this"	2011: Number of Users "talking about this"	2010: Number of Users "talking about this"	2011: Number of Users "were here"	2010: Number of Users "were here"
Executive agencies						
Department of Agriculture	27,060	12,483	527	*	754	*
Department of Commerce	4,173	1,068	4,173	*	—	*
Census Bureau	112,728	*	359	*	—	*
National Oceanic and Atmospheric Agency	65,980	*	1,188	*	—	*
Department of Defense	122,321	57,420	3,226	*	—	*
Air Force	571,522	*	11,301	*	—	*
Army	1,008,661	*	37,950	*	—	*
Coast Guard	81,612	*	2,125	*	—	*
Marines	1,599,687	*	39,371	*	—	*
Navy	388,537	*	11,468	*	—	*
Department of Education	5,355	4,852	145	*	253	*
Department of Energy	9,478	2,678	382	*	5	*
Department of Health and Human Services	—	13,240	—	*	—	*
Centers for Disease Control and Prevention	161,573	62,762	2,502	*	—	*
Food and Drug Administration	15,935	1,581	537	*	—	*
Department of Homeland Security	28,524	11,360	1,216	*	—	*
Federal Emergency Management Agency	63,401	*	1,629	*	—	*
Transportation Security Administration	—	*	—	*	—	*
Department of Housing and Urban Development	22,644	4,685	303	*	6	*
Department of the Interior	3,735	4,390	177	*	559	*

Fish and Wildlife Service	21,197	*	1,777	*	—	*
National Park Service	104,673	*	1,519	*	77,214	*
Department of Justice	29,655	52,886	468	*	—	*
Federal Bureau of Investigation	157,768	*	3,572	*	—	*
Department of Labor	10,967	652	1,097	*	127	*
Department of State	97,846	422	2,604	*	1,764	*
Department of Transportation	8,202	68,426	265	*	—	*
Department of the Treasury	4,342	17,618	144	*	—	*
Department of Veterans Affairs	147,380	3,506	3,331	*	197	*
Independent agencies						
Central Intelligence Agency	—	—	—	—	—	*
Environmental Protection Agency	33,690	1,113	691	*	33	*
Federal Communications Commission	7,342	1,465	167	*	142	*
Federal Deposit Insurance Corporation	2,098	1,465	22	*	—	*
General Services Administration	3,364	155,727	115	*	90	*
National Aeronautics and Space Administration	605,383	286	19,784	*	271	*
National Archives and Records Administration	17,230	155,727	575	*	—	*
Office of Personnel Management	4,878	286	180	*	118	*

Note: None of the surveyed U.S. federal departments and agencies actively promote their use of the social networking platform LinkedIn on their social media hubs or their official websites. There might be informal and closed discussion groups available on LinkedIn that government subunits have set up.
*Data not collected.
— Data not available.

TABLE A.2. USE OF MICROBLOGS BY FEDERAL AGENCIES AND DEPARTMENTS, 2010–2011

Department or Agency	2011: Number of Tweets	2010: Number of Tweets	2011: Number Following	2010: Number Following	2011: Number of Followers	2010: Number of Followers	2011: Number Listed	2010: Number Listed
Executive agencies								
Department of Agriculture	3,061	*	150	48	47,453	14,537	2,384	*
Department of Commerce	3,053	*	113	54	10,532	1,524	569	*
Census Bureau	2,187	*	829	*	16,577	*	1,134	*
National Oceanic and Atmospheric Agency	873	*	70	*	33,140	*	2,238	*
Department of Defense	2,733	*	314	20	54,671	767	3,324	*
Air Force	4,167	*	347	*	29,895	*	1,585	*
Army	8,368	*	312	*	100,310	*	3,740	*
Coast Guard	9,574	*	90	*	15,398	*	851	*
Marines	3,020	*	141	*	63,081	*	2,236	*
Navy	20,000	*	23,508	*	30,426	*	2,008	*
Department of Education	2,413	*	13	7	76,113	29,054	4,300	*
Department of Energy	814	*	84	53	33,900	6,585	1,915	*
Department of Health and Human Services	795	*	116	*	147,423	0	3,071	*
Centers for Disease Control and Prevention	1,968	*	93	44	50,010	7,934	2,133	*
Food and Drug Administration	424	*	8	112	3,268	2,915	178	*
Department of Homeland Security	1,741	*	171	92	51,220	19,813	2,806	*
Federal Emergency Management Agency	5,736	*	452	*	78,897	*	3,774	*
Transportation Security Administration	1,297	*	189	*	17,182	*	1,175	*
Department of Housing and Urban Development	2,223	*	224	82	17,287	5,538	971	*

Department of the Interior	*	774	15,463	4,345	17,129	5,343	1,212	*
Fish and Wildlife Service	*	1,630	574	*	6,538	*	442	*
National Park Service	*	1,374	274	*	25,664	*	1,662	*
Department of Justice	*	425	89	86	428,471	349,749	4,375	*
Federal Bureau of Investigation	*	3,936	963	*	246,249	*	5,482	*
Department of Labor	*	3,078	90	81	27,507	11,840	1,623	*
Department of State	*	11,731	252	161	171,970	40,318	7,595	*
Department of Transportation	*	2,483	865	74	25,065	4,466	2,028	*
Department of the Treasury	*	574	140	586	24,253	10,073	1,379	*
Department of Veterans Affairs	*	1,649	769	706	26,653	8,654	1,507	*
Independent agencies								
Central Intelligence Agency	*	—	—	—	—	—	—	*
Environmental Protection Agency	*	3,891	40	18	51,275	8,450	3,106	*
Federal Communications Commission	*	1,526	35	26	445,123	369,250	4,904	*
Federal Deposit Insurance Corporation	*	947	0	0	4,722	1,748	295	*
General Services Administration	*	806	150	51	2,872	757	149	*
National Aeronautics and Space Administration	*	16,838	151	16	1,507,693	2,422	42,495	*
National Archives and Records Administration	*	2,660	77	16	8,613	639,889	795	*
Office of Personnel Management	*	470	6	—	1,523	—	34	*

Note: None of the surveyed U.S. federal departments and agencies actively promote their use of the social networking platform LinkedIn on their social media hubs or their official websites. There might be informal and closed discussion groups available on LinkedIn that government subunits have set up.

*Data not collected.

—Data not available.

TABLE A.3. USE OF WEB LOGS BY FEDERAL AGENCIES AND DEPARTMENTS, 2010–2011

Department or Agency	Blog Data 2010 and 2011			
	2011: Blog Type	2010: Blog Type	2011: Blog Entry Types	2010: Blog Entry Types
Executive agencies				
Department of Agriculture	Blog	Blog	1,2,3,4	1,2,3,4
Department of Commerce	Blog	Blog	1,2,3,4	1,2,3,4
Census Bureau	Blog	*	1,2,3,4	*
National Oceanic and Atmospheric Agency	RSS	*	1,3	*
Department of Defense	Blog	Blog	1,3	1,3
Air Force	Blog	*	1,2,3,4	*
Army	Blog	*	1,2,3,4	*
Coast Guard	Blog	*	1,2,3,4	*
Marines	Blog	*	1,2,3,4	*
Navy	Blog	*	1,2,3,4	*
Department of Education	Blog	Blog	1,2,3,4	1,2,3,4
Department of Energy	Blog	Blog	1,2,3,4	1,2,3,4
Department of Health and Human Services	—	—	—	—
Centers for Disease Control and Prevention	Blog	Blog	1,2,3,4	1,2,3,4
Food and Drug Administration	Blog	—	1,2,3,4	—
Department of Homeland Security	Blog	Blog	1,2,3,4	1,2,3,4
Federal Emergency Management Agency	Blog	*	1,2,3,4	*
Transportation Security Administration	Blog	*	1,2,3,4	*
Department of Housing and Urban Development	Blog	Blog	1,2,3,4	1,2,3,4
Department of the Interior	RSS	RSS	1,3	1,3
Fish and Wildlife Service	Blog	*	1,2,3,4	*

National Park Service	—	*	—	*
Department of Justice	Blog	Blog	1,2,3,4	1,2,3,4
Federal Bureau of Investigation	Blog	*	1,2,3,4	*
Department of Labor	Blog	Blog	1,2,3,4	1,2,3,4
Department of State	Blog	Blog	1,2,3,4	1,2,3,4
Department of Transportation	Blog	RSS	1,2,3,4	1,3
Department of the Treasury	Blog	—	1,2,3,4	—
Department of Veterans Affairs	Blog	—	1,2,3,4	—
Independent agencies				
Central Intelligence Agency	—	—	—	—
Environmental Protection Agency	Blog	Blog	1,2,3,4	1,2,3,4
Federal Communications Commission	Blog	Blog	1,2,3,4	1,2,3,4
Federal Deposit Insurance Corporation	RSS	RSS	1,3	1,3
General Services Administration	Blog	RSS	1,2,3,4	1,3
National Aeronautics and Space Administration	Blog	Blog	1,2,3,4	1,2,3,4
National Archives and Records Administration	Blog	Blog	1,2,3,4	1,2,3,4
Office of Personnel Management	Blog	RSS	1,2,3,4	1,3

Note: Blog entry types: 1 = press releases; 2 = opinion pieces on issues; 3 = announcements of appearances; 4 = other.
*Data not collected.
—Data not available.

Department or Agency	2011: Number of Subscribers	2010: Number of Subscribers	2011: Number of Channel Views	2010: Number of Channel Views	2011: Number of Total Upload Views	2010: Number of Total Upload Views
Executive agencies						
Department of Agriculture	2,164	1,084	208,640	112,412	368,898	*
Department of Commerce	148	40	31,770	9,123	14,966	*
Census Bureau	1,690	*	251,834	*	949,199	*
National Oceanic and Atmospheric Agency	946	*	20,884	*	89,477	*
Department of Defense	2,497	927	104,638	50,229	312,377	*
Air Force	6,277	*	242,260	*	2,699,468	*
Army	1,995	*	43,363	*	144,801	*
Coast Guard	5,192	*	352,051	*	10,412,587	*
Marine Corps	12,770	*	207,627	*	3,642,951	*
Navy	2,010	*	59,787	*	1,166,946	*
Department of Education	1,563	930	134,037	66,896	571,914	*
Department of Energy	1,348	560	119,151	42,742	660,277	*
Department of Health and Human Services	3,632	24,920	350,092	2,162	—	*
Centers for Disease Control and Prevention	7,416	5,757	353,476	262,275	4,200,613	*
Food and Drug Administration	4,215	2,992	106,131	51,244	1,148,231	*
Department of Homeland Security	2,344	13	124,462	50,844	784,552	*
Federal Emergency Management Agency	4,444	*	215,306	*	373,464	*

YouTube Data 2010 and 2011

Transportation Security Administration	1,706	*	104,727	*	1,145,136	*
Department of Housing and Urban Development	891	302	100,028	32,563	92,446	*
Department of the Interior	279	121	20,263	8,753	39,811	*
Fish and Wildlife Service	285	*	45,591	*	94,368	*
National Park Service	510	*	20,117	*	34,253	*
Department of Justice	593	264	27,889	12,416	18,975	*
Federal Bureau of Investigation	570	*	21,520	*	676,415	*
Department of Labor	786	449	117,820	113,245	185,873	*
Department of State	7,512	4,801	618,322	393,726	2,627,383	*
Department of Transportation	446	360	34,468	6,203	309,182	*
Department of the Treasury	653	33	49,028	15,288	—	*
Department of Veterans Affairs	713	286	51,636	19,718	361,776	*
Independent agencies						
Central Intelligence Agency	2,207	—	136,652	—	268,136	*
Environmental Protection Agency	3,248	2,275	121,399	66,461	214,987	*
Federal Communications Commission	591	388	40,482	20,091	182,515	*
Federal Deposit Insurance Corporation	1,515	1,327	89,543	54,789	285,044	*
General Services Administration	204	81	18,500	5,893	36,380	*
National Aeronautics and Space Administration	82,902	1,370	5,782,612	59,191	26,624,629	*
National Archives and Records Administration	3,077	50,318	148,189	3,966,633	841,943	*
Office of Personnel Management	312	—	22,869	—	278,564	*

*Data not collected.
—Data not available.

TABLE A.5. USE OF FLICKR BY FEDERAL AGENCIES
AND DEPARTMENTS, 2010–2011

	Flickr Data 2010 and 2011	
Department or Agency	2011: Number of Items	2010: Number of Items
Executive agencies		
Department of Agriculture	6,645	2,723
Department of Commerce	—	—
Census Bureau	67	*
National Oceanic and Atmospheric Agency	584	*
Department of Defense	5,057	3,485
Air Force	4,347	*
Army	6,711	*
Coast Guard	4,301	*
Marine Corps	3,245	*
Navy	5,032	*
Department of Education	—	—
Department of Energy	1,573	1,318
Department of Health and Human Services	678	—
Centers for Disease Control and Prevention	—	—
Food and Drug Administration	1,637	208
Department of Homeland Security	—	—
Federal Emergency Management Agency	0	*
Transportation Security Administration	—	*
Department of Housing and Urban Development	260	196
Department of the Interior	752	200
Fish and Wildlife Service	934	*
National Park Service	—	*
Department of Justice	—	—
Federal Bureau of Investigation	—	*
Department of Labor	—	—
Department of State	4,604	2,997
Department of Transportation	1,368	362
Department of the Treasury	585	423
Department of Veterans Affairs	9,845	3,674

(*continued*)

TABLE A.5. (*continued*)

Department or Agency	Flickr Data 2010 and 2011	
	2011: Number of Items	2010: Number of Items
Independent agencies	0	0
Central Intelligence Agency	329	—
Environmental Protection Agency	900	601
Federal Communications Commission	750	535
Federal Deposit Insurance Corporation	—	—
General Services Administration	—	—
National Aeronautics and Space Administration	3,016	5,563
National Archives and Records Administration	8,052	1,714
Office of Personnel Management	1,043	—

*Data not collected.
—Data not available.

TABLE A.6. FEDERAL AGENCIES' AND DEPARTMENTS' HOME PAGES

Department or Agency	Website
Executive agencies	
Department of Agriculture	http://www.usda.gov/wps/portal/usda/usdahome
Department of Commerce	http://www.commerce.gov/
Census Bureau	http://www.census.gov/
National Oceanic and Atmospheric Agency	http://www.noaa.gov/
Department of Defense	http://www.defense.gov/
Air Force	http://www.af.mil/
Army	http://www.army.mil/
Coast Guard	http://www.uscg.mil/
Marine Corps	http://www.marines.mil/Pages/Default.aspx
Navy	http://www.navy.mil/swf/index.asp
Department of Education	http://www.ed.gov/
Department of Energy	http://www.energy.gov/
Department of Health and Human Services	http://www.hhs.gov/

(*continued*)

TABLE A.6. FEDERAL AGENCIES' AND DEPARTMENTS' HOME PAGES
(*continued*)

Department or Agency	Website
Department of Health and Human Services (*cont.*)	
Centers for Disease Control and Prevention	http://www.cdc.gov/
Food and Drug Administration	http://www.fda.gov/
Department of Homeland Security	http://www.dhs.gov/index.shtm
Federal Emergency Management Agency	http://www.fema.gov/
Transportation Security Administration	http://www.tsa.gov/index.shtm
Department of Housing and Urban Development	http://portal.hud.gov/portal/page/portal/HUD
Department of the Interior	http://www.doi.gov/index.cfm
Fish and Wildlife Service	http://www.fws.gov/
National Park Service	http://www.nps.gov/index.htm
Department of Justice	http://www.justice.gov/
Federal Bureau of Investigation	http://www.fbi.gov/
Department of Labor	http://www.dol.gov/
Department of State	http://www.state.gov/
Department of Transportation	http://www.dot.gov/
Department of the Treasury	http://www.ustreas.gov/
Department of Veterans Affairs	http://www.va.gov/
Independent agencies	
Central Intelligence Agency	https://www.cia.gov/
Environmental Protection Agency	http://www.epa.gov/
Federal Communications Commission	http://www.fcc.gov/
Federal Deposit Insurance Corporation	http://www.fdic.gov/
General Services Administration	http://www.gsa.gov/portal/category/100000
National Aeronautics and Space Administration	http://www.nasa.gov/
National Archives and Records Administration	http://www.archives.gov/
Office of Personnel Management	http://www.opm.gov/

TABLE A.7. FEDERAL AGENCIES' AND DEPARTMENTS' YOUTUBE ACCOUNTS

Department or Agency	YouTube
Executive agencies	
Department of Agriculture	http://www.youtube.com/usda
Department of Commerce	http://www.youtube.com/CommerceNews#p/u
Census Bureau	http://www.youtube.com/uscensusbureau
National Oceanic and Atmospheric Agency	http://www.youtube.com/usnoaagov
Department of Defense	http://www.youtube.com/thepentagonchannel#p/u
Air Force	http://www.youtube.com/afbluetube
Army	http://www.youtube.com/usarmy
Coast Guard	http://www.youtube.com/user/USCGImagery
Marine Corps	http://www.youtube.com/marines
Navy	http://www.youtube.com/user/usnavy
Department of Education	http://www.youtube.com/user/usedgov
Department of Energy	http://www.youtube.com/usdepartmentofenergy
Department of Health and Human Services	http://www.youtube.com/USGOVHHS
Centers for Disease Control and Prevention	http://www.youtube.com/user/CDCStreamingHealth
Food and Drug Administration	http://www.youtube.com/user/USFoodandDrugAdmin
Department of Homeland Security	http://www.youtube.com/ushomelandsecurity
Federal Emergency Management Agency	http://www.youtube.com/fema
Transportation Security Administration	http://www.youtube.com/user/TSAHQpublicaffairs
Department of Housing and Urban Development	http://www.youtube.com/HUDchannel#p/u
Department of the Interior	http://www.youtube.com/user/USInterior#p/u
Fish and Wildlife Service	http://www.youtube.com/usfws
National Park Service	http://www.youtube.com/nationalparkservice
Department of Justice	http://www.youtube.com/TheJusticeDepartment
Federal Bureau of Investigation	http://www.youtube.com/user/fbi?ob=5
Department of Labor	http://www.youtube.com/usdepartmentoflabor#p/u

(continued)

TABLE A.7. FEDERAL AGENCIES' AND DEPARTMENTS' YOUTUBE ACCOUNTS (*continued*)

Department or Agency	YouTube
Department of State	http://www.youtube.com/user/statevideo#p/u
Department of Transportation	http://www.youtube.com/usdotgov#p/u
Department of the Treasury	http://www.youtube.com/ustreasgov#p/u
Department of Veterans Affairs	http://www.youtube.com/user/DeptVetAffairs#p/u
Independent agencies	
Central Intelligence Agency	http://www.youtube.com/user/ciagov?ob=5
Environmental Protection Agency	http://www.youtube.com/user/USEPAgov#p/u
Federal Communications Commission	http://www.youtube.com/fccdotgovvideo
Federal Deposit Insurance Corporation	http://www.youtube.com/user/FDICchannel#p/u
General Services Administration	http://www.youtube.com/usgsa#p/u
National Aeronautics and Space Administration	http://www.youtube.com/NASATelevision
National Archives and Records Administration	http://www.youtube.com/USNationalArchives
Office of Personnel Management	http://www.youtube.com/user/USOPM?ob=5#p/u

TABLE A.8. FEDERAL AGENCIES' AND DEPARTMENTS' FACEBOOK ACCOUNTS

Department or Agency	Facebook
Executive agencies	
Department of Agriculture	http://www.facebook.com/USDA
Department of Commerce	http://www.facebook.com/Commercegov
Census Bureau	http://www.facebook.com/uscensusbureau
National Oceanic and Atmospheric Agency	http://www.facebook.com/usnoaagov
Department of Defense	http://www.facebook.com/DeptofDefense?ref=mf
Air Force	http://www.facebook.com/Usairforce
Army	http://www.facebook.com/Usarmy
Coast Guard	http://www.facebook.com/Uscoastguard
Marine Corps	http://www.facebook.com/marines
Navy	http://www.facebook.com/USNavy

(continued)

TABLE A.8. (*continued*)

Department or Agency	Facebook
Department of Education	http://www.facebook.com/ED.gov
Department of Energy	http://www.facebook.com/energygov
Department of Health and Human Services	—
Centers for Disease Control and Prevention	http://www.facebook.com/CDC
Food and Drug Administration	http://www.facebook.com/FDA
Department of Homeland Security	http://www.facebook.com/homelandsecurity
Federal Emergency Management Agency	http://www.facebook.com/FEMA
Transportation Security Administration	—
Department of Housing and Urban Development	http://www.facebook.com/HUD
Department of the Interior	http://www.facebook.com/USInterior
Fish and Wildlife Service	http://www.facebook.com/usfws/
National Park Service	http://www.facebook.com/nationalparkservice
Department of Justice	http://www.facebook.com/DOJ
Federal Bureau of Investigation	https://www.facebook.com/FBI
Department of Labor	http://www.facebook.com/departmentoflabor
Department of State	http://www.facebook.com/usdos
Department of Transportation	http://www.facebook.com/sec.lahood
Department of the Treasury	http://www.facebook.com/ustreasury#!/ustreasury?v=wall
Department of Veterans Affairs	http://www.facebook.com/VeteransAffairs
Independent agencies	
Central Intelligence Agency	—
Environmental Protection Agency	http://www.facebook.com/EPA
Federal Communications Commission	http://www.facebook.com/FCC
Federal Deposit Insurance Corporation	http://www.facebook.com/FDICgov
General Services Administration	http://www.facebook.com/GSA
National Aeronautics and Space Administration	http://www.facebook.com/NASA
National Archives and Records Administration	http://www.facebook.com/usnationalarchives
Office of Personnel Management	http://www.facebook.com/USOPM

—Data not available.

TABLE A.9. FEDERAL AGENCIES' AND DEPARTMENTS' MYSPACE ACCOUNTS

Department or Agency	MySpace
Executive agencies	
Department of Agriculture	—
Department of Commerce	http://www.myspace.com/commercegov
Census Bureau	—
National Oceanic and Atmospheric Agency	—
Department of Defense	—
Air Force	—
Army	—
Coast Guard	—
Marine Corps	—
Navy	—
Department of Education	—
Department of Energy	—
Department of Health and Human Services	—
Centers for Disease Control and Prevention	—
Food and Drug Administration	—
Department of Homeland Security	—
Federal Emergency Management Agency	—
Transportation Security Administration	—
Department of Housing and Urban Development	—
Department of the Interior	—
Fish and Wildlife Service	—
National Park Service	—
Department of Justice	http://www.myspace.com/usdoj
Federal Bureau of Investigation	—
Department of Labor	—
Department of State	—
Department of Transportation	—
Department of the Treasury	—
Department of Veterans Affairs	—

(continued)

TABLE A.9. (*continued*)

Department or Agency	MySpace
Independent agencies	
Central Intelligence Agency	—
Environmental Protection Agency	—
Federal Communications Commission	http://www.myspace.com/fcc
Federal Deposit Insurance Corporation	—
General Services Administration	—
National Aeronautics and Space Administration	—
National Archives and Records Administration	—
Office of Personnel Management	—

—Data not available.

TABLE A.10. FEDERAL AGENCIES' AND DEPARTMENTS' TWITTER ACCOUNTS

Department or Agency	Twitter
Executive agencies	
Department of Agriculture	http://twitter.com/USDA
Department of Commerce	http://twitter.com/CommerceGov
Census Bureau	http://twitter.com/uscensusbureau
National Oceanic and Atmospheric Agency	http://twitter.com/usnoaagov
Department of Defense	http://twitter.com/DeptofDefense
Air Force	http://twitter.com/usairforce
Army	http://twitter.com/USArmy
Coast Guard	http://twitter.com/uscg
Marine Corps	http://twitter.com/usmc
Navy	http://twitter.com/navynews
Department of Education	http://twitter.com/usedgov
Department of Energy	http://twitter.com/energy
Department of Health and Human Services	http://twitter.com/hhsgov
Centers for Disease Control and Prevention	http://twitter.com/CDCgov
Food and Drug Administration	http://twitter.com/US_FDA

(*continued*)

TABLE A.10. FEDERAL AGENCIES' AND DEPARTMENTS'
TWITTER ACCOUNTS (*continued*)

Department or Agency	Twitter
Department of Homeland Security	http://twitter.com/dhsgov
Federal Emergency Management Agency	http://twitter.com/fema
Transportation Security Administration	http://twitter.com/TSABlogTeam
Department of Housing and Urban Development	http://twitter.com/HUDnews
Department of the Interior	http://twitter.com/Interior
Fish and Wildlife Service	http://twitter.com/usfwshq
National Park Service	http://twitter.com/natlparkservice
Department of Justice	http://twitter.com/TheJusticeDept
Federal Bureau of Investigation	https://twitter.com/FBIPressOffice
Department of Labor	http://twitter.com/usdol
Department of State	http://twitter.com/StateDept
Department of Transportation	http://twitter.com/RayLaHood
Department of the Treasury	http://twitter.com/ustreasurydept
Department of Veterans Affairs	http://twitter.com/DeptVetAffairs
Independent agencies	
Central Intelligence Agency	—
Environmental Protection Agency	http://twitter.com/epagov
Federal Communications Commission	http://twitter.com/FCC
Federal Deposit Insurance Corporation	http://twitter.com/FDICgov
General Services Administration	http://twitter.com/usgsa
National Aeronautics and Space Administration	http://twitter.com/nasa
National Archives and Records Administration	http://twitter.com/archivesnews
Office of Personnel Management	http://twitter.com/usopm

—Data not available.

TABLE A.11. FEDERAL AGENCIES' AND DEPARTMENTS' BLOG PAGES

Department or Agency	Blog Page
Executive agencies	
Department of Agriculture	http://blogs.usda.gov/
Department of Commerce	http://www.commerce.gov/blog
Census Bureau	http://blogs.census.gov/
National Oceanic and Atmospheric Agency	http://www.rss.noaa.gov/noaarss.xml

(continued)

TABLE A.11. (*continued*)

Department or Agency	Blog Page
Department of Defense	http://www.dodlive.mil/
Air Force	http://airforcelive.dodlive.mil/
Army	http://armylive.dodlive.mil/
Coast Guard	http://coastguard.dodlive.mil/
Marine Corps	http://marines.dodlive.mil/
Navy	http://navylive.dodlive.mil/
Department of Education	http://www.ed.gov/blog/
Department of Energy	http://blog.energy.gov/
Department of Health and Human Services	—
Centers for Disease Control and Prevention	http://blogs.cdc.gov/healthoutloud/
Food and Drug Administration	http://fdatransparencyblog.fda.gov/
Department of Homeland Security	http://journal.dhs.gov/
Federal Emergency Management Agency	http://blog.fema.gov/
Transportation Security Administration	http://blog.tsa.gov/
Department of Housing and Urban Development	http://portal.hud.gov/portal/page/portal/HUD/press/blog
Department of the Interior	http://www.doi.gov/news/index.cfm
Fish and Wildlife Service	http://www.fws.gov/news/blog/
National Park Service	—
Department of Justice	http://blogs.usdoj.gov/blog/
Federal Bureau of Investigation	https://www.fbi.gov/news/news_blog
Department of Labor	http://social.dol.gov/blog/
Department of State	http://blogs.state.gov/
Department of Transportation	http://fastlane.dot.gov/
Department of the Treasury	http://www.treasury.gov/connect/blog/Pages/default.aspx
Department of Veterans Affairs	http://www.blogs.va.gov/VAntage/
Independent agencies	
Central Intelligence Agency	—
Environmental Protection Agency	http://blog.epa.gov/blog/
Federal Communications Commission	http://reboot.fcc.gov/blog
Federal Deposit Insurance Corporation	http://www.fdic.gov/rss.html
General Services Administration	http://gsablogs.gsa.gov/gsablog/

(*continued*)

TABLE A.11. FEDERAL AGENCIES' AND DEPARTMENTS' BLOG PAGES
(*continued*)

Department or Agency	Twitter
National Aeronautics and Space Administration	http://blogs.nasa.gov/cm/newui/blog/blogs.jsp
National Archives and Records Administration	http://blogs.archives.gov/online-public-access/
Office of Personnel Management	http://www.opm.gov/blogs/openopm/index.aspx

—Data not available.

TABLE A.12. FEDERAL AGENCIES' AND DEPARTMENTS' FLICKR ACCOUNTS

Department or Agency	Flickr
Executive agencies	
Department of Agriculture	http://www.flickr.com/photos/usdagov
Department of Commerce	—
Census Bureau	http://www.flickr.com/photos/uscensusbureau
National Oceanic and Atmospheric Agency	http://www.flickr.com/photos/usoceangov
Department of Defense	http://www.flickr.com/photos/39955793@N07
Air Force	http://www.flickr.com/photos/usairforce
Army	http://www.flickr.com/photos/soldiersmediacenter
Coast Guard	http://www.flickr.com/photos/coast_guard
Marine Corps	http://www.flickr.com/photos/marine_corps
Navy	http://www.flickr.com/photos/usnavy
Department of Education	—
Department of Energy	http://www.flickr.com/photos/departmentofenergy
Department of Health and Human Services	http://www.flickr.com/photos/hhsgov
Centers for Disease Control and Prevention	—
Food and Drug Administration	http://www.flickr.com/photos/fdaphotos
Department of Homeland Security	—
Federal Emergency Management Agency	—
Transportation Security Administration	—

(*continued*)

TABLE A.12. (*continued*)

Department or Agency	Flickr
Department of Housing and Urban Development	http://www.flickr.com/photos/hudopa
Department of the Interior	http://www.flickr.com/photos/usinterior
Fish and Wildlife Service	http://www.flickr.com/photos/usfwshq
National Park Service	—
Department of Justice	—
Federal Bureau of Investigation	—
Department of Labor	—
Department of State	http://www.flickr.com/photos/statephotos
Department of Transportation	http://www.flickr.com/photos/raylahood
Department of the Treasury	http://www.flickr.com/photos/ustreasury
Department of Veterans Affairs	http://www.flickr.com/photos/VeteransAffairs
Independent agencies	
Central Intelligence Agency	http://www.flickr.com/photos/ciagov
Environmental Protection Agency	http://www.flickr.com/photos/usepagov
Federal Communications Commission	http://www.flickr.com/photos/fccdotgov
Federal Deposit Insurance Corporation	—
General Services Administration	—
National Aeronautics and Space Administration	http://www.flickr.com/photos/nasahqphoto
National Archives and Records Administration	http://www.flickr.com/photos/usnationalarchives
Office of Personnel Management	http://www.flickr.com/photos/usopm

—Data not available.

GLOSSARY

Accountability   The acknowledgment or assumption of responsibility for actions, decisions, or products presented.

Blogroll   A blogger's compilation of other blogs that are recommended sources. Blogrolls are usually listed in the sidebar of a blog.

Citizen engagement   The process of connecting citizens more directly with government decision making, enabling them to influence public policy and programs.

Cluster   A group of people within a social network who are connected to one another, but who have few connections with the rest of the network.

Collaboration   Working together to reach common goals through sharing knowledge and learning and building consensus.

Core   The inner group of people who do most of the work in a social network.

Crowdsourcing   Outsourcing a task to a relatively large group of people, each of whom contributes to the end result. Social media tools help to engage people in crowdsourcing activities such as collecting intelligence (as We Are Media does), co-creation (as the Humane Society of the United States' public service announcement video contest does), or voting and fundraising (as America's Giving Challenge does).

Digital natives   Members of the Millennial Generation (born between 1978 and 1993) who since birth have been exposed to the Internet and a constant stream of digital technologies.

Government 2.0   The use of Web 2.0 technologies by government agencies, both internally and externally, to increase collaboration and transparency and to potentially transform the way these agencies relate to citizens and operate.

Hubs   The larger nodes within networks, meaning the people or organizations that have many connections. Hubs are the influencers in the network, the people who know everyone and are known by everyone.

Influencers   People (or websites) who have the relative reach, influence, and social capital to mobilize others. Influence can be gauged by several metrics, including the size of an influencer's network, the number of comments on his or her blog, site traffic, and so forth.

Instant messaging (IM)   Real-time text communication between one or more people via the Internet or a mobile device. Although these conversations function like those in a chat room, IM can take place in pop-up windows on a wide range of websites or by means of an independent application (for example, Meebo).

Listening and measurement tools   Social media tools for assessing websites and online conversations. Most are available free of charge, including the following:

> **Really Simple Syndication (RSS)**   A subscription tool used to deliver feeds (updates) from user-specified blogs and other websites. FeedBurner is a popular tool used to track the number of subscribers to organizational and personal blogs.

> **RSS reader**   An aggregation tool that collects feeds from all user-specified websites (e-mail is another delivery option). Popular RSS readers include Netvibes and Google Reader.

> **Search engines**   Search engines index and rank websites to help Internet users find relevant content through keyword searches. Most search engines favor content that is embedded with URLs and is regularly updated, tagged, and linked to from other websites. This content usually has greater search visibility (a higher position in search results).

> • Traditional search engines (for example, Google and Yahoo) search all public online content (current and historical).

> • Blog search engines search the last six months of blogs and blog posts. Technorati and BlogPulse are two examples of blog search

engines. (Google Blog Search allows searches for content older than six months.) A keyword search on Technorati yields related blogs and blog posts and provides each blog's rank and *authority* (the number of inbound links to that blog).

- Message board search engines search the last six months of discussion forums, threads, and posts. Examples are BoardReader and BoardTracker.

- Twitter Search allows users to search by keyword or hashtag.

Social bookmarking   A way of saving and categorizing links using tags. Whereas traditional bookmarks are saved in the web browser on a personal computer, social bookmarks are accessible from any Internet connection. Additionally, sites that help manage social bookmarks (for example, Delicious.com and StumbleUpon) allow tagged content to be searched and shared.

Tags   User-generated tags allow labeling of online content with codes or keywords. Tags can be general or specific. The more often a specific tag appears (for example, WeAreMedia) the higher it will appear in search engine results and social bookmarking sites. On Twitter, the tagging convention prefixes all tags with a hash mark (for example, #WeAreMedia). These hashtags distinguish tags from other tweeted text.

Tag cloud   A weighted, visual list of the tags in a specific website. In a tag cloud, the size of the tag is proportional to its use, with the most popular tags appearing the largest.

Website analytics   Data about a website's traffic, such as number of unique visitors and page views. Google Analytics is a robust and free analytics tool that helps users analyze and optimize websites, including blogs. PostRank measures additional engagement metrics for blogs, such as comments, bookmarks, and subscriptions.

Nodes   The individuals or organizations connected in a social network.

Power law of distribution   Describes the imbalance between the small number of people in a network who do most of the work on a project and the remaining large number of people who do little. It is otherwise commonly known as the 80/20 rule.

Social media   The peer-to-peer communication and user-generated content made possible through the advent of participatory Web 2.0 tools such as blogs, online social networks, multimedia sites, and text messaging.

Blog   Short for *web log*, a platform that allows an author (a *blogger*) to publish content online. Blog content—whether text, photos, videos, or podcasts—is organized by categories and tags. This content is viewed in reverse chronological order in successive blog *posts*. Others can leave comments on these posts. Millions of blogs exist, and this set of social media is often referred to as the *blogosphere*.

Listserv   An electronic mailing list that distributes messages to subscribers via e-mail. Listservs are usually topical, and in most cases allow anyone to reply or to send a message to the group.

Microblog   A blog composed of "brief text updates or micromedia such as photos or audio clips. . . . These messages can be submitted by a variety of means, including text messaging, instant messaging, e-mail, digital audio or the web" (see http://en.wikipedia.org/wiki/Micro_blog). Twitter is a popular microblogging platform that limits text-based *tweets* (posts) to 140 characters.

Multimedia   Nontext-based digital content, from MP3s to videos to photos, that can be published, shared, and tagged online. Online music-sharing sites include Napster and iTunes. Online video-sharing sites include YouTube, Vimeo, and Google Video. Online photo-sharing sites include Flickr, Picasa, and Photobucket.

Social network   An online community of individuals (nodes) who are connected to each other via ties (friending, following, group membership, and so on). Social networks form through many types of social media platforms, including blog networks, listservs, and Google Groups. Larger social networks, such as Facebook, MySpace, and LinkedIn, serve a wide variety of interests and geographical areas. Niche social networks, such as Change.org and independent Ning networks, are typically focused on a specific topic.

Social news site   A website, such as Digg, that enables people to submit and rank news stories, listing the most popular stories first.

Virtual world   A computer-simulated environment—or cyber world—that enables users to interact with each other and manipulate the digital ecosystem via their personalized avatars (Second Life is a well-known virtual world).

Wiki   A website that can be easily edited by many people simultaneously, allowing them to think, strategize, share documents, and create plans together. Wikis facilitate microplanning, the process of enabling more people to participate in the creation and implementation of an effort much less expensively and over longer periods of time than would otherwise be possible.

Social media policy   Organizational guidelines for participating in social media. Policies often include hard-and-fast rules for confidentiality, disclaimers, and disclosures in order to protect the organization, employees, and stakeholders, but should ultimately facilitate effective and authentic social media engagement. Blogging guidelines might include best practices. A comment policy might include criteria for blog comments (for example, no profanity).

Social media strategy   An organizational approach to using social media to increase collaboration and innovation.

Ties   The connections between people and organizations, or nodes, in a social network.

Transparency   Honest and authentic information, communication, and actions. Transparency is a core tenet of social media engagement, requiring disclosure of affiliations and biases that—if omitted—could diminish credibility. Organizations that have transparency as a fundamental value are called *transparents*.

Uniform resource locator (URL)   A web address. Also referred to as *links*, URLs are often embedded in hyperlinked text on websites to enable click-throughs to other websites.

Viral   A term used to describe the organic and rapid spread of online content resulting from many individuals engaging in electronic communication.

Web 1.0   The first era of the Internet, which began in the early 1990s with the advent of the World Wide Web and e-mail.

Web 2.0   The second era of the Internet, starting in the late 1990s, through which online information became inexpensively storable, shareable, and participatory through the advent of social media tools.

REFERENCES

Chapter One

Bretschneider, S. I., & Mergel, I. (2010). Technology and public management information systems: Where we have been and where we are going. In D. C. Menzel & H. J. White (Eds.), *The state of public administration: Issues, challenges, and opportunities* (pp. 187–203). New York: M. E. Sharpe.

Lazer, D., & Mergel, I. (2011). *Tying the network together: evaluating the impact of an intervention into the advice network of public managers* [Working paper]. Retrieved from http://papers.ssrn.com/sol3/papers.cfm?abstract_id=1881674

Lazer, D., Mergel, I., Ziniel, C., Esterling, K., & Neblo, M. (2011). The multiple institutional logics of innovation. *International Public Management Journal, 14*(3), 311–340.

Mergel, I. (2005). *The influence of multiplex network ties on the adoption of eLearning practices: A social network analysis* (Doctoral dissertation, University of St. Gallen, St. Gallen, Switzerland, No. 3026). Available from IDS St. Gallen.

Mergel, I. (2010). *Informal networks in the public sector using social media applications* [Unpublished manuscript]. Maxwell School of Citizenship and Public Affairs, Syracuse University, New York.

Mergel, I. (2011, October 10). Crowdsourced ideas make participating in government cool again. *From bureaucratic to cool: A call for public service* [Special issue]. *PA Times, 34*(4), 4, 6.

Mergel, I. (2012). The public manager 2.0: Preparing the social media generation for the networked workplace. *Journal of Public Affairs Education, 18*(3), 467–492.

Mergel, I., Lazer, D., & Binz-Scharf, M. (2008). Lending a helping hand: Voluntary engagement in a network of professionals. *International Journal of Learning and Change, 3*(1), 5–22.

Obama, B. (2009). Transparency and open government (Memorandum for the heads of executive departments and agencies). Retrieved from http://www.whitehouse .gov/the_press_office/TransparencyandOpenGovernment

Pew Research Center for the People & the Press. (2010). *Distrust, discontent, anger and partisan rancor: The people and their government.* Retrieved from http://pewresearch .org/pubs/1569/trust-in-government-distrust-discontent-anger-partisan-rancor

Schweik, C., Mergel, I., Sanford, J., & Zhao, J. (2011). Toward open public administration scholarship. *Journal of Public Administration Research and Theory, 21*(Suppl. 1: Minnowbrook III), i175–i198.

Chapter Two

Aitoro, J. R. (2009, March 25). *GSA signs deals for agencies to use social networking sites.* Retrieved from http://www.nextgov.com/nextgov/ng_20090325_5490 .php?oref=search

Boyd, D. M., & Ellison, N. B. (2007). Social network sites: Definition, history, and scholarship. *Journal of Computer-Mediated Communication, 13*(1). Retrieved from http:// jcmc.indiana.edu/vol13/issue1/boyd.ellison.html

Bretschneider, S. I., & Mergel, I. (2010). Technology and public management information systems: Where we have been and where we are going. In D. C. Menzel & H. J. White (Eds.), *The state of public administration: Issues, challenges, and opportunities* (pp. 187–203). New York: M. E. Sharpe.

Carpenter, C. A. (2009). The Obamachine: Techno-politics 2.0. In *Conference proceedings: YouTube and the 2008 election cycle* (pp. 189–190). Amherst, MA: ScholarWorks@ UMassAmherst.

Cormode, G., & Krishnamurthy, B. (2008). Key differences between Web 1.0 and Web 2.0. *First Monday, 13*(6). Retrieved from http://firstmonday.org/htbin/cgiwrap/ bin/ojs/index.php/fm/article/view/2125

Dawes, S. S., Cresswell, A. M., & Pardo, T. A. (2009). From "need to know" to "need to share": Tangled problems, information boundaries, and the building of public sector knowledge networks. *Public Administration Review, 69*(3), 392–402.

DeRosa, A. (2011). A social media timeline of the London riots [Web log post]. Retrieved from http://blogs.reuters.com/anthony-derosa/2011/08/11/a-social-media-timeline-of-the-london-riots-2

Eggers, W. D. (2005). *Government 2.0: Using technology to improve education, cut red tape, reduce gridlock, and enhance democracy.* Lanham, MD: Rowman & Littlefield.

Eggers, W. D., & Dovely, T. (2008). Government 2.0's inauguration. *Governing.* Retrieved from http://www.governing.com/mgmt_insight.aspx?id=6062

Facebook. (2011a). Statistics. Retrieved from http://www.facebook.com/press/info .php?statistics

Facebook. (2011b). What does memorializing an account mean? Does it deactivate or delete it? [Frequently asked question]. Retrieved from http://www.facebook.com/

help/?faq=103897939701143—What-does-memorializing-an-account-mean?-Does-it-deactivate-or-delete-it?

Granovetter, M. (1983). The strength of weak ties: A network theory revisited. *Sociological Theory, 1*, 201–233.

Granovetter, M., & Soong, R. (1983). Threshold models of diffusion and collective behavior. *Journal of Mathematical Sociology, 9*(3), 165–179.

Halliday, J. (2011). London riots: How BlackBerry Messenger played a key role: Police looking on Facebook and Twitter for signs of unrest spreading will have missed out—they should have watched BBM. *The Guardian.* Retrieved from http://www.guardian.co.uk/media/2011/aug/08/london-riots-facebook-twitter-blackberry

Haythornthwaite, C. (2001). Exploring multiplexity: Social network structures in a computer-supported distance learning class. *The Information Society, 17*, 211–226.

Horowitz, B. (2011). Google+ [Web log post about real name policy]. Retrieved from https://plus.google.com/113116318008017777871/posts/VJoZMS8zVqU

Kamentz, A. (2010, December/January). How an army of techies is taking on city hall. *FastCompany.* Retrieved from http://www.fastcompany.com/magazine/151/icitizen bonus.html?page=0%2C2

Lakhani, K. R., & Wolf, R. G. (2005). Why hackers do what they do: Understanding motivation and effort in free/open source software. In J. Feller, B. Fitzgerald, A. S. Hissam, & K. R. Lakhani (Eds.), *Perspectives on free and open source software* (pp. 3–22). Cambridge, MA: MIT Press.

Mergel, I. (2010). Government 2.0 revisited: Social media strategies in the public sector. *PA Times, 33*(3), 7, 10.

Mergel, I. (2011). The use of social media to dissolve knowledge silos in government. In R. O'Leary, S. Kim, & D. VanSlyke (Eds.), *The future of public administration, public management, and public service around the world* (pp. 177–187). Washington, DC: Georgetown University Press.

Mergel, I. (2012). *Working the network: A manager's guide for the use of Twitter in government.* Washington, DC: IBM Center for The Business of Government.

Narayanan, A., & Shmatikov, V. (2010). *De-anonymizing social networks.* Retrieved from http://arxiv.org/pdf/0903.3276

Obama, B. (2009). Transparency and open government (Memorandum for the heads of executive departments and agencies). Retrieved from http://www.whitehouse.gov/the_press_office/TransparencyandOpenGovernment

O'Reilly, T. (2005, September 30). *What is Web 2.0: Design patterns and business models for the next generation of software.* Retrieved from http://www.oreillynet.com/pub/a/oreilly/tim/news/2005/09/30/what-is-web-20.html

O'Reilly, T. (2010). *Government as a platform.* Retrieved from http://ofps.oreilly.com/titles/9780596804350

Shea, C. M., & Garson, D. G. (Eds.). (2010). *Handbook of public information systems* (3rd ed.). Boca Raton, FL: CRC Press.

Stanton, K. J. (2012, May 2–4). Twitter joining the conversation. Paper presented at *re:publica,* Berlin, Germany.

Sulzberger, A. O., Jr. (2011, March 17). A letter to our readers about digital subscriptions. *The New York Times.* Retrieved from http://www.nytimes.com/2011/03/18/opinion/l18times.html

Tolbert, C. J., & Mossberger, K. (2006). The effects of e-government on trust and confidence in government. *Public Administration Review, 66*(3), 354–369.

Twitter. (2012). Twitter turns six [Web log post]. Retrieved from http://blog.twitter.com/2012/03/twitter-turns-six.html

U.S. General Services Administration. (2010, March 25). *Landmark agreements clear path for government new media* (News release, GSA #10572). Retrieved from http://www.gsa.gov/portal/content/103496

U.S. Government Accountability Office. (2011). *U.S. Postal Service: Mail trends highlight need to fundamentally change business model* (GAO-12-159SP). Retrieved from http://www.gao.gov/new.items/d12159SP.pdf

von Hippel, E. (2005a). *Democratizing innovation.* Cambridge, MA: MIT Press.

von Hippel, E. (2005b). Open source software projects as user innovation networks. In J. Feller, B. Fitzgerald, S. A. Hissam, & K. R. Lakhani (Eds.), *Perspectives on free and open source software* (pp. 267–278). Cambridge, MA: MIT Press.

Watts, D. J., Dodds, P. S., & Newman, M.E.J. (2008). *Identity and search in social networks.* Retrieved from http://arxiv.org/pdf/cond-mat/0205383

The White House. (2009, March 26). *Online town hall: Open for questions* [Video uploaded by the White House]. Retrieved from http://www.youtube.com/watch?v=YPPT9pWhivM

Wolf, G. (2009). How the Internet invented Howard Dean. *Wired.* Retrieved from http://www.wired.com/wired/archive/12.01/dean.html

Wyld, D. C. (2007). *The blogging revolution: Government in the age of Web 2.0.* Retrieved from http://www.businessofgovernment.org/sites/default/files/WyldReportBlog.pdf

YouTube. (2011). Thanks, YouTube community, for two BIG gifts on our sixth birthday! [Web log post]. Retrieved from http://youtube-global.blogspot.com/2011/05/thanks-youtube-community-for-two-big.html

Chapter Three

Anderson, C. (2008). *The long tail: Why the future of business is selling less of more* (Rev. and updated ed.). New York: Hyperion.

Benkler, Y. (2006). *The wealth of networks: How social production transforms markets and freedom.* New Haven, CT: Yale University Press.

Boyd, D. M., & Ellison, N. B. (2007). Social network sites: Definition, history, and scholarship. *Journal of Computer-Mediated Communication, 13*(1). Retrieved from http://jcmc.indiana.edu/vol13/issue1/boyd.ellison.html

Brabham, D. (2008a). Crowdsourcing as a model for problem solving: An introduction and cases. *Convergence, 14*(1), 75–90.

Brabham, D. (2008b). Moving the crowd at iStockphoto: The composition of the crowd and motivations for participation in a crowdsourcing application. *FirstMonday, 13*(6). Retrieved from http://www.uic.edu/htbin/cgiwrap/bin/ojs/index.php/fm/article/view/2159/1969

Creative Commons. (2008). *Creative Commons.* Retrieved from http://creativecommons.org

Dawes, S. S., Cresswell, A. M., & Pardo, T. A. (2009). From "need to know" to "need to share": Tangled problems, information boundaries, and the building of public sector knowledge networks. *Public Administration Review, 69*(3), 392–402.

Deek, F. P., & McHugh, J.A.M. (2008). *Open source technology and policy.* New York: Cambridge University Press.

Fountain, J. E. (2001). *Building the virtual state: Information technology and institutional change.* Washington, DC: Brookings Institution Press.

Fretwell, L. (2010). *10 Entrepreneurs changing the way government works.* Retrieved from http://govfresh.com/2010/04/10-entrepreneurs-changing-the-way-government-works

Gasser, U., & Palfrey, J. (2008). *Born digital: Understanding the first generation of digital natives.* New York: Basic Books.

Ghosh, R. A. (2005). Understanding free software developers: Findings from the FLOSS study. In J. Feller, B. Fitzgerald, S. A. Hissam, & K. R. Lakhani (Eds.), *Perspectives on free and open source software* (pp. 23–46). Cambridge, MA: MIT Press.

Gillmore, D. (2006). *We the media: Grassroots journalism by the people, for the people.* Sebastopol, CA: O'Reilly Media.

Granovetter, M. (1973). The strength of weak ties. *American Journal of Sociology, 78*(6), 1360–1380.

Granovetter, M. (1983). The strength of weak ties: A network theory revisited. *Sociological Theory, 1,* 201–233.

Howe, J. P. (2008, December). Mumbai and the media. *Wired.*

Johnson, J. (2011). Tweets about Bowie State dorm stabbing traveled faster than university text messages [Web log post]. Retrieved from http://www.washingtonpost.com/blogs/campus-overload/post/tweets-about-bowie-state-dorm-stabbing-traveled-faster-than-university-text-messages/2011/09/19/gIQAq0z6fK_blog.html

Joinson, A. N. (2008). *"Looking at," "looking up" or "keeping up with" people? Motives and uses of Facebook.* Paper presented at CHI 2008, Florence, Italy.

Jordan, M. (2009). *Transit 2.0 at BART.gov* [Audio and slide show from Gov 2.0 Expo Showcase '09]. Retrieved from http://www.youtube.com/watch?v=cQAByeeqOpU

Krishnamurthy, S. (2002). Cave or community? An empirical examination of 100 mature open source projects. *First Monday, 7*(6). Retrieved from http://firstmonday.org/issues/issue7_6/krishnamurthy

Lakhani, K. R., & Wolf, R. G. (2005). Why hackers do what they do: Understanding motivation and effort in free/open source software projects. In J. Feller, B. Fitzgerald, S. A. Hissam, & K. R. Lakhani (Eds.), *Perspectives on free and open source software* (pp. 3–22). Cambridge, MA: MIT Press.

Lazer, D., & Mergel, I. (2011). *Tying the network together: Evaluating the impact of an intervention into the advice network of public managers.* Retrieved from http://papers.ssrn.com/sol3/papers.cfm?abstract_id=1881674

Lazer, D., Mergel, I., Ziniel, C., Esterling, K., & Neblo, M. (2011). The multiple institutional logics of innovation. *International Public Management Journal, 14*(3). doi: 10.1080/10967494.10962011.10618308

Liikanen, J., Stoneman, P., & Toivanen, O. (2004). Intergenerational effects in the diffusion of new technology: The case of mobile phones. *International Journal of Industrial Organization, 22,* 1137–1154.

Lipowicz, A. (2011, October 18). Government workers using mobile to access social media, survey shows. *Federal Computer Week.* Retrieved from http://fcw.com/articles/2011/10/18/government-workers-using-mobile-to-access-social-media-survey-shows.aspx

Lukensmeyer, C. J., & Torres, L. H. (2008). Citizensourcing: Citizen participation in a networked nation. In K. Yang & E. Bergrud (Eds.), *Civic engagement in a networked society* (pp. 207–233). Charlotte, NC: Information Age Publishing .

Madden, M. (2011). *State of social media 2011* [Slide show]. Pew Research Center. Retrieved from http://www.pewinternet.org/Presentations/2011/Dec/State-of-Social-Media-2011.aspxs

Marks, J. (2011). Members of Congress join the rush to social media. Retrieved from http://www.nextgov.com/technology-news/2011/10/members-of-congress-join-the-rush-to-social-media/50031

McCarthy, C. (2007, October 24). *Microsoft acquires equity stake in Facebook, expands ad partnership.* Retrieved from http://news.cnet.com/8301-13577_3-9803872-36.html

Mergel, I. (2012). The public manager 2.0: Preparing the social media generation for the networked workplace. *Journal of Public Affairs Education, 18*(3).

O'Reilly, T. (2005, September 30). *What is Web 2.0: Design patterns and business models for the next generation of software.* Retrieved from http://www.oreillynet.com/pub/a/oreilly/tim/news/2005/09/30/what-is-web-20.html

Page, L., Brin, S., Motwani, R., & Winograd, T. (1999). *The PageRank citation ranking: Bringing order to the web* (Technical Report, Stanford InfoLab). Retrieved from http://ilpubs.stanford.edu:8090/422

Pew Internet & American Life Project. (2007). *A typology of information and communication technology users.* Retrieved from http://www.pewinternet.org/pdfs/PIP_ICT_Typology.pdf

Pew Internet & American Life Project. (2010). *Updated: Change in internet access by age group, 2000–2010.* Retrieved from http://pewinternet.org/Infographics/2010/Internet-acess-by-age-group-over-time-Update.aspx

Pew Research Center for the People & the Press. (2011). *Internet gains on television as public's main news source.* Retrieved from http://www.people-press.org/2011/01/04/internet-gains-on-television-as-publics-main-news-source

Pew Research Center's Project for Excellence in Journalism. (2011). *The state of the news media 2011: An annual report on American journalism.* Retrieved from http://stateofthemedia.org/overview-2011

Riehle, D. (2007, April). *The economic motivation of open source software: Stakeholder perspectives.* Washington, DC: IEEE Computer Society.

Rittel, H. W., & Webber, M. M. (1973). Dilemmas in a general theory of planning. *Policy Sciences, 4,* 155–169.

Schweik, C. M., & English, R. (2007). Conceptualizing the institutional designs of free/libre and open source software projects. *First Monday, 12*(2). Retrieved from http://www.firstmonday.org/issues/issue12_2/schweik/index.html

Stebbins, R. A. (2001). Serious leisure. *Society, 38*(4), 53–57.

Surowiecki, J. (2005). *The wisdom of crowds.* New York: Doubleday.

Tolbert, C. J., Mossberger, K., & McNeal, R. (2008). Institutions, policy innovation, and e-government in the American states. *Public Administration Review, 68*(3), 549–563.

U.S. Government Accountability Office. (2011). *U.S. Postal Service mail trends highlight need to fundamentally change business model* (GAO-12-159S). Retrieved from http://www.gao.gov/new.items/d12159sp.pdf

von Hippel, E. (2005a). *Democratizing innovation.* Cambridge, MA: MIT Press.

von Hippel, E. (2005b). Open source software projects as user innovation networks. In J. Feller, B. Fitzgerald, S. A. Hissam, & K. R. Lakhani (Eds.), *Perspectives on free and open source software* (pp. 267–278). Cambridge, MA: MIT Press.

von Hippel, E., & von Krogh, G. (2003). Open source software and the "private-collective" innovation model: Issues for organization science. *Organization Science, 14*(2), 209–223.

The White House. (2009). The Open Government Initiative. Retrieved from http://www.whitehouse.gov/open

Chapter Four

Associated Press. (2011). Twitter hiccup leads Inslee to follow racy site. *Seattle Times.* Retrieved from http://seattletimes.nwsource.com/html/localnews/2016734513_apwainsleetwitter.html

Behn, R. D. (1995, July/August). The big questions of public management. *Public Administration Review, 55,* 313–324.

Beizer, D. (2009a, August 4). Marines: Facebook is not for the few good men. *Federal Computer Week.* Retrieved from http://fcw.com/Articles/2009/08/04/Marines-ban-social-networking.aspx

Beizer, D. (2009b, August 21). Social media and DOD: To be or not to be? DOD's indecision on social-media tools continues. *Federal Computer Week.* Retrieved from http://fcw.com/articles/2009/08/24/week-dod-social-media-debate.aspx

Benkler, Y. (2006). *The wealth of networks: How social production transforms markets and freedom.* New Haven, CT: Yale University Press.

Bretschneider, S. I., & Mergel, I. (2010). Technology and public management information systems: Where we have been and where we are going. In D. C. Menzel & H. J. White (Eds.), *The state of public administration: Issues, challenges, and opportunities* (pp. 187–203). New York: M. E. Sharpe.

Brewin, B. (2008, January 29). FDA panel cites shortfalls in technology, staffing. *Government Executive.* Retrieved from http://www.govexec.com/story_page.cfm?articleid=39153&printerfriendlyvers=1

Bughin, J., Byers, A. H., & Chui, M. (2011). How social technologies are extending the organization. *McKinsey Quarterly.* Retrieved from http://www.mckinseyquarterly.com/High_Tech/Strategy_Analysis/How_social_technologies_are_extending_the_organization_2888

Carr, D. (2008, October 29). Mourning old media's decline. *The New York Times.* Retrieved from http://www.nytimes.com/2008/10/29/business/worldbusiness/29iht29carr.17331056.html

Dawes, S. S., Cresswell, A. M., & Pardo, T. A. (2009). From "need to know" to "need to share": Tangled problems, information boundaries, and the building of public sector knowledge networks. *Public Administration Review, 69*(3), 392–402.

ForeSee. (2011). *Federal social media usage and citizen satisfaction update. Foresee ASCI E-Government Satisfaction Index (Q3) 2011.* Retrieved from http://www.nrc.gov/public-involve/open/evaluating-progress/foresee-satisfaction-index.pdf

Fountain, J. (2001). *Building the virtual state: Information technology and institutional change.* Washington, DC: Brookings Institution Press.

Fountain, J. (2007). Challenges to organizational change: Multi-level integrated information structures (MIIS). In V. M. Schönberger & D. Lazer (Eds.), *Governance and information technology: From electronic government to information government* (pp. 63–93). Cambridge, MA: MIT Press.

Goode, L. (2009). Social news, citizen journalism and democracy. *New Media & Society, 11*(8), 1287–1305. doi: 1461444809341393v1461444809341391

Gross, G. (2006, October 31). US Intelligence Community's wiki aids info sharing. *InfoWorld*. Retrieved from http://www.infoworld.com/article/06/10/31/HNusintelligencewiki_1.html

Kettl, D. F. (2006). Managing boundaries in American administration: The collaboration imperative. *Public Administration Review, 66*(Suppl. 1), 10–19.

Kettl, D. F., & Fesler, J. W. (2009). *The politics of the administrative process*. Washington, DC: CQ Press.

Kirlin, J. J. (1996). The big questions of public administration in a democracy. *Public Administration Review, 56*(5), 416–423.

Mergel, I. (2011). The use of social media to dissolve knowledge silos in government. In R. O'Leary, S. Kim, & D. VanSlyke (Eds.), *The future of public administration, public management, and public service around the world* (pp. 177–187). Washington, DC: Georgetown University Press.

Mergel, I., Lazer, D., & Binz-Scharf, M. (2008). Lending a helping hand: Voluntary engagement in a network of professionals. *International Journal of Learning and Change, 3*(1), 5–22.

Moon, M. J. (2002). The evolution of e-government among municipalities: Rhetoric or reality? *Public Administration Review, 62*, 424–433.

Morozov, E. (2009, April 25). Swine flu: Twitter's power to misinform [Web log post]. *Foreign Policy*. Retrieved from http://neteffect.foreignpolicy.com/posts/2009/04/25/swine_flu_twitters_power_to_misinform

Nabatchi, T., & Reeher, G. (In press). Public relations in the United States government: Fragmentation, democratic tension, and the puzzle of public trust. In *Comparative government public relations*. Seoul, South Korea: Korean Institute of Public Administration (KIPA).

Office of the Director of National Intelligence. (2008). *United States Intelligence Community: Information sharing strategy*. Retrieved from http://www.dni.gov/reports/IC_Information_Sharing_Strategy.pdf

O'Reilly, T. (2004, June). *The architecture of participation*. Retrieved from http://www.oreillynet.com/pub/a/oreilly/tim/articles/architecture_of_participation.html

Pew Research Center's Project for Excellence in Journalism. (2008). *2007 State of the news media report—newspapers*. Retrieved from http://www.journalism.org/node/7218

Rainie, L., Purcell, K., Siesfeld, T., & Patel, M. (2011). *How the public perceives community information systems*. Retrieved from http://pewinternet.org/Reports/2011/08-Community-Information-Systems.aspx

Schweik, C. M., Mergel, I., Sanford, J. R., & Zhao, Z. J. (2011). Toward open public administration scholarship. *Journal of Public Administration Research and Theory, 21*(Suppl. 1: Minnowbrook III), i175-i198.

Schweik, C. M., Stepanov, A., & Grove, J. M. (2005). The open research system: A web-based metadata and data repository for collaborative research. *Computers and Electronics in Agriculture, 47*, 221–242.

Surowiecki, J. (2004). *The wisdom of crowds: Why the many are smarter than the few and how collective wisdom shapes business, economies, societies and nations*. New York: Random House.

Sutter, J. (2009, April 30). *Swine flu creates controversy on Twitter.* Retrieved from http://www.cnn.com/2009/TECH/04/27/swine.flu.twitter

Thottam, G. (1999). The future of newspapers: Survival or extinction? *Media Asia, 26*(4), 216–221.

U.S. Army. (2008). *Army knowledge management principles.* Retrieved from http://www.army.mil/ciog6/docs/AKMPrinciples.pdf

U.S. Department of State. (n.d.). U.S. Department of State Freedom of Information Act (FOIA) [Instructions for requesting State Department records]. Retrieved from http://www.state.gov/m/a/ips

U.S. Government Accountability Office. (2009). *Information technology: FDA needs to establish key plans and processes for guiding systems modernization efforts* (GAO-09-523). Washington, DC: Author.

U.S. Government Accountability Office. (2011). *IT Dashboard: Accuracy has improved, and additional efforts are under way to better inform decision making* (GAO-12-210). Retrieved from http://www.gao.gov/products/GAO-12-210

Veteritti, J. P. (2008). The environmental context of communication: Public sector organizations. In M. Lee (Ed.), *Government public relations: A reader* (pp. 319–341). Boca Raton, FL: CRC Press.

Wells, L., Sorenson, J. A., Justice, N., Castilo, C., & Lin, P. (2009, September 10). *Innovation from within: Apps for security program in armed forces.* Paper presented at the Gov 2.0 Expo Showcase, Washington, DC. Retrieved from http://www.gov2summit.com/public/schedule/detail/10427

The White House. (2011). TooManyWebsites.gov [Web log post]. Retrieved from http://www.whitehouse.gov/blog/2011/06/13/toomanywebsitesgov

Wildstrom, S. (2009, April 27). Updated: Twitter and swine flu: All noise, no signal. *BusinessWeek.* Retrieved from http://www.businessweek.com/the_thread/techbeat/archives/2009/04/twitter_swi9ne.html

Wylie, S. (2007, May 26). The 2.0 agenda: Transparency, sharing, access—are you ready for enterprise 2.0? *Information Week.* Retrieved from http://www.informationweek.com/news/infrastructure/management/showArticle.jhtml?articleID=199702156

Zeleny, J., & Thee-Brenan, M. (2011, October 26). New poll finds a deep distrust of government. *The New York Times.* Retrieved from http://www.nytimes.com/2011/10/26/us/politics/poll-finds-anxiety-on-the-economy-fuels-volatility-in-the-2012-race.html?_r=1

Chapter Five

Bertot, J. C., Jaeger, P. T., & Hansen, D. L. (2011). The impact of policies on government social media usage: Issues, challenges, and recommendations. *Government Information Quarterly, 29*(1), 30–40. doi: 10.1016/j.giq.2011.04.004

Bretschneider, S. I., & Mergel, I. (2010). Technology and public management information systems: Where we have been and where we are going. In D. C. Menzel & H. J. White (Eds.), *The state of public administration: Issues, challenges, and opportunities* (pp. 187–203). New York: M. E. Sharpe.

Carpenter, C. A. (2009). The Obamachine: Techno-politics 2.0. *Knowledge Politics Quarterly, 2*(1), 216–225.

Creative Commons. (2008). *Creative Commons*. Retrieved from http://creativecommons.org

E-Government Act of 2002, Pub. L. No. 107-347, encoded in multiple titles of the U.S.C., including 44 U.S.C. §§ 2108 et seq. (2002).

General Services Administration. (2010, July 22). Dave McClure, Associate Administrator for Citizen Services and Innovative Technologies, Testifies on Federal Agency Use of Web 2.0 Technologies. Retrieved from: http://www.gsa.gov/portal/content/158009

Lerner, J., & Tirole, J. (2005). Economic perspectives on open source. In J. Feller, B. Fitzgerald, S. A. Hissam, & K. R. Lakhani (Eds.), *Perspectives on free and open source software*, pp. 33–69. Cambridge, MA: MIT Press.

Library of Congress. (2010, April 14). [Tweet about acquisition of Twitter archive.] Retrieved from http://twitter.com/#!/librarycongress/status/12169442690

Obama, B. (2009a, September 8). *Prepared remarks of President Barack Obama: Back to school event.* Retrieved from http://www.whitehouse.gov/MediaResources/PreparedSchoolRemarks

Obama, B. (2009b). Transparency and open government (Memorandum for the heads of executive departments and agencies). Retrieved from http://www.whitehouse.gov/the_press_office/TransparencyandOpenGovernment

Office of Management and Budget. (2004, December 17). Policies for federal agency public websites (Memorandum for the heads of executive departments and agencies). Retrieved from http://www.whitehouse.gov/sites/default/files/omb/memoranda/fy2005/m05-04.pdf

Office of Management and Budget. (2009, December 8). Open Government Directive (Memorandum for the heads of executive departments and agencies and independent regulatory agencies). Retrieved from http://www.whitehouse.gov/sites/default/files/omb/assets/memoranda_2010/m10-06.pdf

Office of Management and Budget. (2010a, June 25). Guidance for online use of web measurement and customization technologies (Memorandum for the heads of executive departments and agencies). Retrieved from http://www.whitehouse.gov/sites/default/files/omb/assets/memoranda_2010/m10-22.pdf

Office of Management and Budget. (2010b, April 7). Information collection under the Paperwork Reduction Act (Memorandum for the heads of executive departments and agencies and independent regulatory agencies). Retrieved from http://www.whitehouse.gov/sites/default/files/omb/assets/inforeg/PRAPrimer_04072010.pdf

Office of Management and Budget. (2010c, April 7). Social media, web-based interactive technologies, and the Paperwork Reduction Act (Memorandum for the heads of executive departments and agencies and independent regulatory agencies). Retrieved from http://www.whitehouse.gov/sites/default/files/omb/assets/inforeg/SocialMediaGuidance_04072010.pdf

Phillips, M. (2009). Reality check: The Presidential Records Act of 1978 meets web-based social media of 2009 [Web log post]. Retrieved from http://www.whitehouse.gov/blog/Reality-Check-The-Presidential-Records-Act

Presidential Records Act, 44 U.S.C. §§2201–2207 (1978).

Price, C. (2010). Why don't my students think I'm groovy? The new "R"s for engaging millennial learners. *Essays from E-xcellence in Teaching, 9*, 29–34. Retrieved from http://teachpsych.org/resources/e-books/eit2009/index.php

U.S. General Services Administration. (2010, March 25). *Landmark agreements clear path for government new media* (News release, GSA #10572). Retrieved from http://www .gsa.gov/portal/content/103496

U.S. Government Accountability Office. (2010). *Information management: Challenges in federal agencies' use of Web 2.0 technologies* (GAO-10-872T). Retrieved from http:// www.gao.gov/products/GAO-10-872T

U.S. Government Accountability Office. (2011). *Social media: Federal agencies need policies and procedures for managing and protecting information they access and disseminate* (GAO-11-605). Retrieved from http://www.gao.gov/products/GAO-11-605

U.S. National Archives and Records Administration. (2010). *Guidance on managing records in Web 2.0/social media platforms* (NARA Bulletin 2011-02). Retrieved from http:// www.archives.gov/records-mgmt/bulletins/2011/2011-02.html

The White House. (2009). The Open Government Initiative. Retrieved from http:// www.whitehouse.gov/open

The White House (2010, September 14). Presidential memorandum—Accountable Government Initiative. Retrieved from http://www.whitehouse.gov/the-press-office/2010/09/14/presidential-memorandum-accountable-government-initiative

Chapter Six

Dunn, B. (2010, December). Best Buy's CEO on learning to love social media. *Harvard Business Review*, pp. 43–48.

Dutta, S. (2010, November). Managing yourself: What's your personal social media strategy? *Harvard Business Review*. Retrieved from http://hbr.org/2010/11/managing-yourself-whats-your-personal-social-media-strategy/ar/1

Guidelines for Ensuring and Maximizing the Quality, Objectivity, Utility, and Integrity of Information Disseminated by Federal Agencies (Republication), 67 Fed. Reg. 36, 8452 (2002). Retrieved from http://www.whitehouse.gov/sites/default/files/omb/fedreg/reproducible2.pdf

Hrdinova, J., Helbig, N., & Peters, C. S. (2010). *Designing social media policy for government: Eight essential elements.* Albany: State University of New York, University at Albany, Center for Technology in Government.

Ignatius, A. (2011, July/August). Disney CEO Robert A. Iger: Technology, tradition & the mouse. *Harvard Business Review*, pp. 112–117.

Narayanan, A., & Shmatikov, V. (2010). *De-anonymizing social networks.* Retrieved from http://arxiv.org/pdf/0903.3276

Office of Management and Budget. (2011). Implementing Executive Order 13571 on streamlining service delivery and improving customer service (Memorandum for heads of executive departments and agencies). Retrieved from http://www.white house.gov/sites/default/files/omb/memoranda/2011/m11-24.pdf

Schellong, A. (2008). *Citizen relationship management: A study of CRM in government.* Frankfurt am Main: Lang.

Spenner, P. (2010, December). Why you need a new-media "ringmaster." *Harvard Business Review*, pp. 78–79.

U.S. Government Accountability Office. (2010a). *Information management: Challenges in federal agencies' use of Web 2.0 technologies* (GAO-10-872T). Retrieved from http://www.gao.gov/products/GAO-10-872T

U.S. Government Accountability Office. (2010b). *Managing for results: Opportunities to strengthen agencies' customer service efforts* (GAO-11-44). Retrieved from http://www.gao.gov/new.items/d1144.pdf

U.S. Government Accountability Office. (2011). *Social media: Federal agencies need policies and procedures for managing and protecting information they access and disseminate* (GAO-11-605). Retrieved from http://www.gao.gov/products/GAO-11-605

U.S. Navy. (2010a). *Navy command social media handbook—online version* [Slide show]. Retrieved from http://www.slideshare.net/USNavySocialMedia/navy-command-social-media-handbook-web

U.S. Navy. (2010b). *U.S. Navy social media content guide* [Slide show]. Retrieved from http://www.slideshare.net/USNavySocialMedia/navy-social-media-content-guide

U.S. Navy. (2011). *U.S. Navy: Social media handbook for Navy PAOs* [Slide show]. Retrieved from http://www.slideshare.net/USNavySocialMedia/sm-handbook-print

The White House. (2011). Executive Order 13571—Streamlining service delivery and improving customer service. Retrieved from http://www.whitehouse.gov/the-press-office/2011/04/27/executive-order-streamlining-service-delivery-and-improving-customer-ser

Wilson, H. J., Guinan, P. J., Parise, S., & Weinberg, B. D. (2011 July/August). What's your social media strategy? *Harvard Business Review*, pp. 23–25.

Chapter Seven

Bretschneider, S. I., & Mergel, I. (2010). Technology and public management information systems: Where we have been and where we are going. In D. C. Menzel & H. J. White (Eds.), *The state of public administration: Issues, challenges, and opportunities* (pp. 187–203). New York: M. E. Sharpe.

Carr, D. F. (2011, June 21). Social software needs metrics that matter. *Information Week*. Retrieved from http://www.informationweek.com/thebrainyard/news/community_management_development/231000075

Centers for Disease Control and Prevention. (2009). Social media at CDC: Buttons and badges gallery. Retrieved from http://www.cdc.gov/socialmedia

Hazlett, S.-A., & Hill, F. (2003). E-government: The realities of using IT to transform the public sector. *Managing Service Quality*, *13*(6), 445–452.

Hicks, R. (2010, November 22). Singapore to mine citizen sentiment in social media. *FutureGov*. Retrieved from http://www.futuregov.asia/articles/2010/nov/22/singapore-mine-citizen-sentiment-social-media

Hoffman, D., & Fodor, M. (2010). Can you measure the ROI of your social media marketing? *MIT Sloan Management Review*, *52*(1), 41–49. Retrieved from http://sloanreview.mit.edu/the-magazine/2010-fall/52105/can-you-measure-the-roi-of-your-social-media-marketing

Isett, K., Mergel, I., Leroux, K., Mischen, P., & Rethemeyer, K. (2011). Networks in public administration scholarship: Understanding where we are and where we need to go. *Journal of Public Administration Research and Theory*, *21*(Suppl. 1), i157–i173.

Klout. (n.d.). NASA is a taste maker. Retrieved from http://www.klout.com/#/nasa/kloutstyle

Lazer, D., Pentland, A., Adamic, L., Aral, S., Barabási, A.-L., Brewer, D., . . . Alstyne, M. V. (2009). Computational social science. *Science, 323*(5915), 721–723.

Melitski, J. (2003). Capacity and e-government performance: An analysis based on early adopters of Internet technologies in New Jersey. *Public Performance & Management Review, 26*(4), 376–390.

Mislove, A., Lehmann, S., Ahn, Y.-Y., Onnela, J.-P., & Rosenquist, J. N. (2010). *Pulse of the nation: U.S. mood throughout the day inferred from Twitter.* Retrieved from http://www.ccs.neu.edu/home/amislove/twittermood

Moon, M. J. (2002). The evolution of e-government among municipalities: Rhetoric or reality? *Public Administration Review, 62,* 424–433.

Naaman, M., Boase, J., & Lai, C.-H. (2010). Is it really about me? Message content in social awareness streams. In *Proceedings of the 2010 ACM conference on computer supported cooperative work.* New York: ACM. Available from http://dl.acm.org/citation.cfm?id=1718918

Office of Management and Budget. (2010). Guidance for agency use of third-party websites and applications (Memorandum for the heads of executive departments and agencies). Retrieved from http://www.whitehouse.gov/sites/default/files/omb/assets/memoranda_2010/m10-23.pdf

Pew Research Center for the People & the Press. (2010). *Distrust, discontent, anger and partisan rancor: The people and their government.* Retrieved from http://pewresearch.org/pubs/1569/trust-in-government-distrust-discontent-anger-partisan-rancor

Rocheleau, B. (2007). Whither e-government? *Public Administration Review, 67*(3), 584–588.

Stowers, G.N.L. (2004). *Measuring the performance of e-government.* Washington, DC: IBM Center for the Business of Government.

Titmuss, R. M. (1971). *The gift relationship: From human blood to social policy.* London: Allen & Unwin.

Tolbert, C. J., & Mossberger, K. (2006). The effects of e-government on trust and confidence in government. *Public Administration Review, 66*(3), 354–369.

West, D. M. (2004). E-government and the transformation of service delivery and citizen attitudes. *Public Administration Review, 64*(1), 15–27.

Chapter Eight

Bretschneider, S. I., & Mergel, I. (2010). Technology and public management information systems: Where we have been and where we are going. In D. C. Menzel & H. J. White (Eds.), *The state of public administration: Issues, challenges, and opportunities* (pp. 187–203). New York: M. E. Sharpe.

Chesbrough, H. W. (2003). *Open innovation: The new imperative for creating and profiting from technology.* Cambridge, MA: Harvard Business Press.

Cormode, G., & Krishnamurthy, B. (2008). Key differences between Web 1.0 and Web 2.0. *First Monday, 13*(6). Retrieved from http://firstmonday.org/htbin/cgiwrap/bin/ojs/index.php/fm/article/view/2125

Crosseau, C. (2011). The fix: SeeClickFix has a brand new Facebook widget [Web log post]. Retrieved from http://tucsoncitizen.com/social-citizen/2011/04/12/the-fix-seeclickfix-has-a-facebook-widget

Fast Company Staff. (2010). Fixing a pothole with your iPhone. *Fast Company*. Retrieved from http://www.fastcompany.com/magazine/151/upright-citizens-brigade.html

Fretwell, L. (2010). *10 Entrepreneurs changing the way government works*. Retrieved from http://govfresh.com/2010/04/10-entrepreneurs-changing-the-way-government-works

Goodnoe, E. (2005, August 29). Wikis make collaboration easier. *Information Week*. Retrieved from http://www.informationweek.com/shared/printableArticle.jhtml;jsessionid=ZBHP4HNEXGTV5QE1GHPSKHWATMY32JVN?articleID=170100392

Howard, A. (2010). *What is SeeClickFix and Gov2.0, Ben Berkowitz?* Retrieved from http://gov20.govfresh.com/what-is-seeclickfix-and-gov-2-0-ben-berkowitz

Howe, J. P. (2006, June). The rise of crowdsourcing. *Wired*. Retrieved from http://www.wired.com/wired/archive/14.06/crowds.html

Kamenetz, A. (2010). How an army of techies is taking on city hall. *Fast Company*. Retrieved from http://www.fastcompany.com/magazine/151/icitizen-bonus.html

Kennedy, D. (2010). The wisdom of crowdsourcing: Far from the nasty comments found on many sites, projects such as SeeClickFix channel participation in constructive, useful ways. *The Guardian*. Retrieved from http://www.guardian.co.uk/commentisfree/cifamerica/2010/jun/01/crowdsourcing-internet

Leighninger, M. (2011). *Using online tools to engage—and be engaged by—the public*. Retrieved from http://www.businessofgovernment.org/report/using-online-tools-engage-public

Lukensmeyer, C. (2010). Learning from the past, looking into the future: A practitioner's view of our democracy. *Public Administration Review, 70*(Suppl.), S273–S283.

Mergel, I. (2010). *Social media: Digital divide, digital access and digital literacy*. http://inesmergel.wordpress.com/2010/09/21/social-media-digital-divide-digital-access-and-digital-literacy

Mergel, I. (2011). The use of social media to dissolve knowledge silos in government. In R. O'Leary, S. Kim, & D. VanSlyke (Eds.), *The future of public administration, public management, and public service around the world* (pp. 177–187). Washington, DC: Georgetown University Press.

National Public Radio. (2010, January 30). *The pros and cons of a YouTube democracy*. Retrieved from http://www.npr.org/templates/story/story.php?storyId=123164827

North Carolina Center for Voter Education. (2011, February 9). Center to honor citizens, journalists and public servants at 2011 Spectrum of Democracy Awards (Press release). Retrieved from http://www.ncvotered.com/releases/2011/2_9_11_sda_recipients.php

O'Reilly, T. (2007). What is Web 2.0: Design patterns and business models for the next generation of software. *Communications & Strategies*, No. 1, pp. 17–37.

Simon, M. (2009). Island DIY: Kauai residents don't wait for state to repair road. Retrieved from: http://articles.cnn.com/2009-04-09/us/hawaii.volunteers.repair_1_repairs-wait-business-owners?_s=PM:US

Slotnick, D. (2010, January 4). News sites dabble with a web tool for nudging local officials. *The New York Times*. Retrieved from http://www.nytimes.com/2010/01/04/business/media/04click.html

Veen, C. V. (2009). *San Jose, Calif.'s Wikiplanning project on course*. Retrieved from http://www.govtech.com/gt/719878?topic=290174

Chapter Nine

Aitoro, J. R. (2009, March 25). GSA signs deals for agencies to use social networking sites. *NextGov*. Retrieved from http://www.nextgov.com/nextgov/ng_20090325_5490 .php?oref=search

Anand, V., Glick, W. H., & Manz, C. C. (2002). Thriving on the knowledge of outsiders: Tapping organizational social capital. *Academy of Management Executive, 16*(1), 87–101.

Anderson, N. (2010). *State Department moves from telegrams to wiki*. Retrieved from http:// arstechnica.com/tech-policy/news/2010/05/diplopedia-how-the-state-dept-embraced-wiki-diplomacy.ars

Andrus, D. C. (2005). The wiki and the blog: Toward a complex adaptive intelligence community. *Studies in Intelligence, 49*(3). Retrieved from https://www.cia.gov/ library/center-for-the-study-of-intelligence/csi-publications/csi-studies/studies/ vol49no3/html_files/Wik_and_%20Blog_7.html

Blau, P., & Scott, W. R. (1962). *Formal organizations*. San Francisco: Chandler.

Bretschneider, S. I., & Mergel, I. (2010). Technology and public management information systems: Where we have been and where we are going. In D. C. Menzel & H. J. White (Eds.), *The state of public administration: Issues, problems and challenges* (pp. 187–203). New York: M. E. Sharpe.

Brewer, J. (2010). *Civic hackers for Haiti*. Retrieved from http://www.huffingtonpost .com/jake-brewer/civic-hackers-for-haiti_b_425176.html

Bronk, C., & Smith, T. (2010). *Diplopedia imagined: Building State's diplomacy wiki*. Paper presented at the 2010 International Symposium on Collaborative Technologies and Systems, Chicago, Illinois.

Burke, D. (2008). *CIA presenting Intellipedia—Social media for govt conference* [Video]. Retrieved from http://www.youtube.com/watch?v=wuSrbZpXu40

Calabresi, M. (2009, April 8). Wikipedia for spies: The CIA discovers Web 2.0. *Time*.

Chang, A.-M., & Kannan, P. K. (2008). *Leveraging Web 2.0 in government*. Retrieved from http://www.businessofgovernment.org/pdfs/ChangReport2.pdf

Cohen, N. (2008, August 3). On Web, U.S. diplomats learn to share information. *International Herald Tribune*. Retrieved from http://www.iht.com/arti cles/2008/08/03/technology/link04.php

Cross, R., Borgatti, S. P., & Parker, A. (2001). Beyond answers: Dimensions of the advice network. *Social Networks, 23*(3), 215–235.

Cross, R., Rice, R. E., & Parker, A. (2001). Information seeking in social context: Structural influences and receipt of information benefits. *IEEE Transactions on Systems, Man, and Cybernetics, Part C: Applications and Reviews, 31*(4), 438–448.

Dawes, S. S., Cresswell, A. M., & Pardo, T. A. (2009). From "need to know" to "need to share": Tangled problems, information boundaries, and the building of public sector knowledge networks. *Public Administration Review, 69*(3), 392–402.

Demil, B., & Lecocq, X. (2006). Neither market nor hierarchy nor network: The emergence of bazaar governance. *Organization Studies, 27*(10), 1447–1466.

Eggers, W. D. (2005). *Government 2.0: Using technology to improve education, cut red tape, reduce gridlock, and enhance democracy*. Lanham, MD: Rowman & Littlefield.

Goetz, K. (2010). *Hackathon: 2 days, 1,000 developers, lots of caffeine*. Retrieved from http://www.npr.org/2010/12/06/131853415/hackathon-2-days-1-000-developers-lots-of-caffeine

Grant, R. M. (1996). Toward a knowledge-based theory of the firm. *Strategic Management Journal, 17*, 109–122.

Guy, M. (2006, October). Wiki or won't he? A tale of public sector wikis. *Ariadne, 49*. Retrieved from http://www.ariadne.ac.uk/issue49/guy

Hindman, M. S. (2008). *The myth of digital democracy.* Princeton, NJ: Princeton University Press.

Janelle, R. (2009). GCPedia a success, says Government of Canada CIO [Web log post]. Retrieved from http://www.techvibes.com/blog/gcpedia-a-success-says-government-of-canada-cio

Krackhardt, D., & Hanson, J. (1993, July). Informal networks: The company behind the charts. *Harvard Business Review*, 104–111.

Kram, K. E., & Isabella, L. A. (1985). Mentoring alternatives: The role of peer relationships in career development. *Academy of Management Journal, 28*(1), 110–132.

Lawlor, M. (2008). Web 2.0 intelligence. *Signal, 62*(8), 63.

Massey, L. L. (2009). *Despite wikis and other Web 2.0 tools, government collaboration is still slow to catch on.* Retrieved from http://www.govtech.com/gt/715791

Mergel, I. (2010). Government 2.0 revisited: Social media strategies in the public sector. *PA Times, 33*(3), 7, 10.

Mergel, I. (2011). The use of social media to dissolve knowledge silos in government. In R. O'Leary, S. Kim, & D. VanSlyke (Eds.), *The future of public administration, public management, and public service around the world* (pp. 177–187). Washington, DC: Georgetown University Press.

Mergel, I., Schweik, C. M., & Fountain, J. (2009). *The transformational effect of Web 2.0 technologies on government.* Retrieved from http://ssrn.com/abstract=1412796

Morrison, E. W. (2002). Newcomers' relationships: The role of social network ties during socialization. *Academy of Management Journal, 45*(6), 1149–1160.

Nonaka, I., & Takeuchi, H. (1995). *The knowledge-creating company.* New York: Oxford University Press.

Nonaka, I., & Takeuchi, H. (1996). The knowledge-creating company: How Japanese companies create the dynamics of innovation. *Long Range Planning, 29*(4), 592.

Noveck, B. (2009). Open government laboratories of democracy [Web log post]. http://www.whitehouse.gov/blog/2009/11/19/open-government-laboratories-democracy

Obama, B. (2009). Transparency and open government (Memorandum for the heads of executive departments and agencies). Retrieved from http://www.whitehouse.gov/the_press_office/TransparencyandOpenGovernment

Office of Management and Budget. (2009, December 8). Open Government Directive (Memorandum for the heads of executive departments and agencies and independent regulatory agencies). Retrieved from http://www.whitehouse.gov/sites/default/files/omb/assets/memoranda_2010/m10-06.pdf

Powell, W. W. (1990). Neither market nor hierarchy—network forms of organization. *Research in Organizational Behavior, 12*, 295–336.

Rasmussen, C. (2009). *Living intelligence* [Video]. Retrieved from http://www.youtube.com/watch?v=nbgQ1V2BLEs

Simon, H. (1982). From substantive to procedural rationality. In S. J. Latsis (Ed.), *Method and appraisal in economics.* New York: Cambridge University Press. (Original work published 1976).

Terdiman, D. (2005). *Study: Wikipedia as accurate as Britannica.* Retrieved from http://news.cnet.com/Study-Wikipedia-as-accurate-as-Britannica/2100-1038_3-5997332.html

Trkman, M., & Trkman, P. (2009). A wiki as intranet: A critical analysis using the Delone and McLean model. *Online Information Review, 33*(6), 1087–1102.

U.S. Department of State. (2009). About Diplopedia. Retrieved from http://www.state.gov/m/irm/ediplomacy/115847.htm

U.S. General Services Administration. (2010, March 25). *Landmark agreements clear path for government new media* [News release]. Retrieved from http://www.gsa.gov/portal/content/103496

Chapter Ten

Dawes, S. S. (1996). Interagency information sharing: Expected benefits, manageable risks. *Journal of Policy Analysis and Management, 15*(3), 377–394.

Dawes, S. S., Cresswell, A. M., & Pardo, T. A. (2009). From "need to know" to "need to share": Tangled problems, information boundaries, and the building of public sector knowledge networks. *Public Administration Review, 69*(3), 392–402.

Data.gov. (n.d.). About. Retrieved from http://www.data.gov/about

Entner, R. (2011). Smartphones to overtake feature phone in U.S. by 2011 [Web log post]. Retrieved from http://blog.nielsen.com/nielsenwire/consumer/smartphones-to-overtake-feature-phones-in-u-s-by-2011

Federal Communications Commission. (2011). Executive summary. In *National broadband plan—connecting America*. Retrieved from http://www.broadband.gov/plan/executive-summary

FlyOnTime. (n.d.). About FlyOnTime.us. Retrieved from FlyOnTime.us/about

Kettl, D. (2008). *The next government of the United States: Why our institutions fail us and how to fix them.* New York: Norton.

Kundra, V. (2011). *Reflections on public service* [Working paper]. Retrieved from http://www.hks.harvard.edu/presspol/publications/papers/kundra_reflections_on_public_service_2011.pdf

Madden, M., & Zickuhr, K. (2011). *65% of online adults use social networking sites.* Retrieved from http://pewinternet.org/Reports/2011/Social-Networking-Sites.aspx

Meinrath, S., & Losey, J. (2010, April 28). Denial of service: Don't believe the telecoms; broadband access in the United States is even worse than you think. *Slate.* Retrieved from http://www.slate.com/id/2252141

Mergel, I. (2011, October 10). Crowdsourced ideas make participating in government cool again. *From bureaucratic to cool: A call for public service* [Special issue]. *PA Times, 34*(4), 4, 6.

Mergel, I. (2012, January/February/March). Open data goes global: Challenges and solutions. *PA Times* (International suppl.), 7–8.

National Aeronautics and Space Administration. (n.d.). NASA Visualization Explorer: App description. Retrieved from http://apps.usa.gov/nasa-visualization-explorer.shtml

Obama, B. (2009). Transparency and open government (Memorandum for the heads of executive departments and agencies). Retrieved from http://www.whitehouse.gov/the_press_office/TransparencyandOpenGovernment

O'Reilly, T. (2010). *Government as a platform.* Retrieved from http://ofps.oreilly.com/titles/9780596804350

Pew Research Center for the People & the Press. (2010). *Distrust, discontent, anger and partisan rancor: The people and their government.* Retrieved from http://pewresearch .org/pubs/1569/trust-in-government-distrust-discontent-anger-partisan-rancor

Stern, A. (2009). Making government cool again [Web log post]. Retrieved from http:// www.governing.com/blogs/bfc/Making-Government-Cool-Again.html

Thaler, R. (2011, March 13). Are statistics practical? Count the ways, online. *The New York Times.* Retrieved from http://www.nytimes.com/2011/03/13/business/13sview .html

Chapter Eleven

Andersen, K. (2011, December 14). The protester [Person of the year]. *Time.* Retrieved from http://www.time.com/time/specials/packages/article/ 0,28804,2101745_ 2102132_2102373,00.html

Baird, D. E., & Fisher, M. (2005–2006). Neomillennial user experience design strategies: Utilizing social-networking media to support "always on" learning styles. *Journal of Educational Technology Systems, 34*(1), 5–32.

Chen, H., Thoms, S., & Fu, T. (2008). Cyber extremism in Web 2.0: An exploratory study of international Jihadist groups. In *Proceedings of Intelligence and Security Informatics ISI, 2008,* pp. 98–103. Washington, DC: IEEE.

Dawes, S. S., Cresswell, A. M., & Pardo, T. A. (2009). From "need to know" to "need to share": Tangled problems, information boundaries, and the building of public sector knowledge networks. *Public Administration Review, 69*(3), 392–402.

Director of National Intelligence. (2008). *United States intelligence community: Information sharing strategy.* Retrieved from http://www.dni.gov/reports/IC_Information_ Sharing_Strategy.pdf

Google.org. (2008). Flu trends. Retrieved from http://www.google.org/about/flu trends/how.html

Hazlett, S.-A., & Hill, F. (2003). E-government: The realities of using IT to transform the public sector. *Managing Service Quality, 13*(6), 445–452.

Lazer, D., Pentland, A., Adamic, L., Aral, S., Barabási, A.-L., Brewer, D., . . . Alstyne, M. V. (2009). Computational social science. *Science, 323*(5915), 721–723.

Mello, J. P., Jr. (2011, December 26). Confidential client list safe from Anonymous, Stratfor says: The magnitude of a Christmas Eve attack on Stratfor appears exaggerated by the data bandits. *Computerworld.* Retrieved from http://www.computerworld.com/s/ article/9223025/Confidential_client_list_safe_from_Anonymous_Stratfor_says

Mergel, I. (2012). Measuring the impact of social media use in the public sector. In E. Downey & M. Jones (Eds.), *Public service, governance and Web 2.0 technologies* (pp. 48–64). Hershey, PA: IGI-Global.

Mergel, I., Lazer, D., & Binz-Scharf, M. (2008). Lending a helping hand: Voluntary engagement in a network of professionals. *International Journal of Learning and Change, 3*(1), 5–22.

Moon, M. J. (2002). The evolution of e-government among municipalities: Rhetoric or reality? *Public Administration Review, 62,* 424–433.

Nagesh, G. (2009, February 9). *Agencies used social media to manage salmonella outbreak.* Retrieved from http://www.nextgov.com/nextgov/ng_20090209_7840.php

Noyes, K. (2007, April 4). Campaign 2.0. *TechNewsWorld*. Retrieved from http://www.technewsworld.com/story/56682.html

Oliphant, J. (2011, June 16). The Anthony Weiner scandal: How it all went wrong. *The Los Angeles Times*. Retrieved from http://articles.latimes.com/2011/jun/16/news/la-pn-weiner-scandal-timeline-20110616

Sunlight Foundation. (2009). Apps for America. Retrieved from http://sunlightlabs.com/contests/appsforamerica

Sutter, J. (2009, April 27). *Swine flu creates controversy on Twitter*. Retrieved from http://www.cnn.com/2009/TECH/04/27/swine.flu.twitter

U.S. Army. (2008). *Army knowledge management principles*. Retrieved from http://www.army.mil/ciog6/docs/AKMPrinciples.pdf

U.S. Department of State. (n.d.). *U.S. Department of State Freedom of Information Act (FOIA)* [Instructions for requesting State Department records]. Retrieved from http://www.state.gov/m/a/ips

Wasik, B. (2011, December). Gladwell vs. Shirky: A year later, scoring the debate over social-media revolutions. *Wired*. Retrieved from http://www.wired.com/threatlevel/2011/12/gladwell-vs-shirky

Wildstrom, S. (2009, April 28). Twitter and swine flu: All noise, no signal [Updated]. *BusinessWeek*. Retrieved from http://www.businessweek.com/the_thread/techbeat/archives/2009/04/twitter_swi9ne.html

INDEX

Page references followed by *fig* indicate an illustrated figure; followed by *t* indicate a table.